ALTERNATIVE TITLE:
MOR. PART1, FEAST OF FIELDS

FEAST
OF FIELDS

BY SEAN KAREMAKER

For my Mother
Hanne Nim Karemaker,

You have given me literally everything.
I love and admire you deeply.

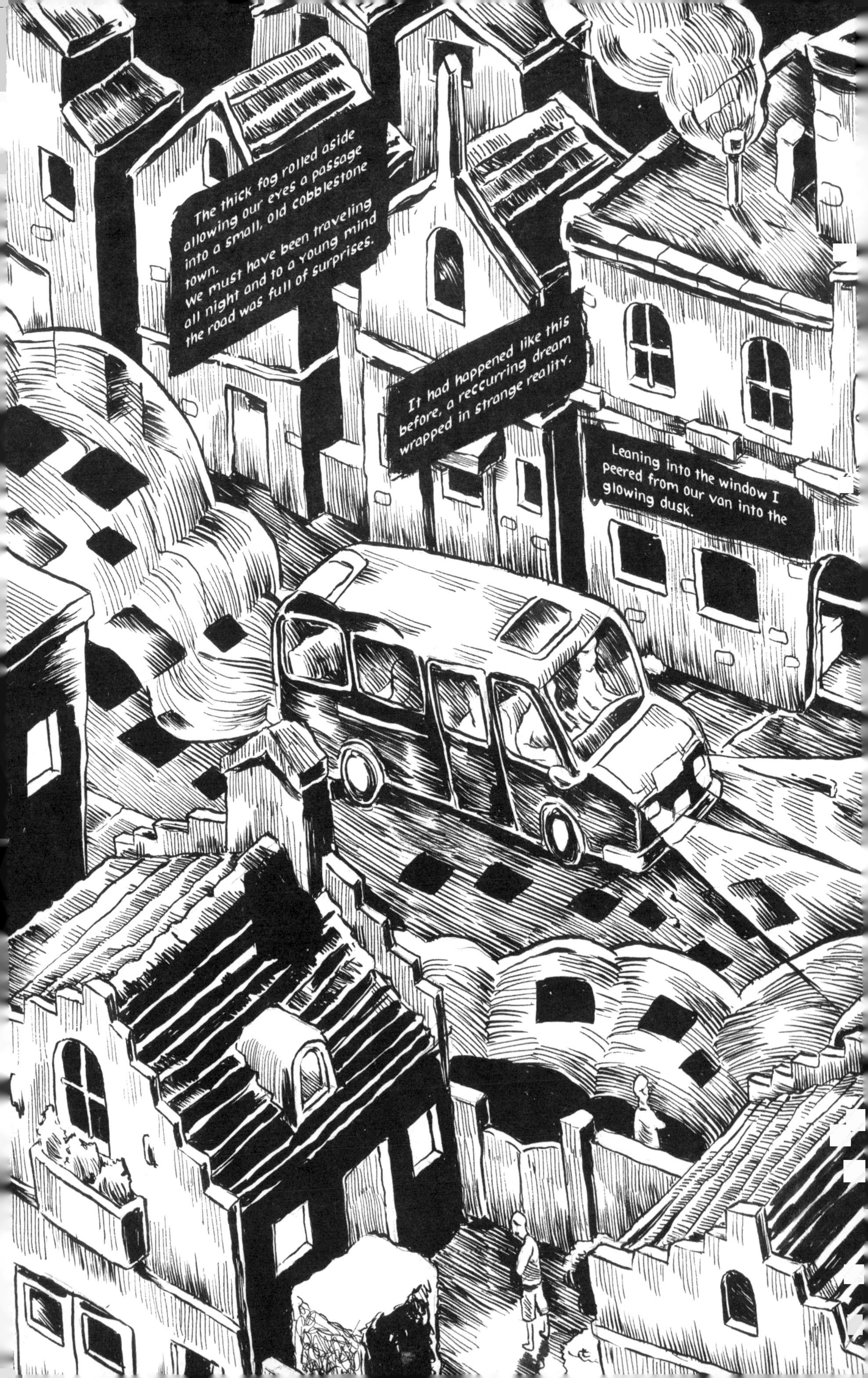
The thick fog rolled aside allowing our eyes a passage into a small, old cobblestone town.
We must have been traveling all night and to a young mind the road was full of surprises.
It had happened like this before, a reccurring dream wrapped in strange reality.
Leaning into the window I peered from our van into the glowing dusk.

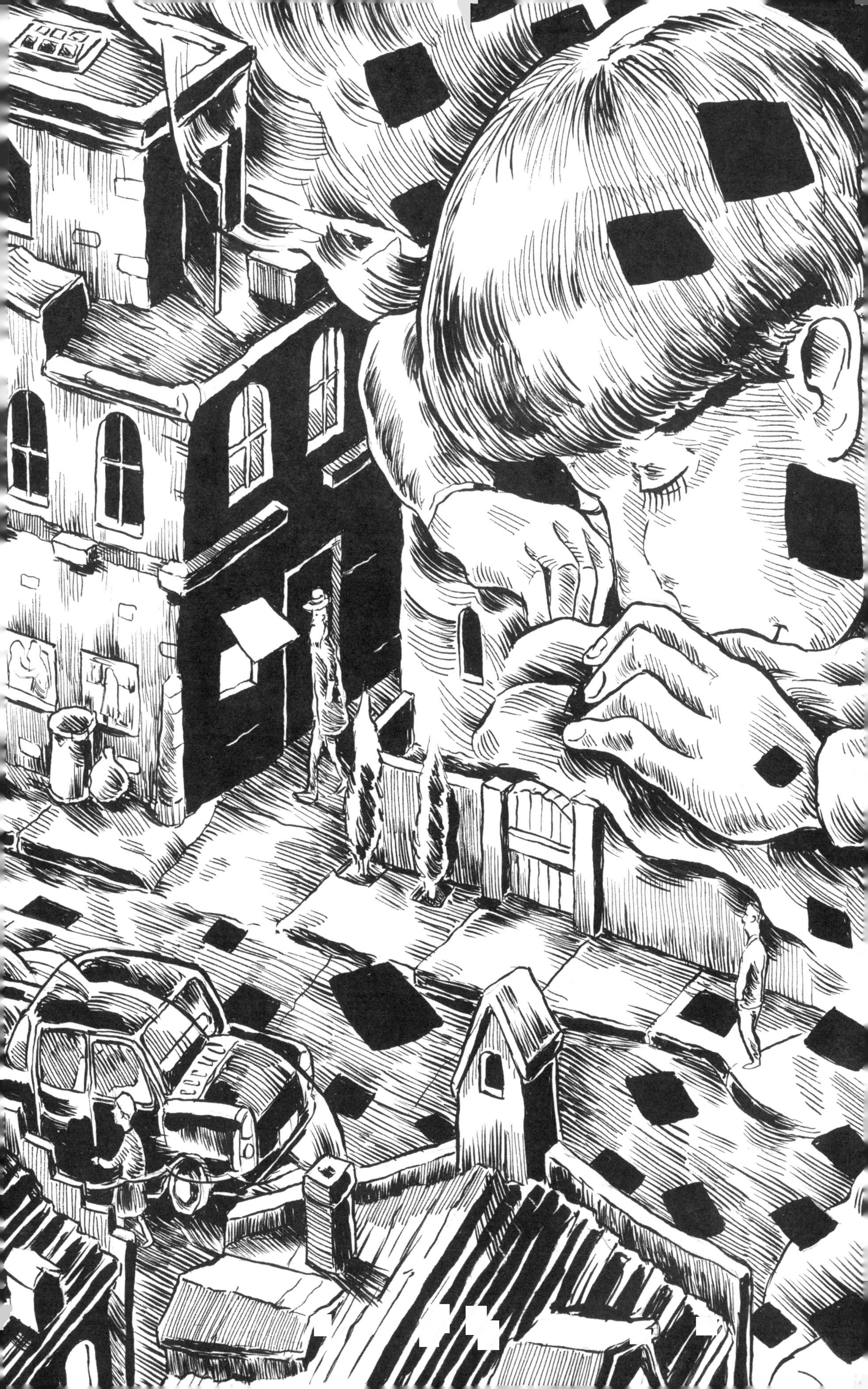

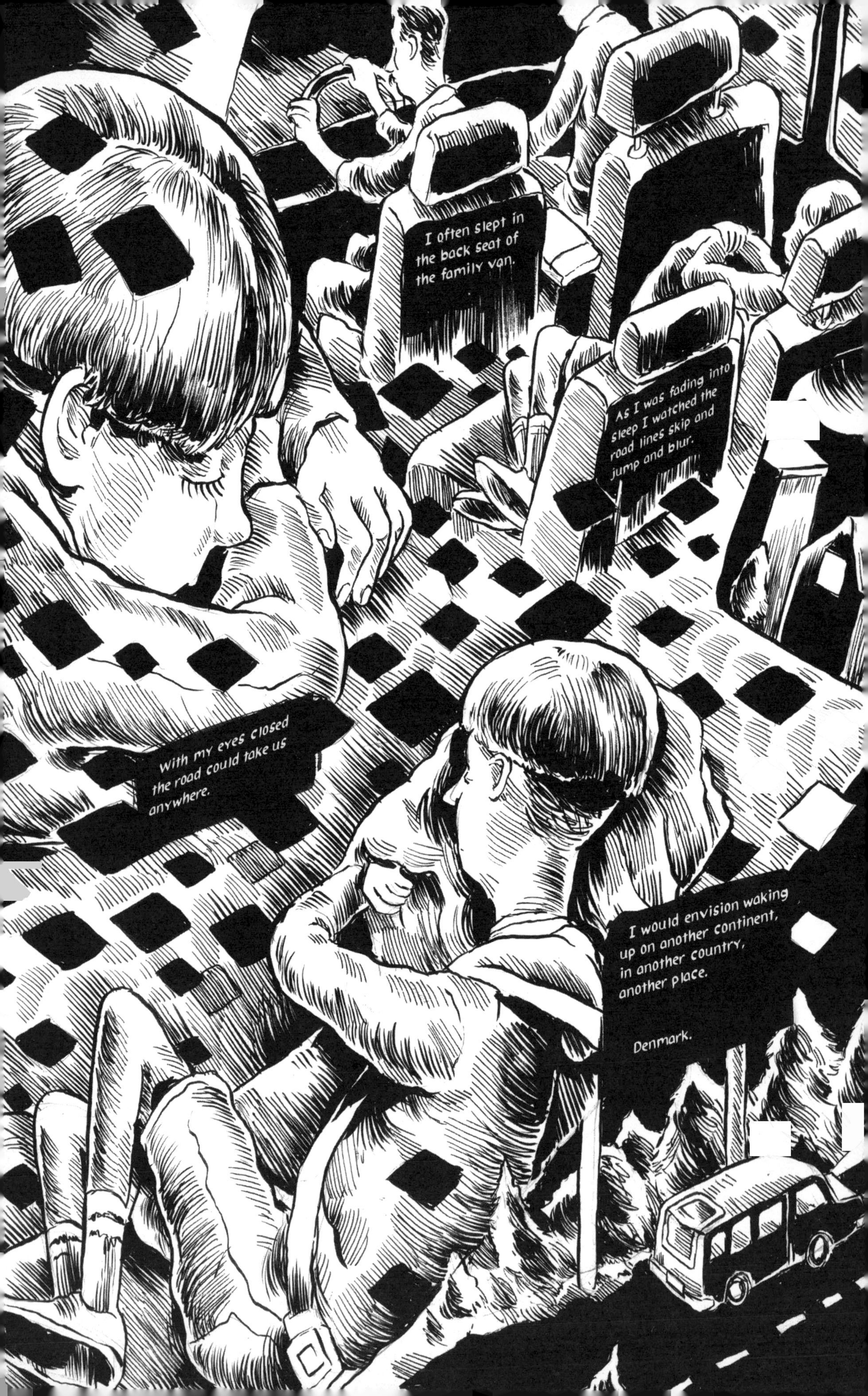
I often slept in the back seat of the family van.
As I was fading into sleep I watched the road lines skip and jump and blur.
With my eyes closed the road could take us anywhere.
I would envision waking up on another continent, in another country, another place.
Denmark.

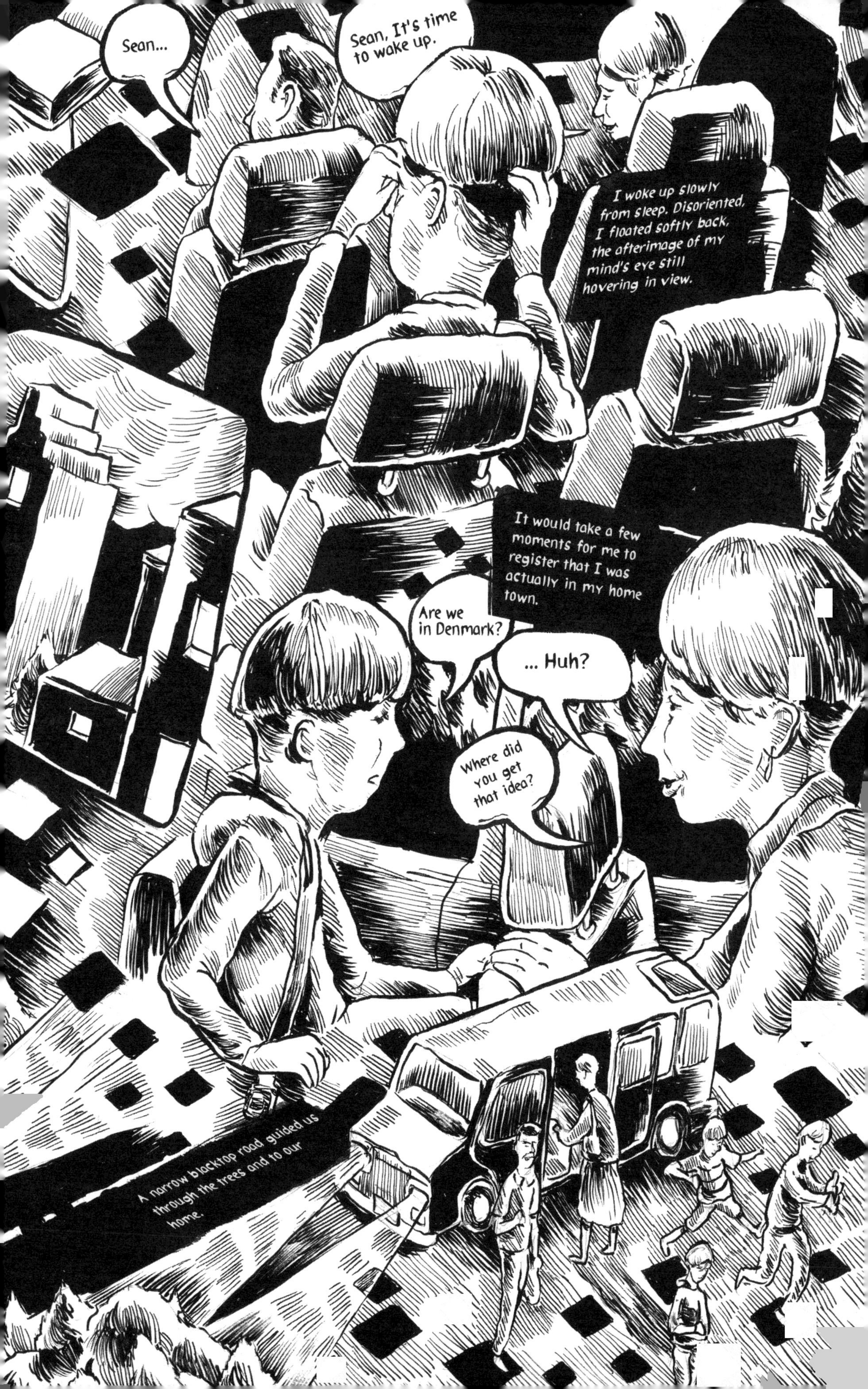
Sean...
Sean, It's time to wake up.
I woke up slowly from sleep. Disoriented, I floated softly back, the afterimage of my mind's eye still hovering in view.
It would take a few moments for me to register that I was actually in my home town.
Are we in Denmark?
... Huh?
Where did you get that idea?
A narrow blacktop road guided us through the trees and to our home.

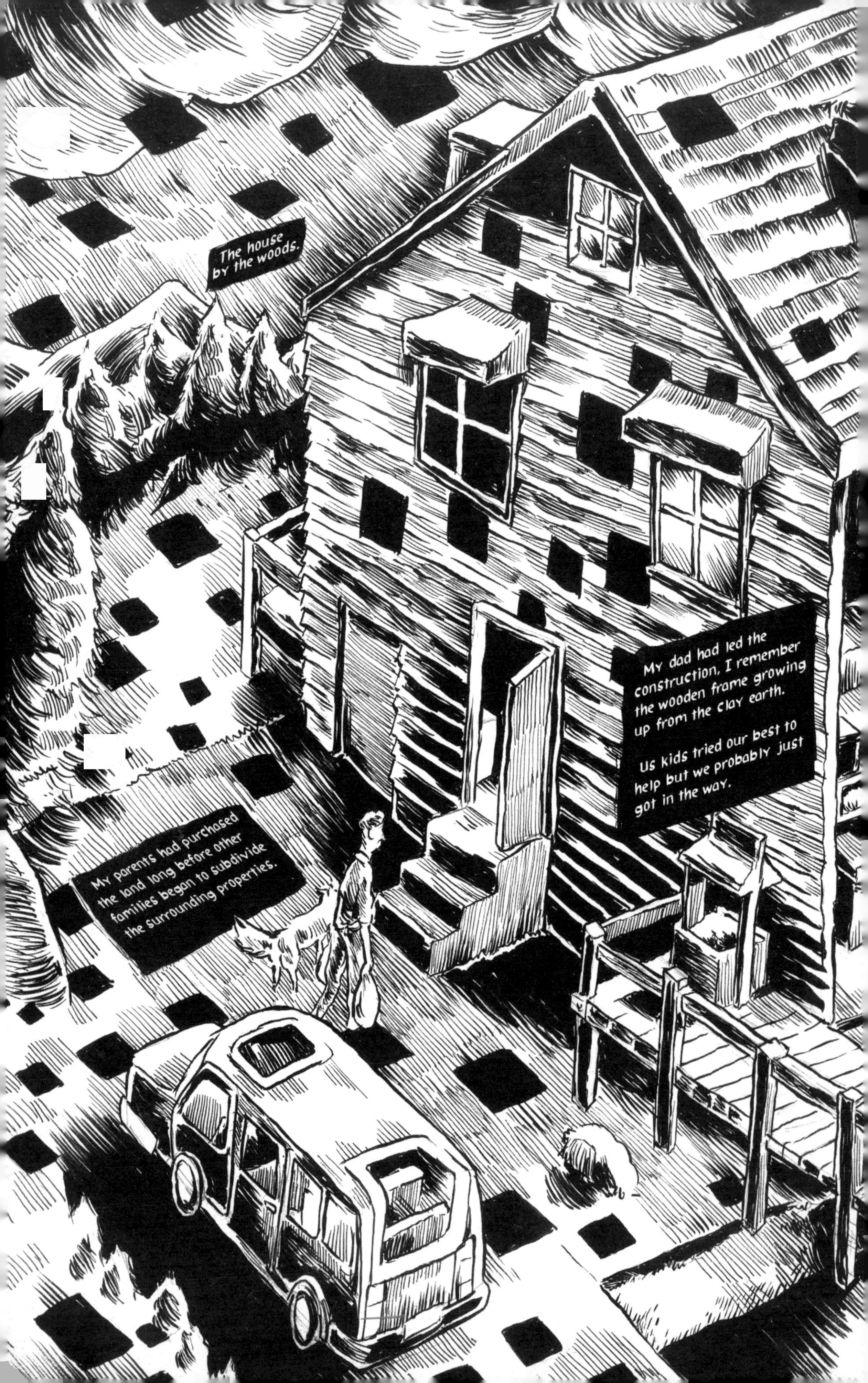
The house by the woods.
My dad had led the construction, I remember the wooden frame growing up from the clay earth.
Us kids tried our best to help but we probably just got in the way.
My parents had purchased the land long before other families began to subdivide the surrounding properties.

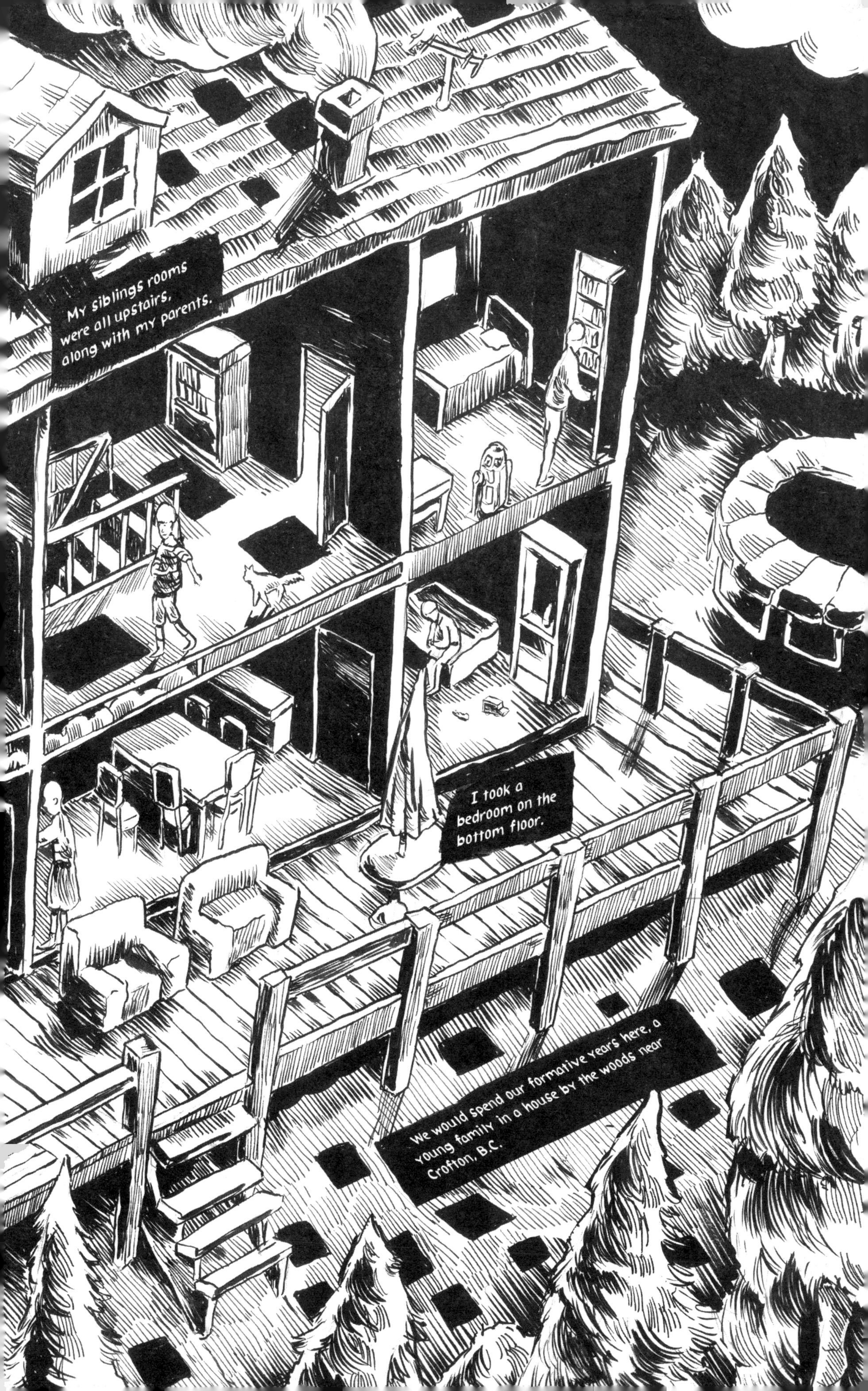
My siblings rooms were all upstairs, along with my parents.
I took a bedroom on the bottom floor.
We would spend our formative years here, a young family in a house by the woods near Crofton, B.C.

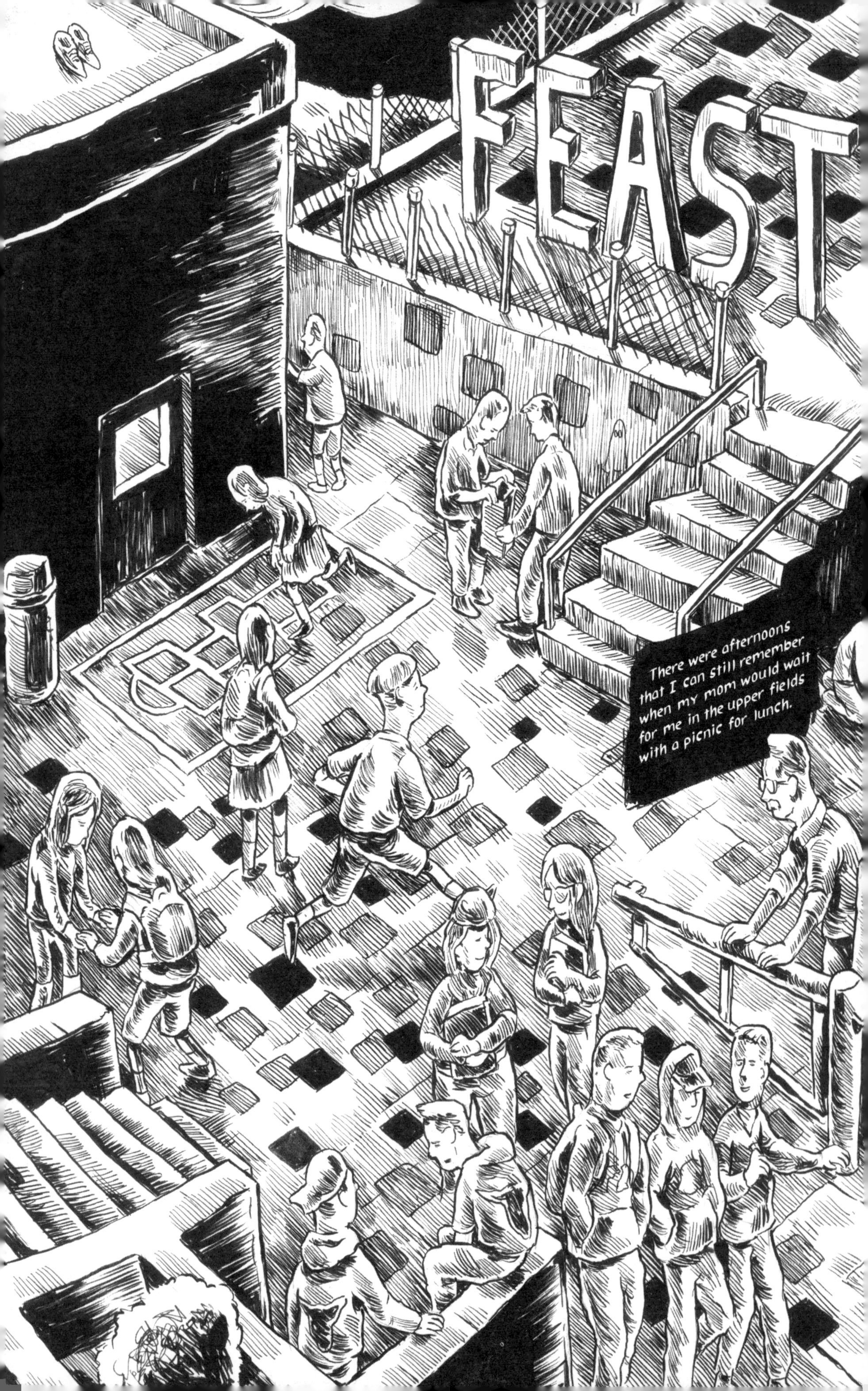
FEAST
There were afternoons that I can still remember when my mom would wait for me in the upper fields with a picnic for lunch.

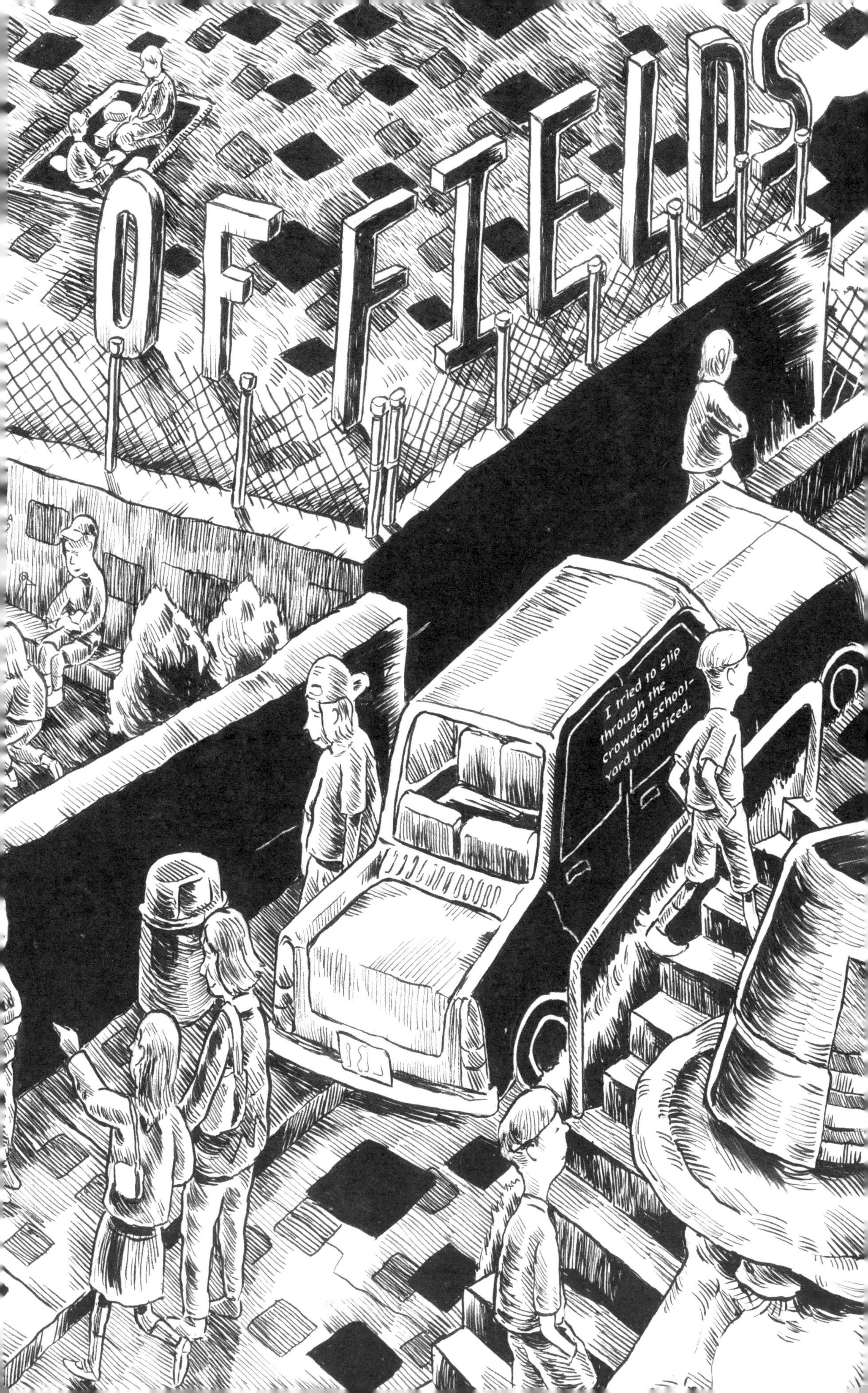
OF FIELDS
I tried to slip through the crowded school-yard unnoticed.

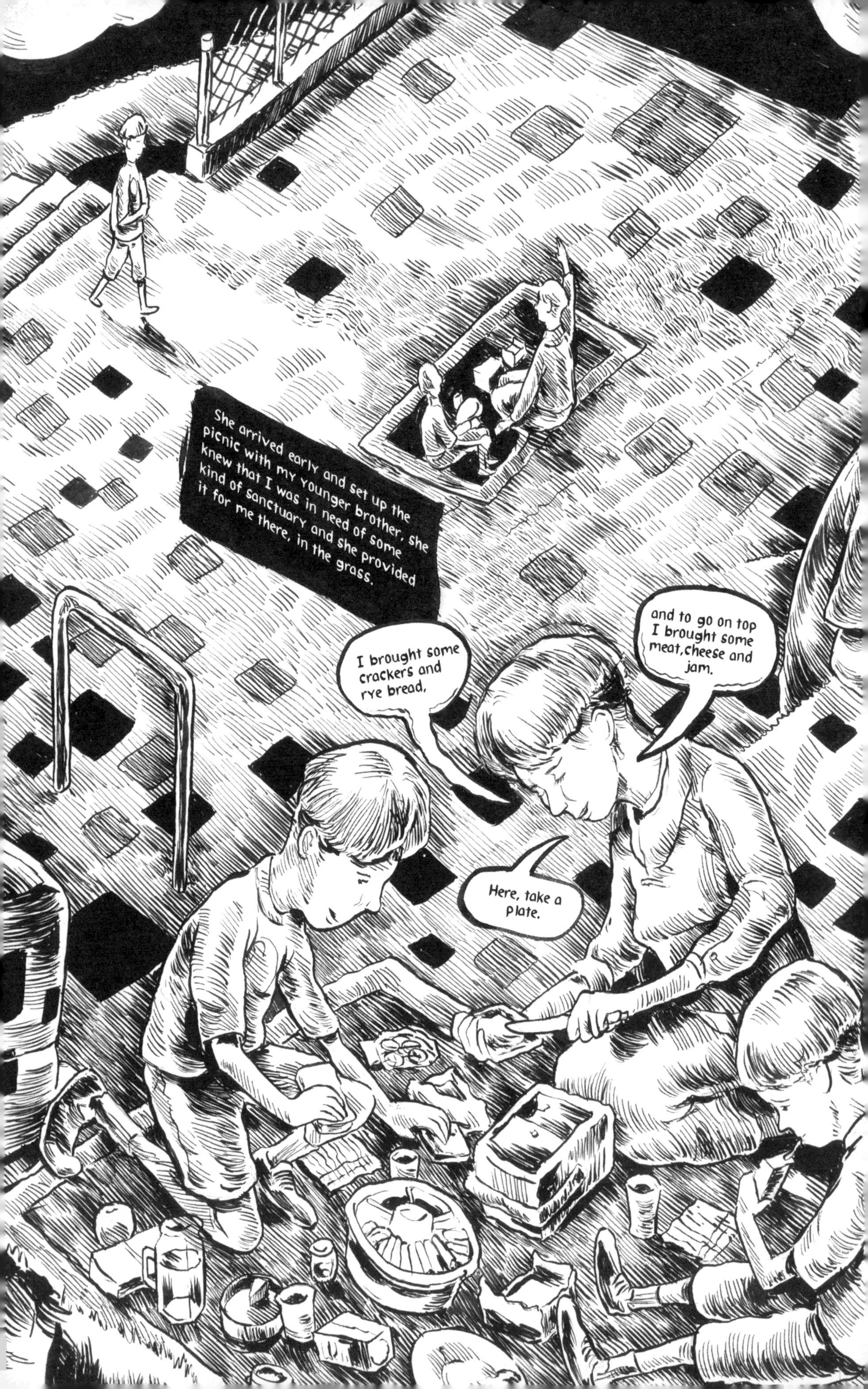
She arrived early and set up the picnic with my younger brother, she knew that I was in need of some kind of sanctuary and she provided it for me there, in the grass.
I brought some crackers and rye bread,
and to go on top I brought some meat, cheese and jam.
Here, take a plate.

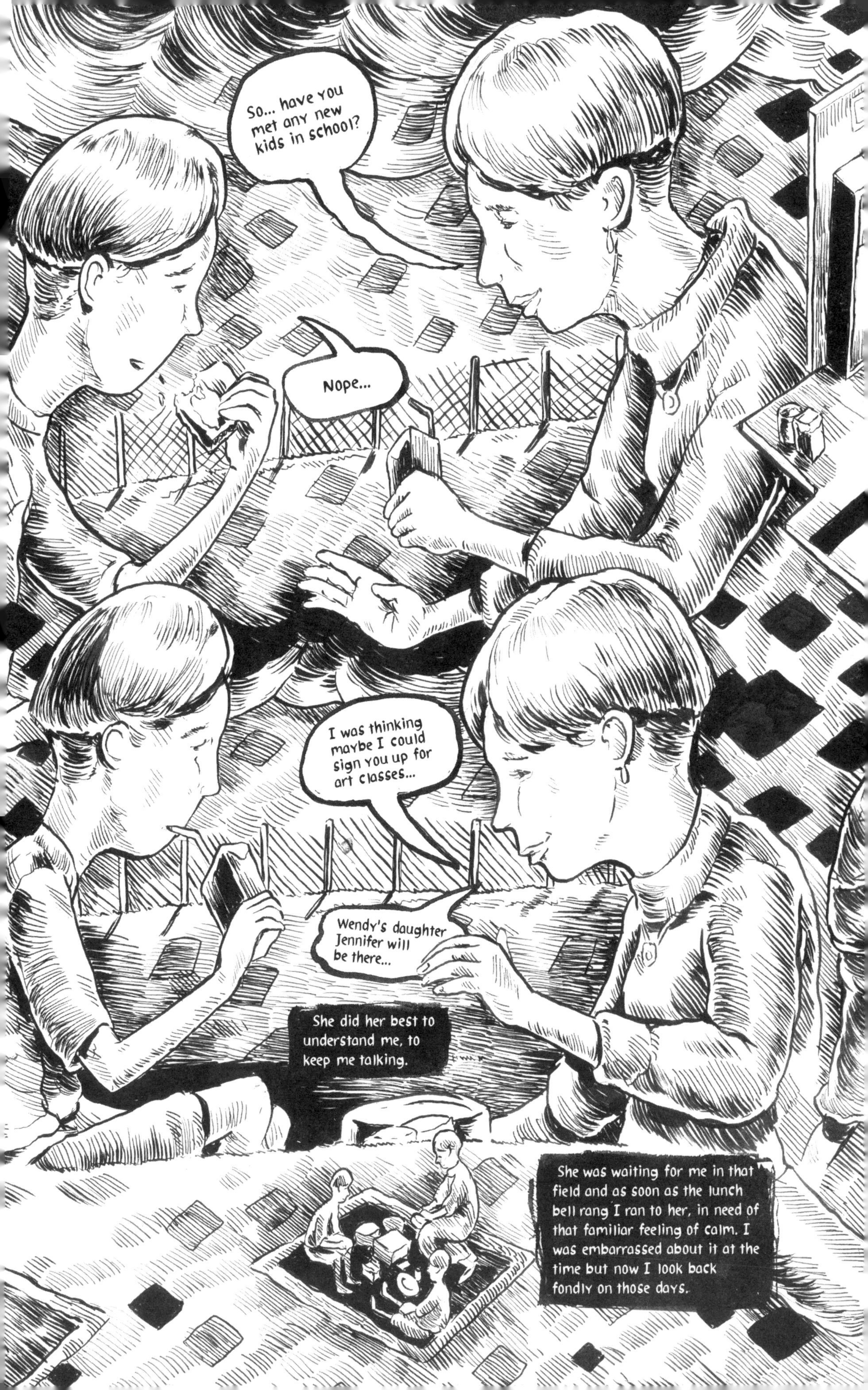
So... have you met any new kids in school?
Nope...
I was thinking maybe I could sign you up for art classes...
Wendy's daughter Jennifer will be there...
She did her best to understand me, to keep me talking.
She was waiting for me in that field and as soon as the lunch bell rang I ran to her, in need of that familiar feeling of calm. I was embarrassed about it at the time but now I look back fondly on those days.

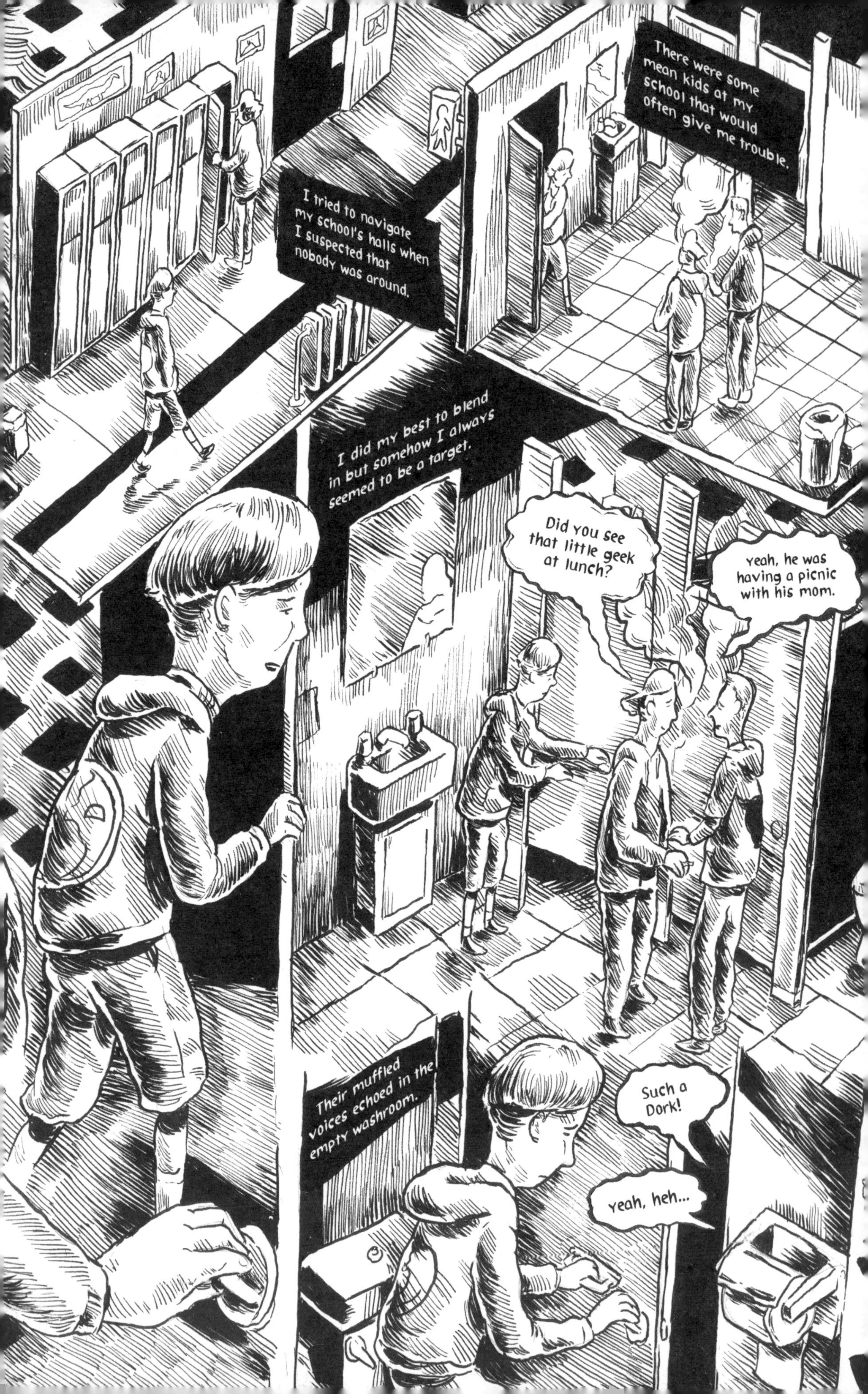
I tried to navigate my school's halls when I suspected that nobody was around.
There were some mean kids at my school that would often give me trouble.
I did my best to blend in but somehow I always seemed to be a target.
Did you see that little geek at lunch?
Yeah, he was having a picnic with his mom.
Their muffled voices echoed in the empty washroom.
Such a Dork!
Yeah, heh...

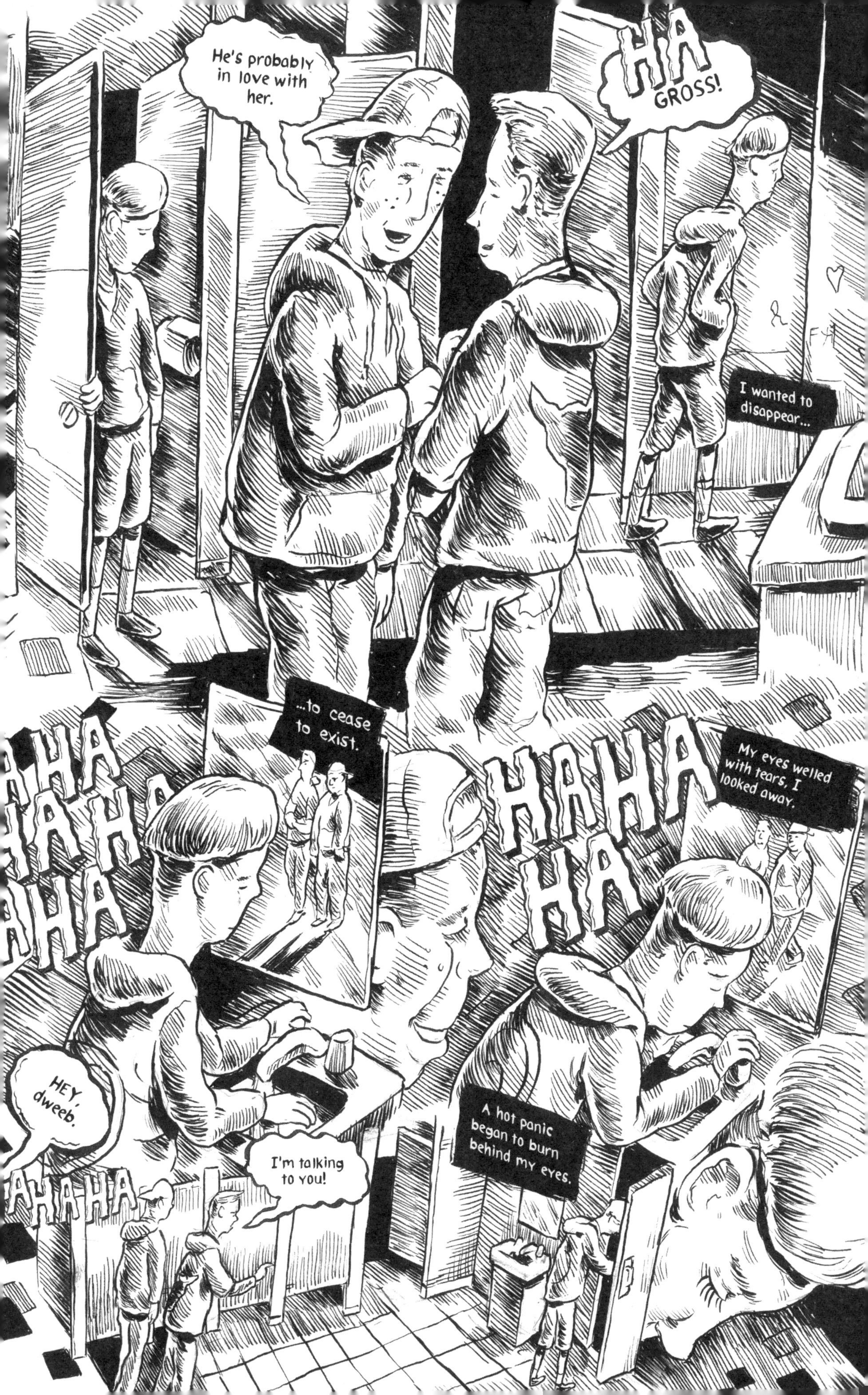
He's probably in love with her.
HA GROSS!
I wanted to disappear...
...to cease to exist.
HA HA HA HA
HEY, dweeb.
HAHAHA
I'm talking to you!
HAHAHA HA
My eyes welled with tears, I looked away.
A hot panic began to burn behind my eyes.

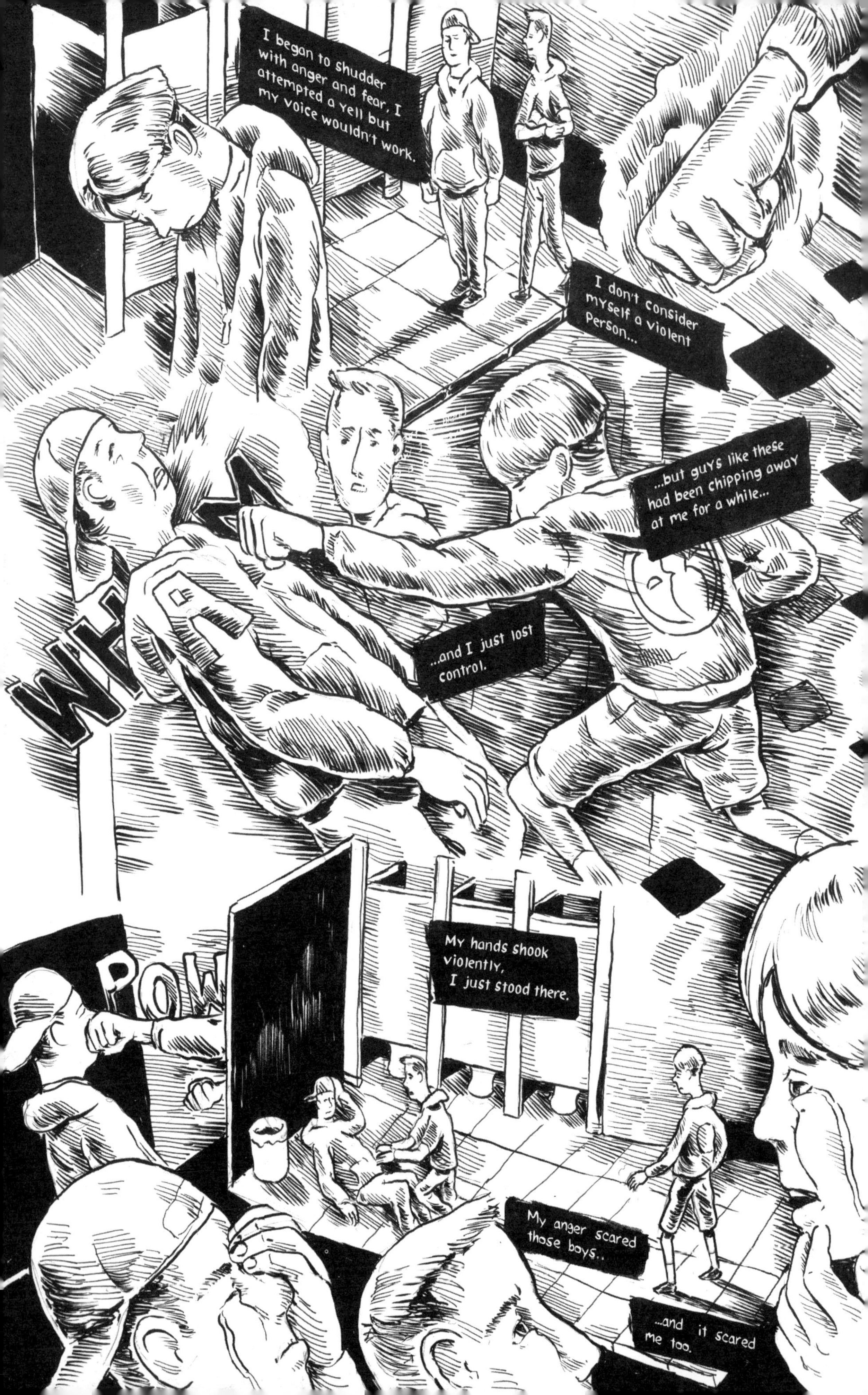
I began to shudder with anger and fear, I attempted a yell but my voice wouldn't work.
I don't consider myself a violent Person...
...but guys like these had been chipping away at me for a while...
...and I just lost control.
WHA
POW
My hands shook violently, I just stood there.
My anger scared those boys..
...and it scared me too.

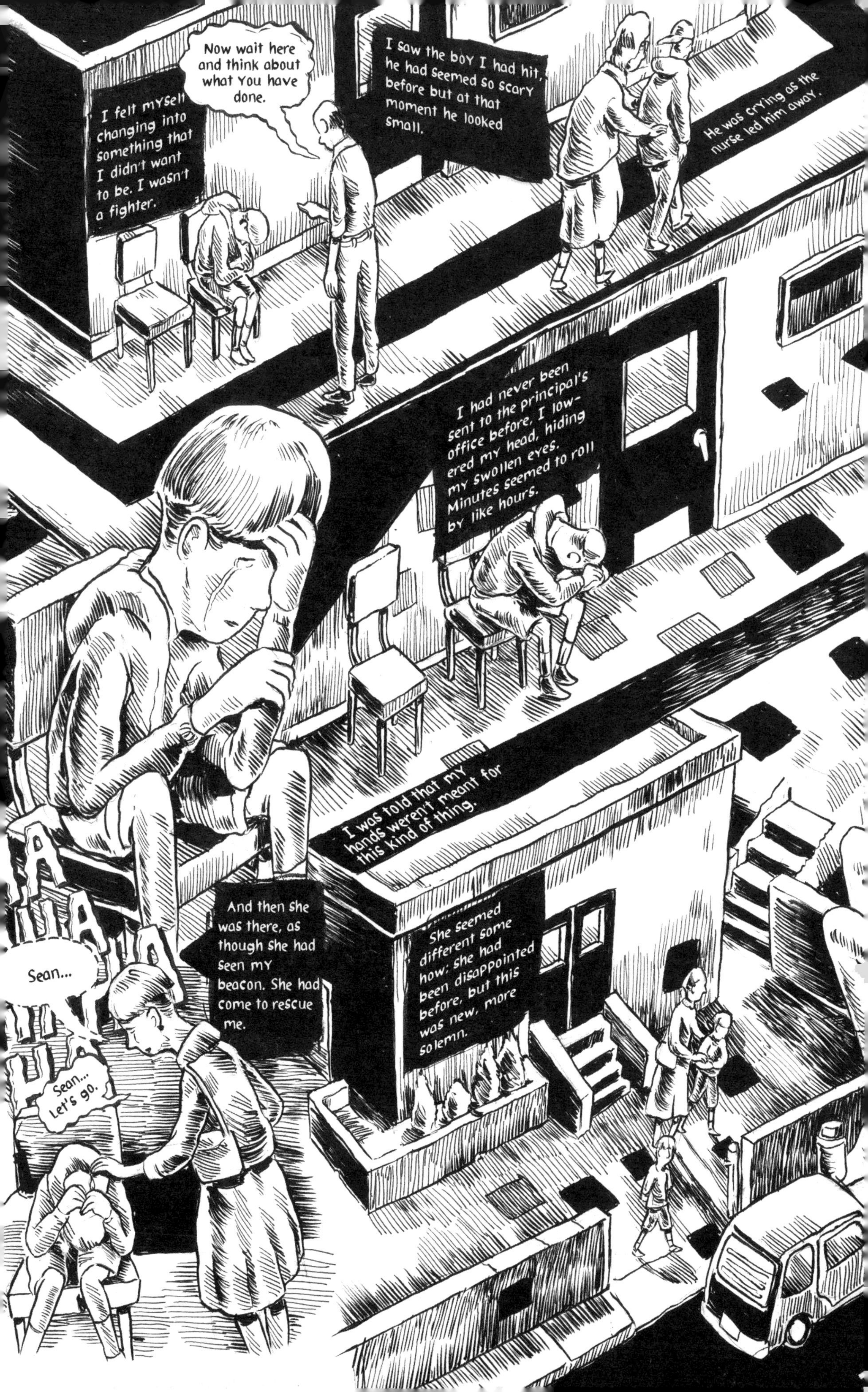
I felt myself changing into something that I didn't want to be. I wasn't a fighter.
Now wait here and think about what you have done.
I saw the boy I had hit, he had seemed so scary before but at that moment he looked small.
He was crying as the nurse led him away.
I had never been sent to the principal's office before, I lowered my head, hiding my swollen eyes. Minutes seemed to roll by like hours.
I was told that my hands weren't meant for this kind of thing.
And then she was there, as though she had seen my beacon. She had come to rescue me.
She seemed different somehow; she had been disappointed before, but this was new, more solemn.
Sean...
Sean... Let's go.

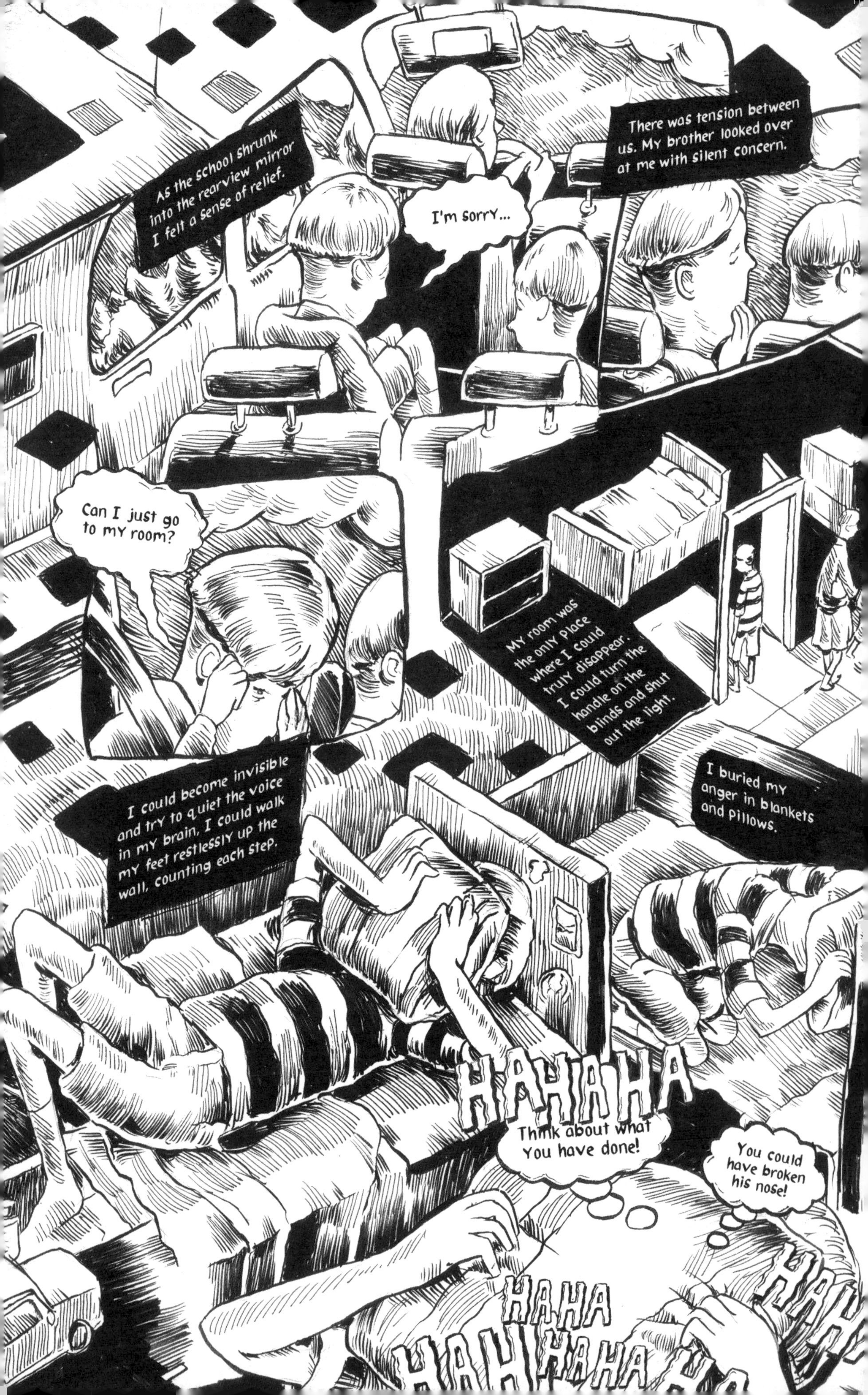
As the school shrunk into the rearview mirror I felt a sense of relief.
I'm sorry...
There was tension between us. My brother looked over at me with silent concern.
Can I just go to my room?
My room was the only place where I could truly disappear. I could turn the handle on the blinds and shut out the light.
I could become invisible and try to quiet the voice in my brain, I could walk my feet restlessly up the wall, counting each step.
I buried my anger in blankets and pillows.
HAHAHA
Think about what you have done!
You could have broken his nose!
HAHA
HAHHAHAHA

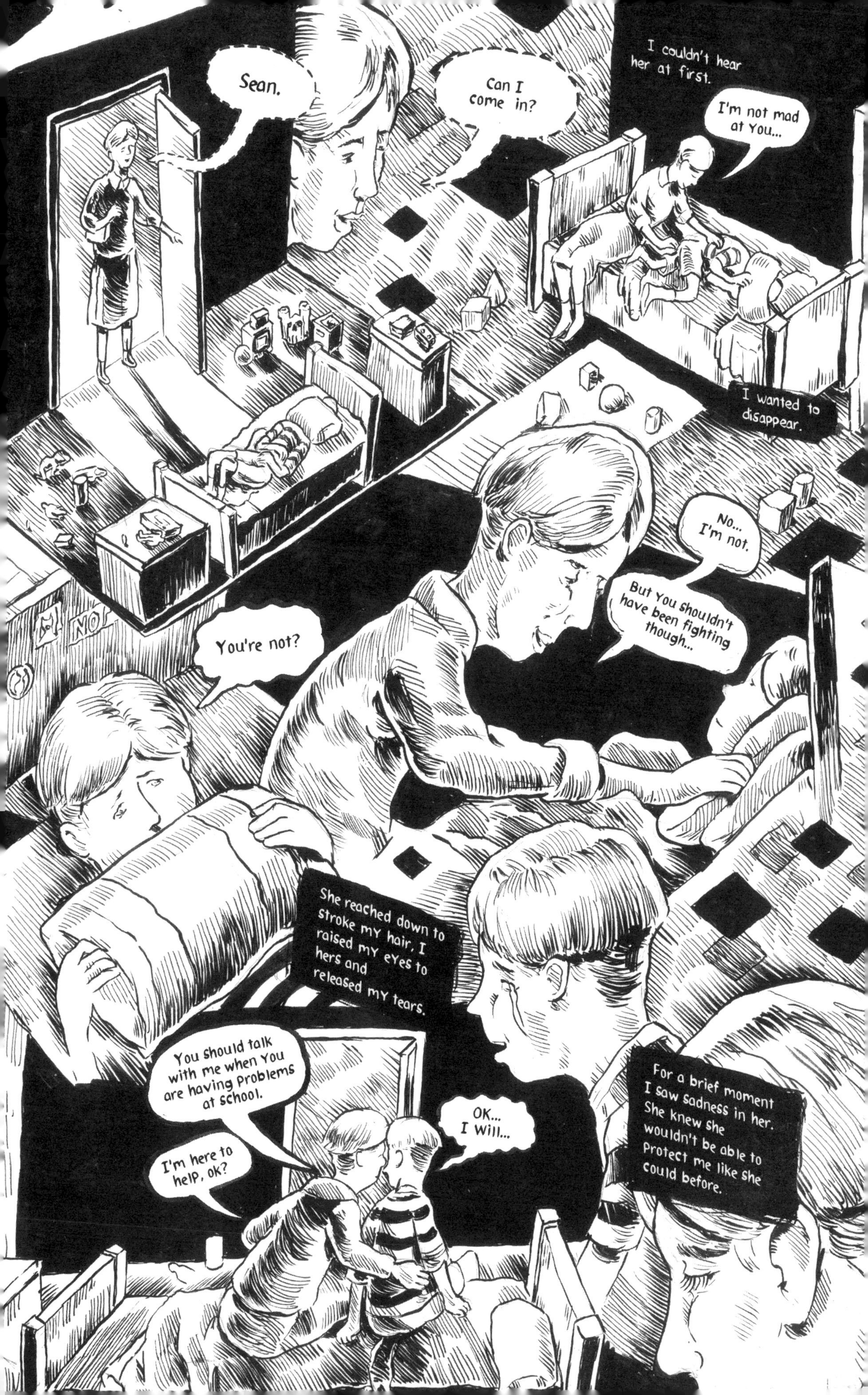
Sean.
Can I come in?
I couldn't hear her at first.
I'm not mad at You...
I wanted to disappear.
No... I'm not.
But You shouldn't have been fighting though...
You're not?
She reached down to stroke MY hair, I raised MY eYes to hers and released MY tears.
You should talk with me when You are having Problems at school.
I'm here to help, ok?
OK... I will...
For a brief moment I saw sadness in her. She knew she wouldn't be able to protect me like she could before.

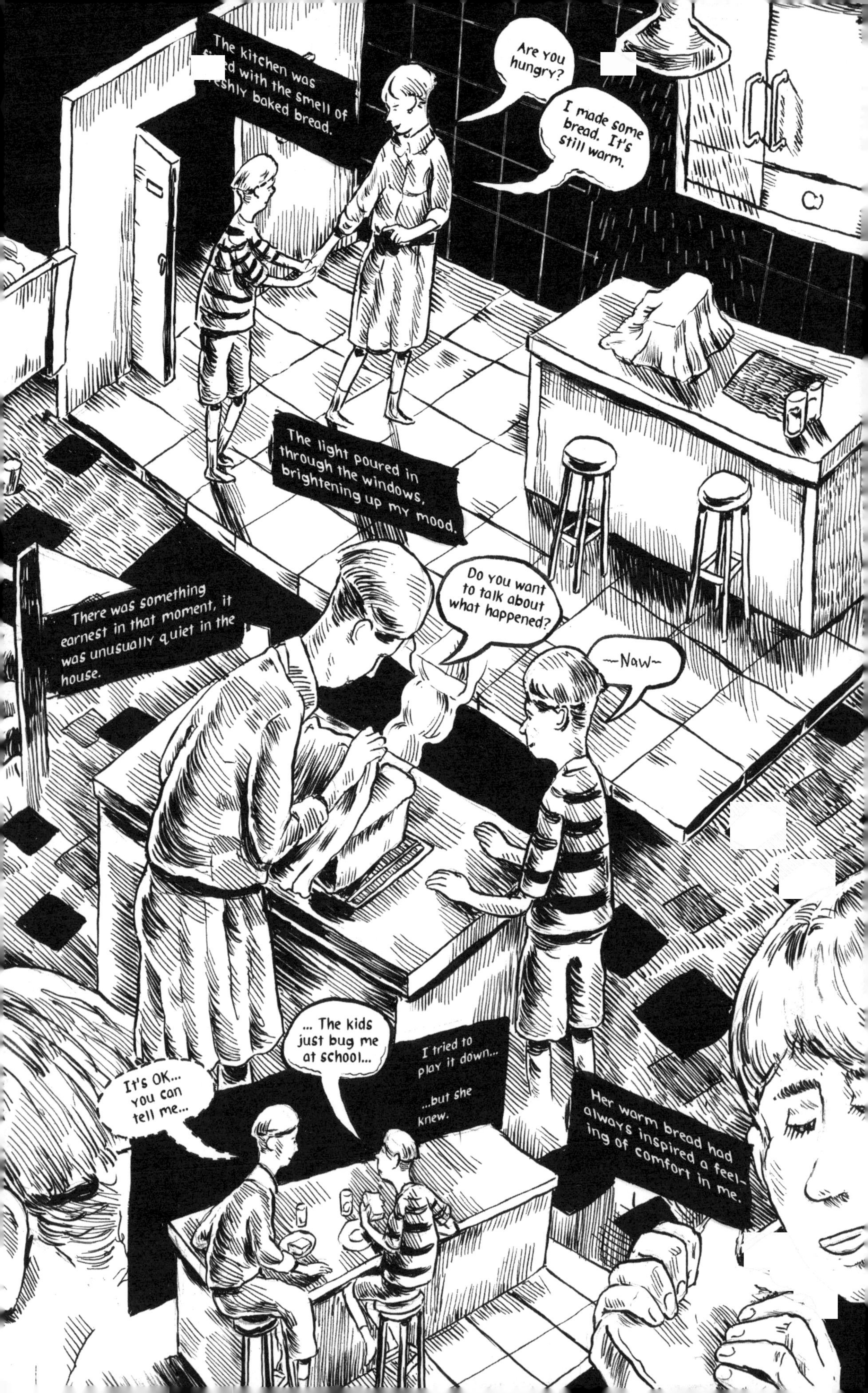
The kitchen was
d with the smell of
eshly baked bread.
Are you hungry?
I made some bread. It's still warm.
The light poured in through the windows, brightening up my mood.
There was something earnest in that moment, it was unusually quiet in the house.
Do you want to talk about what happened?
~Naw~
It's OK... you can tell me...
... The kids just bug me at school...
I tried to play it down...
...but she knew.
Her warm bread had always inspired a feel-ing of comfort in me.

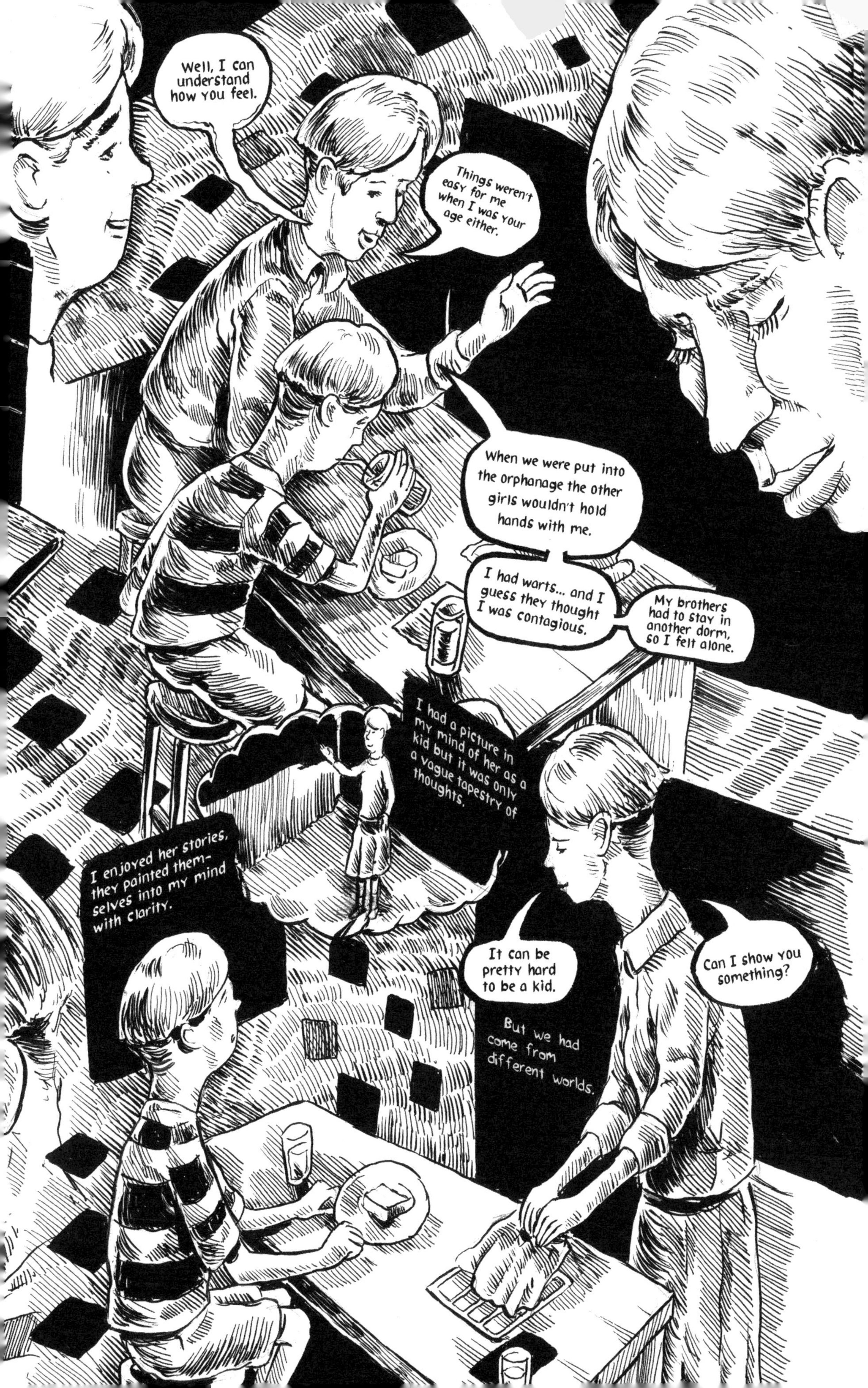

Well, I can understand how you feel.
Things weren't easy for me when I was your age either.
When we were put into the orphanage the other girls wouldn't hold hands with me.
I had warts... and I guess they thought I was contagious.
My brothers had to stay in another dorm, so I felt alone.
I had a picture in my mind of her as a kid but it was only a vague tapestry of thoughts.
I enjoyed her stories, they painted themselves into my mind with clarity.
It can be pretty hard to be a kid.
Can I show you something?
But we had come from different worlds.

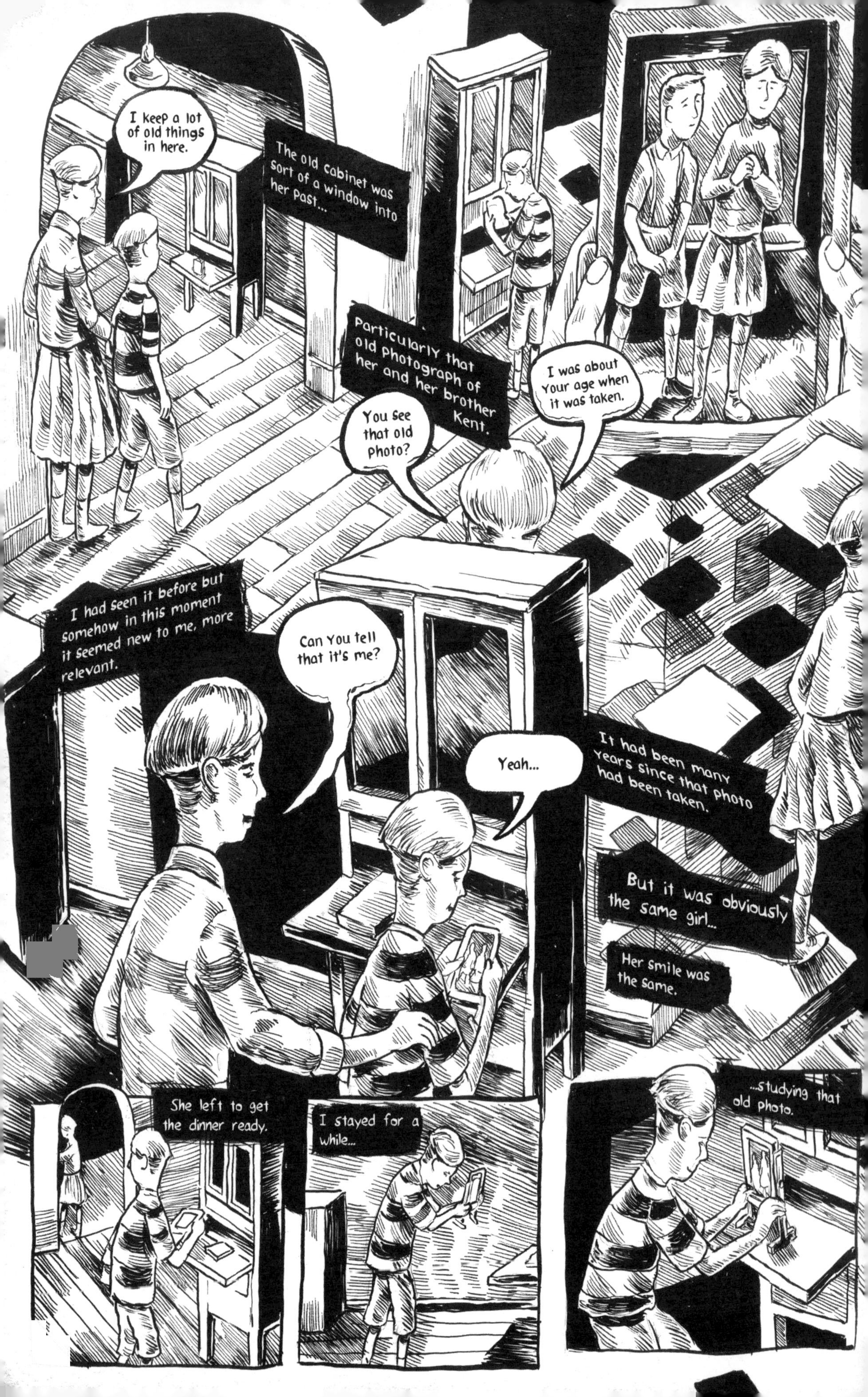
I keep a lot of old things in here.
The old cabinet was sort of a window into her past...
Particularly that old photograph of her and her brother Kent.
You see that old photo?
I was about your age when it was taken.
I had seen it before but somehow in this moment it seemed new to me, more relevant.
Can you tell that it's me?
Yeah...
It had been many years since that photo had been taken.
But it was obviously the same girl...
Her smile was the same.
She left to get the dinner ready.
I stayed for a while...
...studying that old photo.

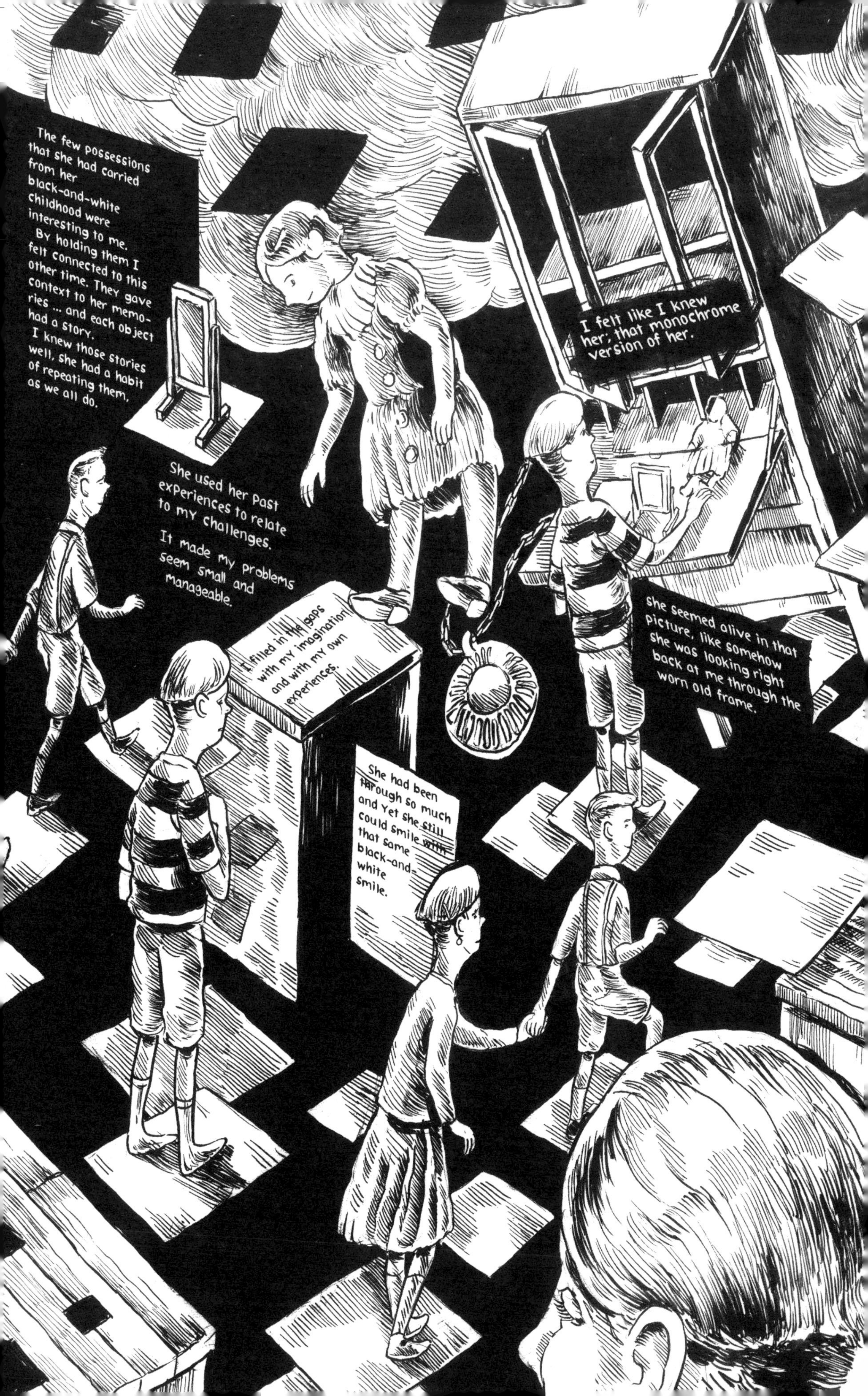
The few possessions that she had carried from her black-and-white childhood were interesting to me. By holding them I felt connected to this other time. They gave context to her memories ... and each object had a story. I knew those stories well, she had a habit of repeating them, as we all do.
I felt like I knew her; that monochrome version of her.
She used her past experiences to relate to my challenges.
It made my problems seem small and manageable.
I filled in the gaps with my imagination and with my own experiences.
She seemed alive in that picture, like somehow she was looking right back at me through the worn old frame.
She had been through so much and yet she still could smile with that same black-and-white smile.

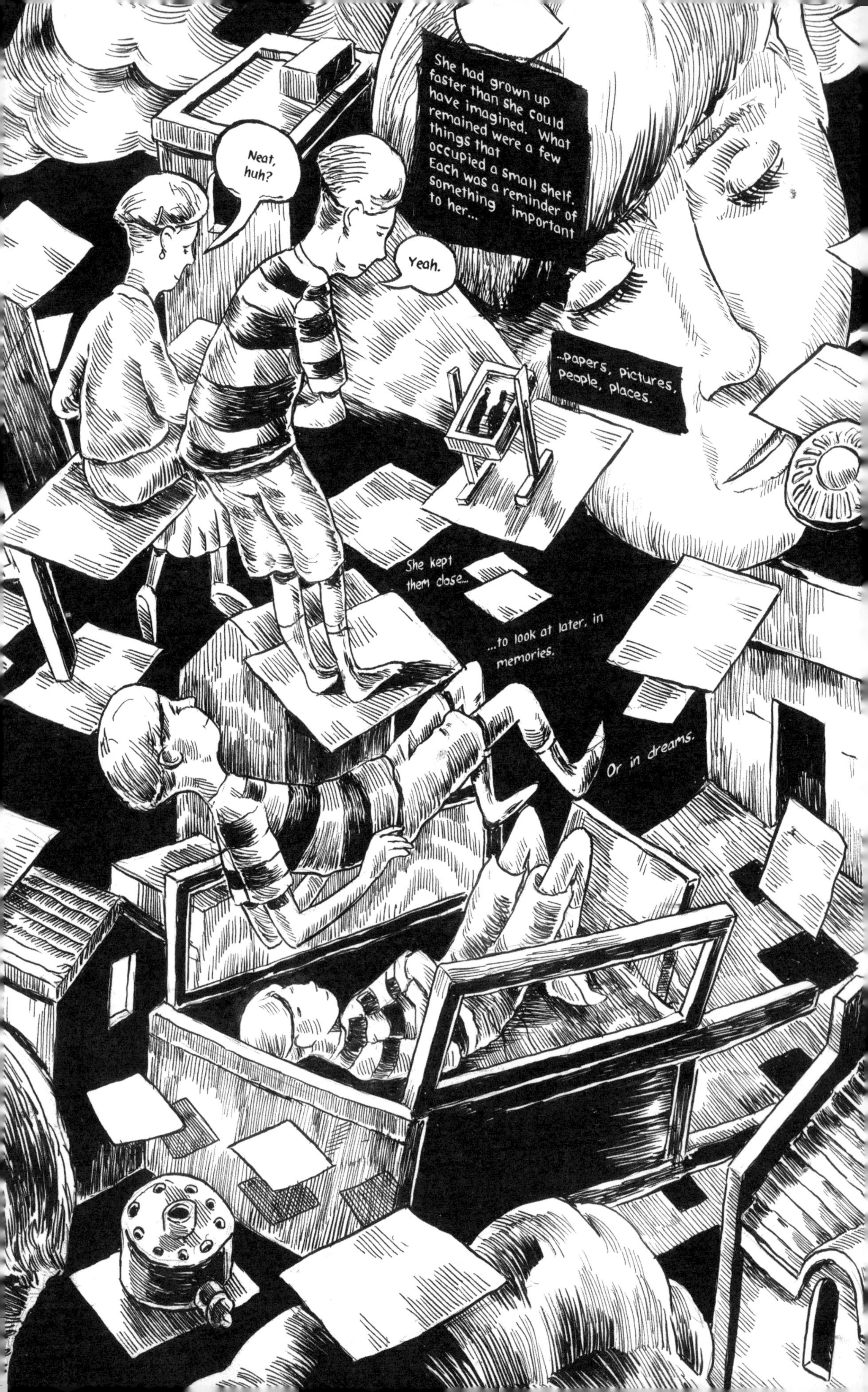
She had grown up faster than she could have imagined. What remained were a few things that occupied a small shelf. Each was a reminder of something important to her...
Neat, huh?
Yeah.
...papers, pictures, people, places.
She kept them close...
...to look at later, in memories.
Or in dreams.

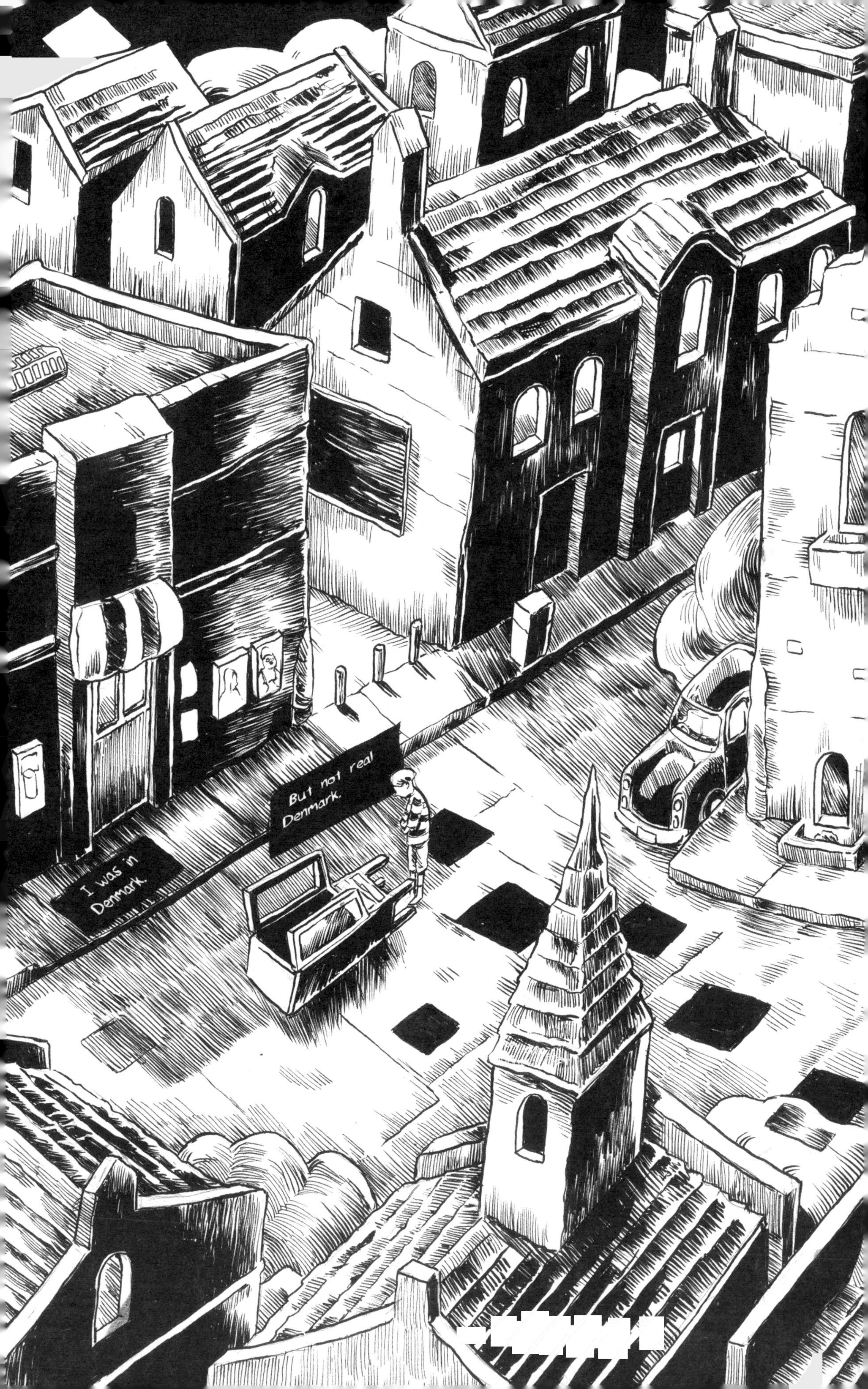
I was in Denmark.
But not real Denmark.

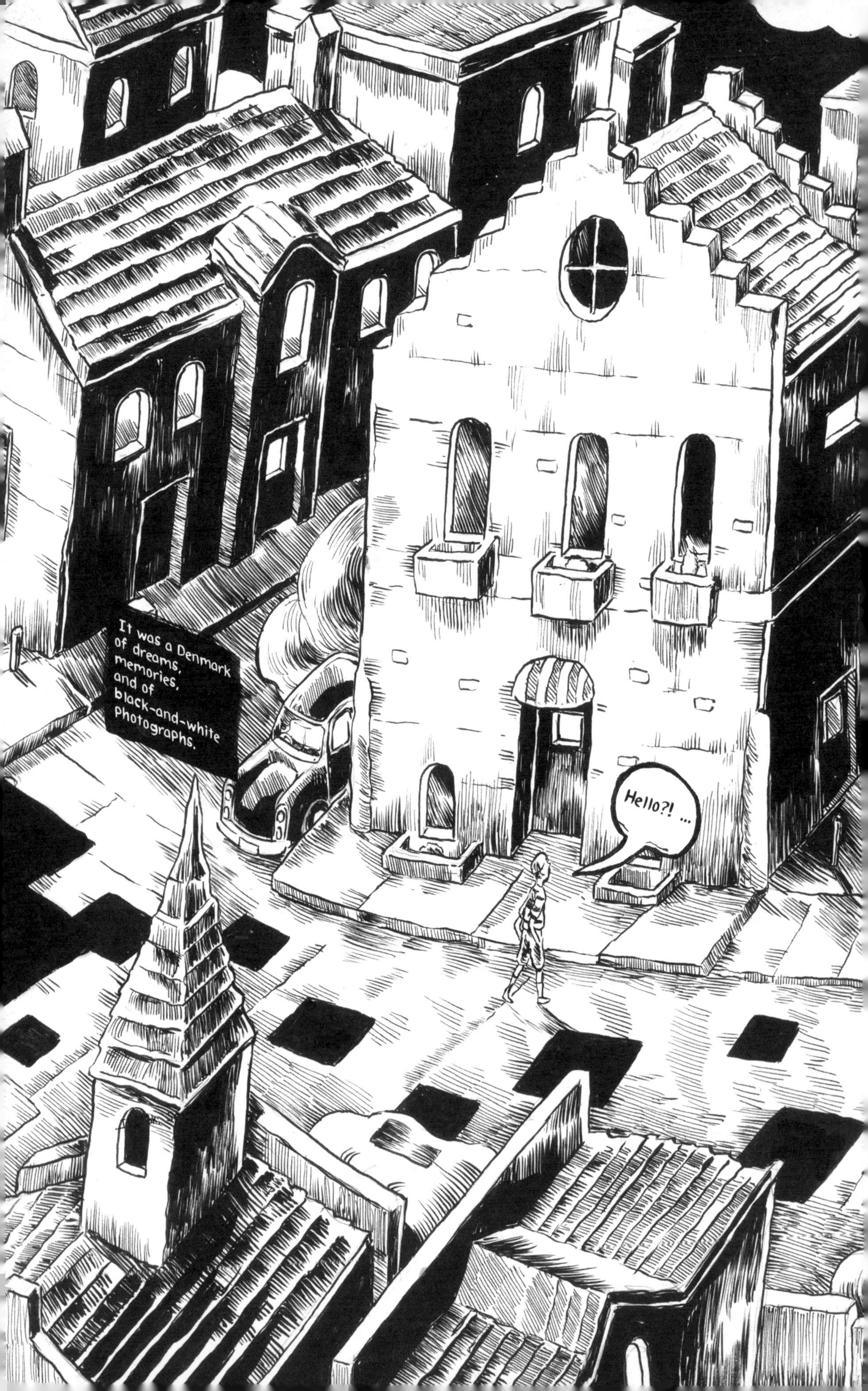
It was a Denmark of dreams, memories, and of black-and-white photographs.
Hello?! ...

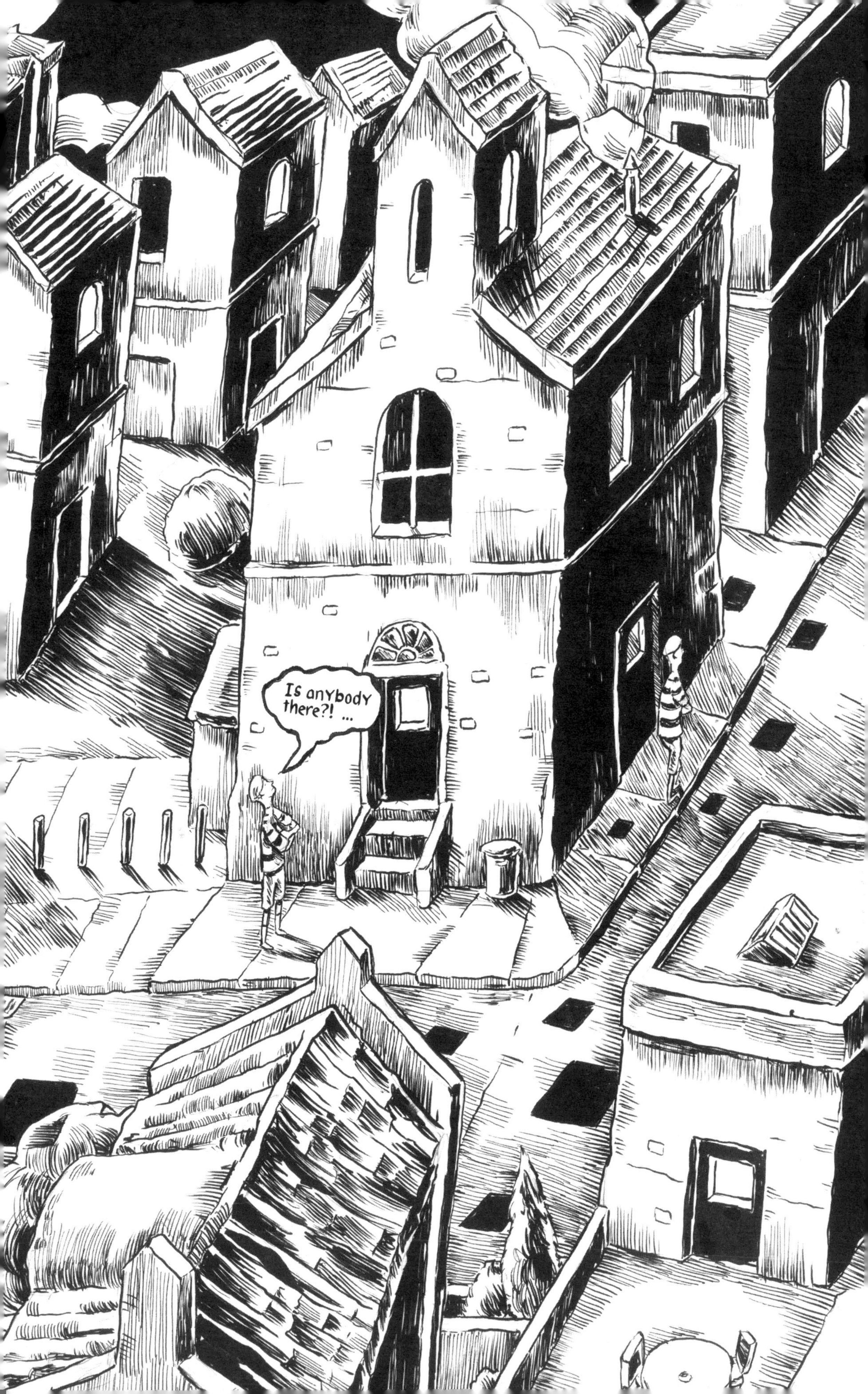
Is anybody there?! ...

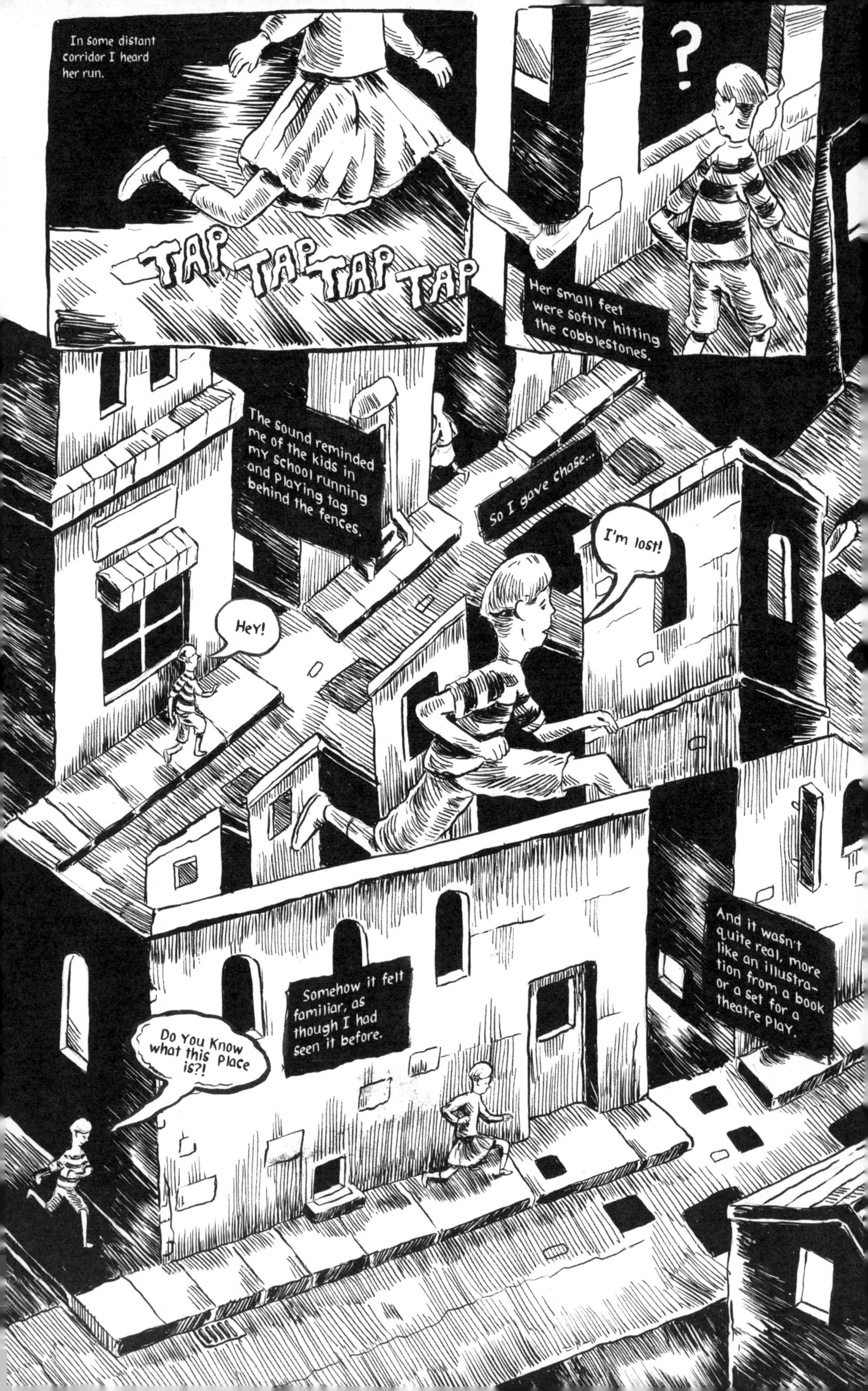
In some distant corridor I heard her run.
TAP TAP TAP TAP
?
Her small feet were softly hitting the cobblestones.
The sound reminded me of the kids in my school running and playing tag behind the fences.
So I gave chase...
I'm lost!
Hey!
And it wasn't quite real, more like an illustration from a book or a set for a theatre play.
Somehow it felt familiar, as though I had seen it before.
Do You Know what this Place is?!

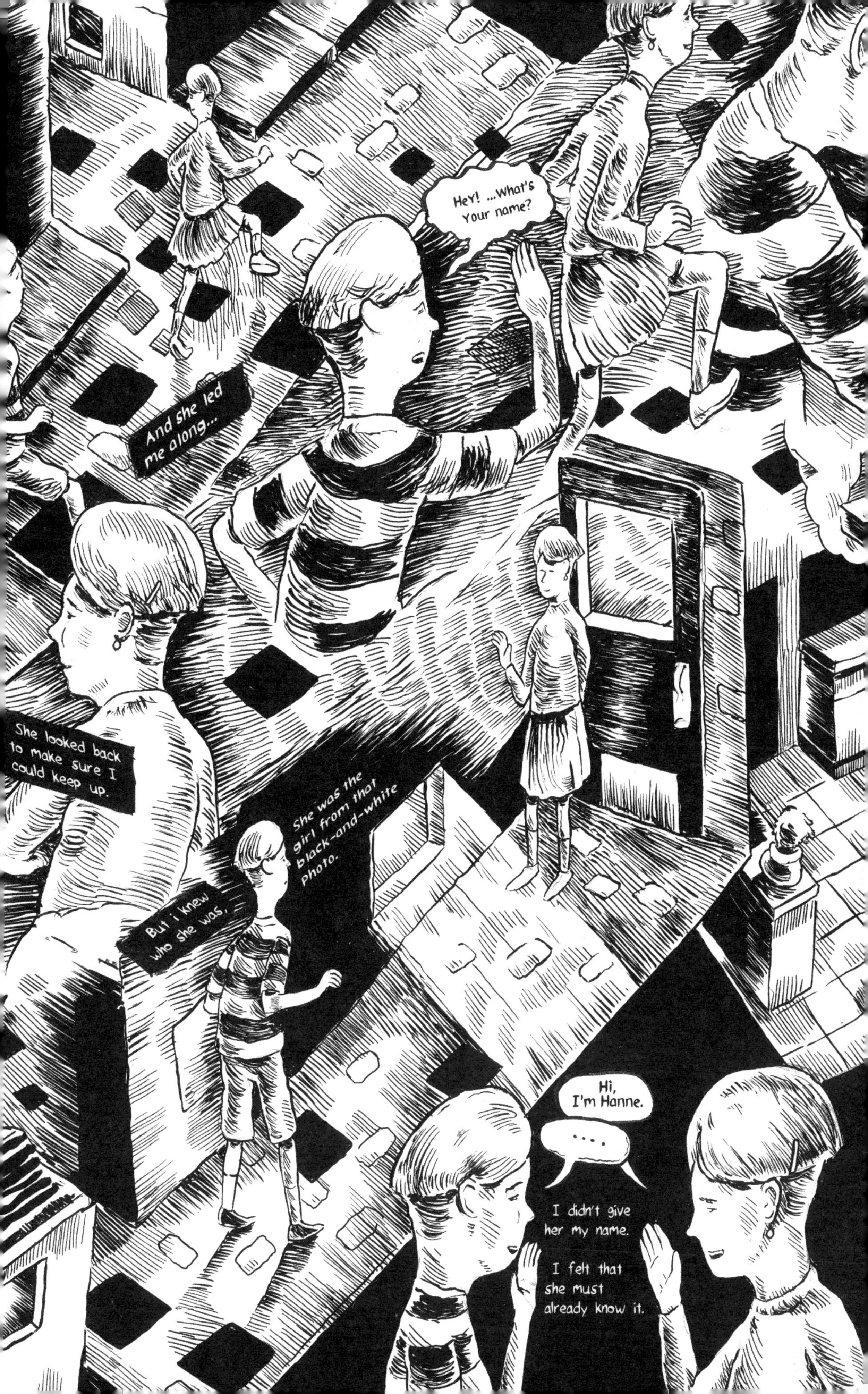
And she led me along...
Hey! ...What's your name?
She looked back to make sure I could keep up.
She was the girl from that black-and-white photo.
But i knew who she was.
Hi, I'm Hanne.
....
I didn't give her my name.
I felt that she must already know it.

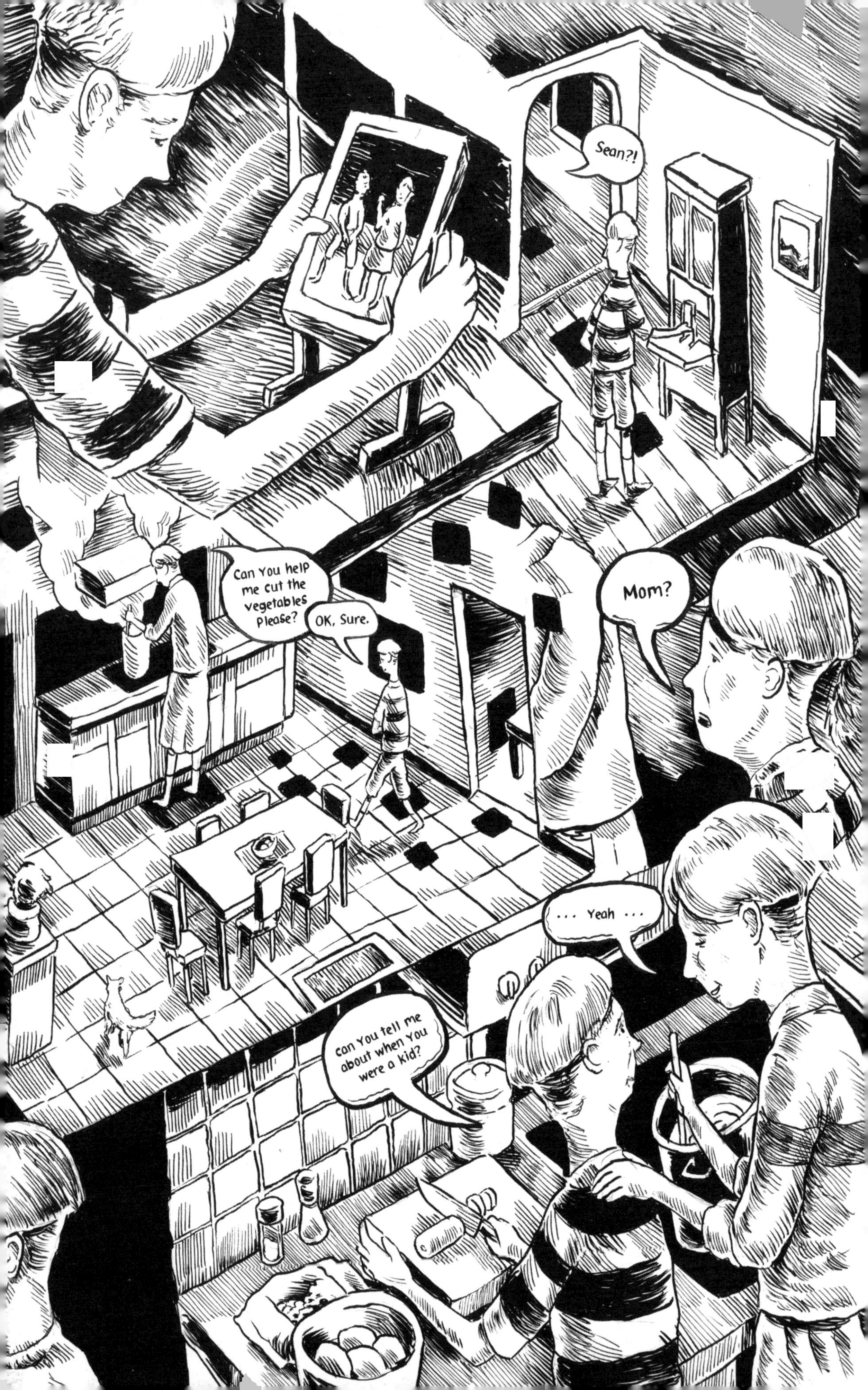
Sean?!
Can You help me cut the vegetables Please?
OK, Sure.
Mom?
... Yeah ...
Can You tell me about when You were a kid?

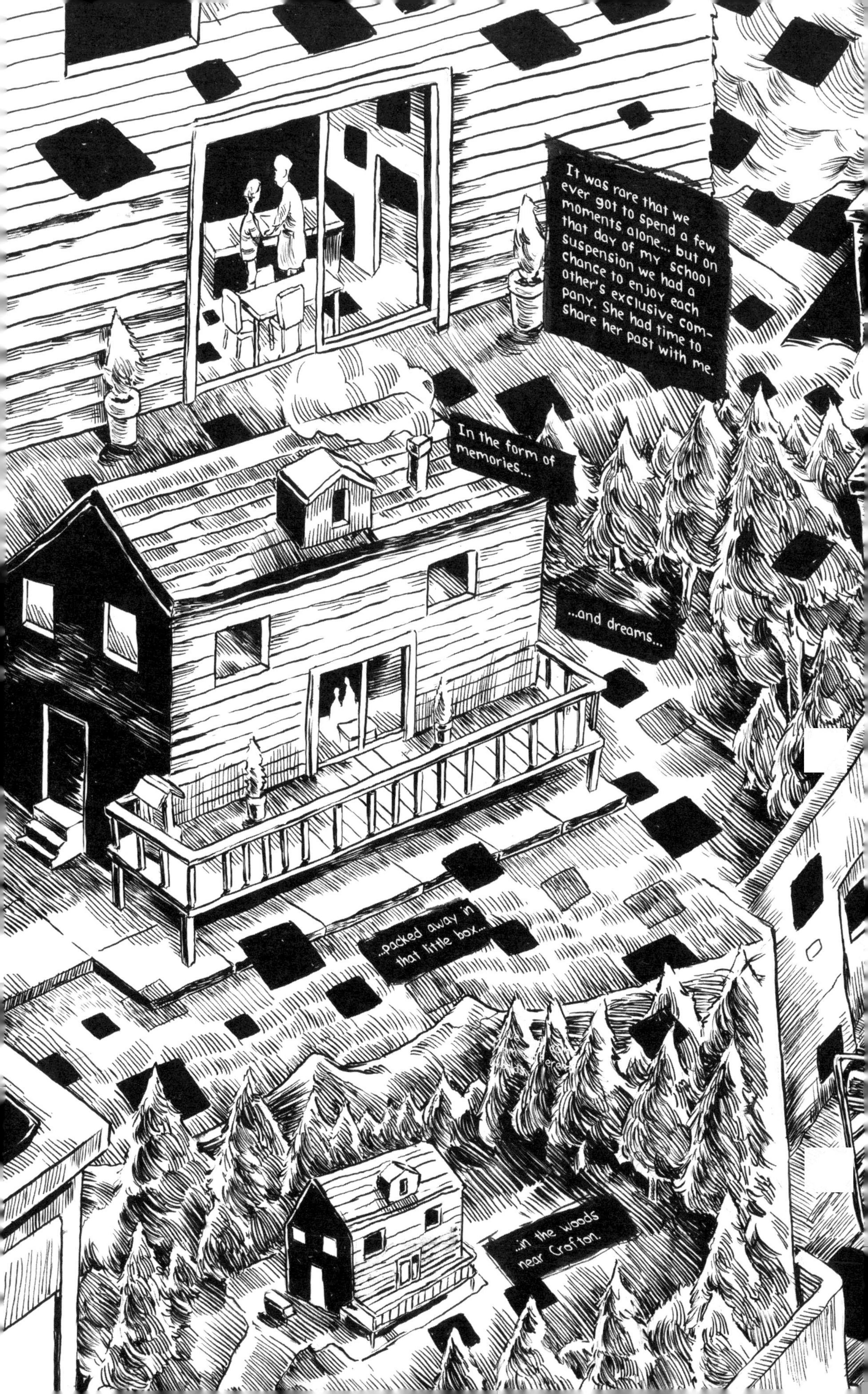
It was rare that we ever got to spend a few moments alone... but on that day of my school suspension we had a chance to enjoy each other's exclusive company. She had time to share her past with me.
In the form of memories...
...and dreams...
...packed away in that little box...
...in the woods near Crofton.

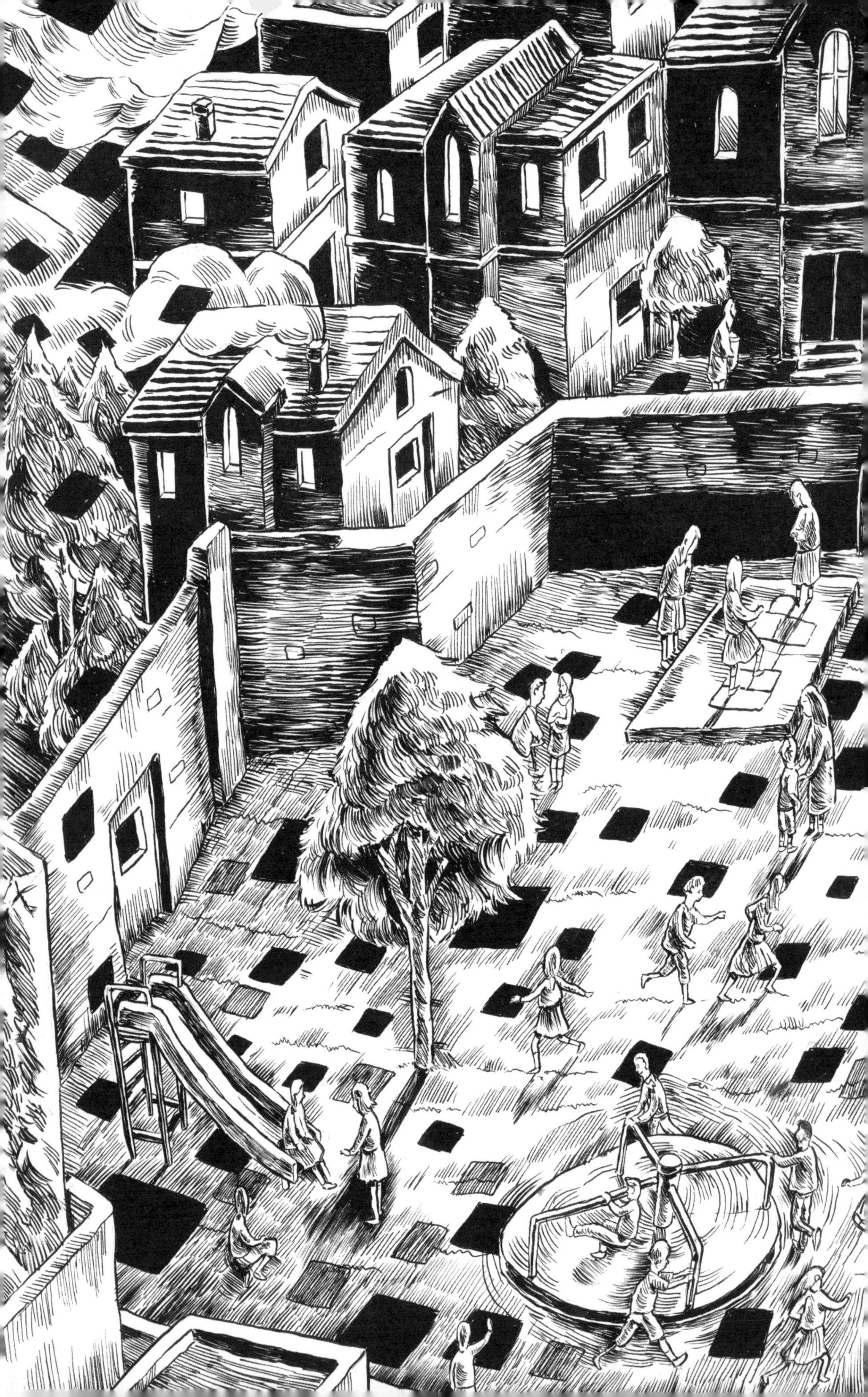

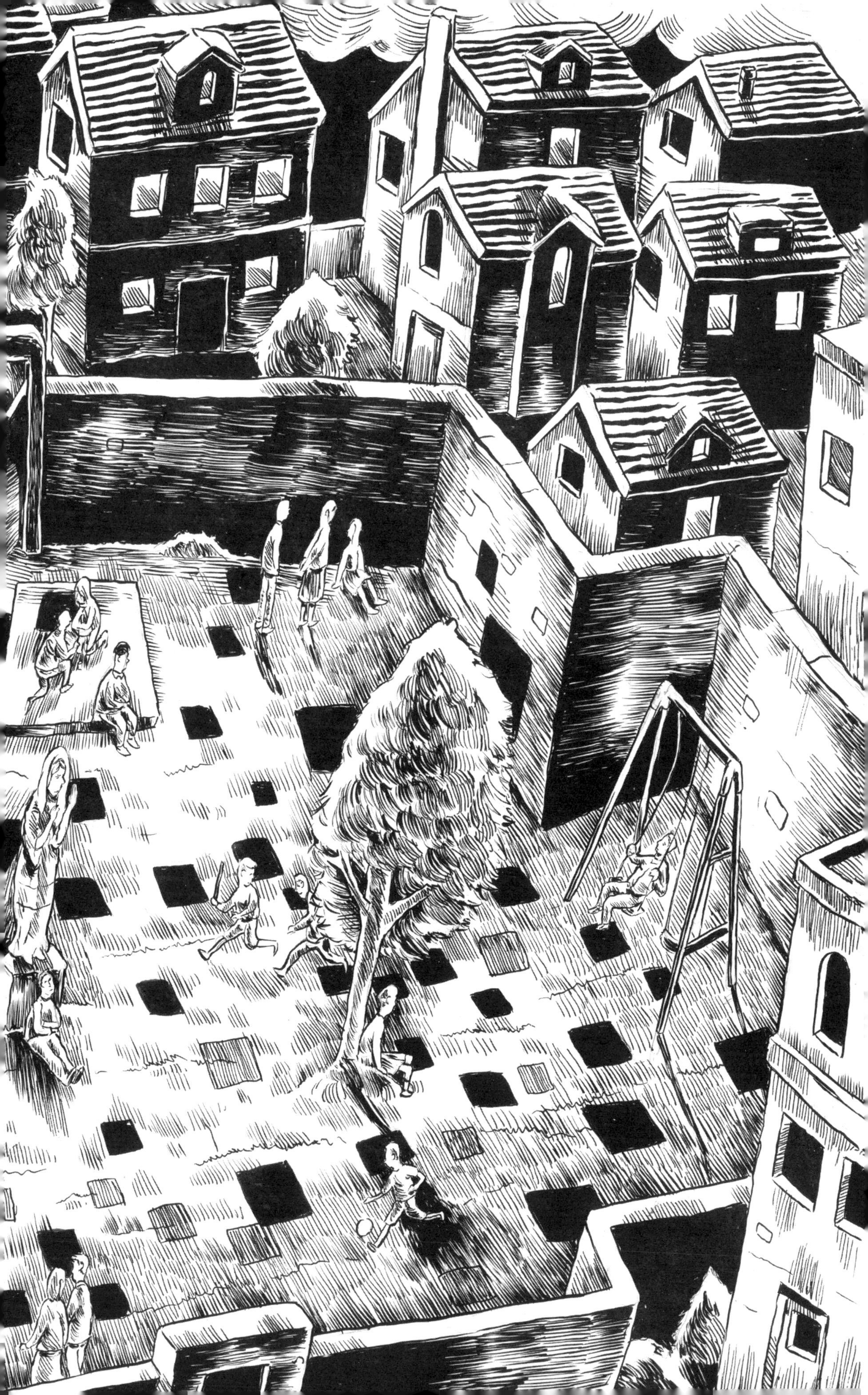

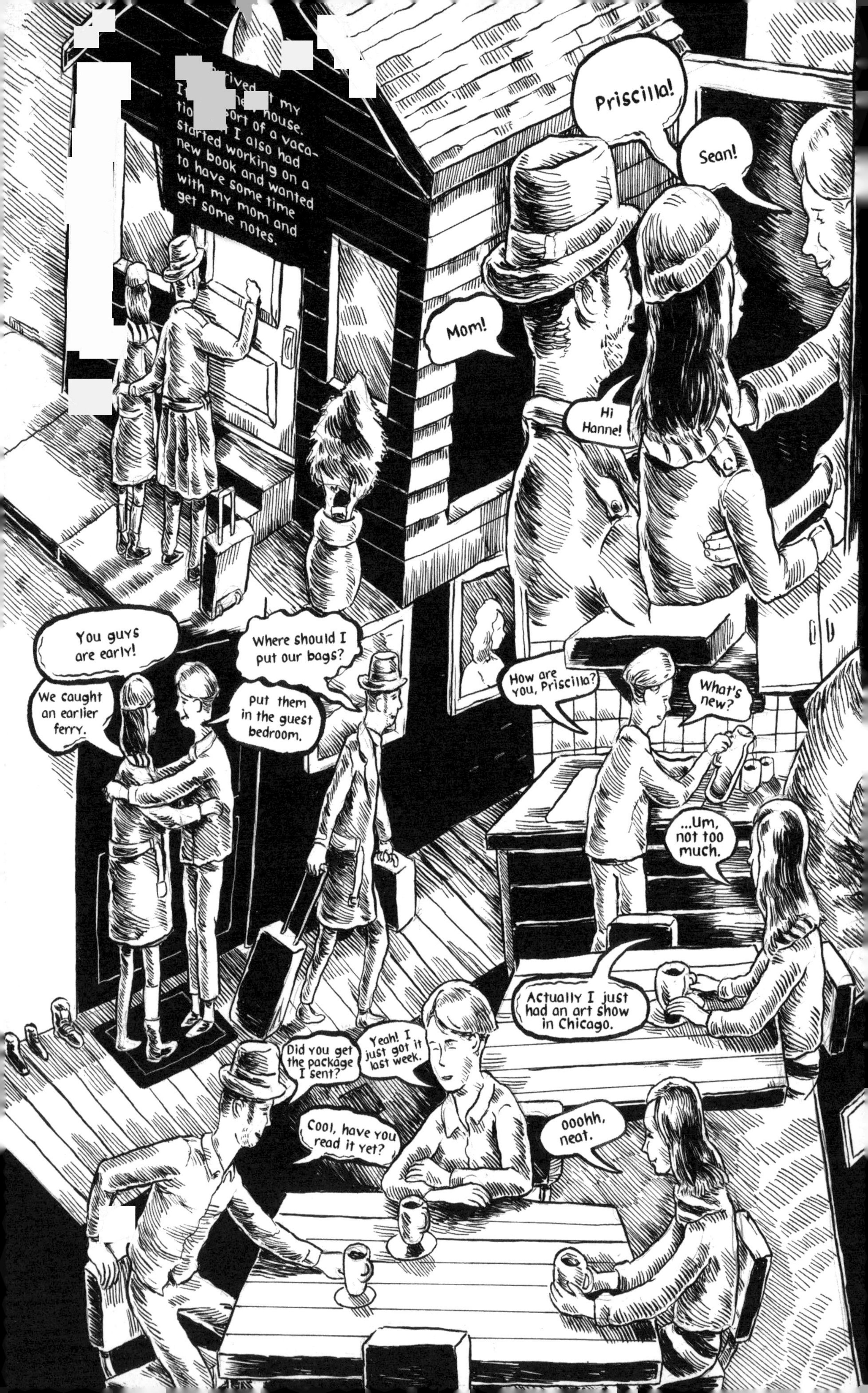
rrived
my
house.
ort of a vaca-
I also had
started working on a
new book and wanted
to have some time
with my mom and
get some notes.
Priscilla!
Sean!
Mom!
Hi Hanne!
You guys are early!
We caught an earlier ferry.
Where should I put our bags?
put them in the guest bedroom.
How are you, Priscilla?
What's new?
...Um, not too much.
Actually I just had an art show in Chicago.
Did you get the package I sent?
Yeah! I just got it last week.
Cool, have you read it yet?
oooh, neat.

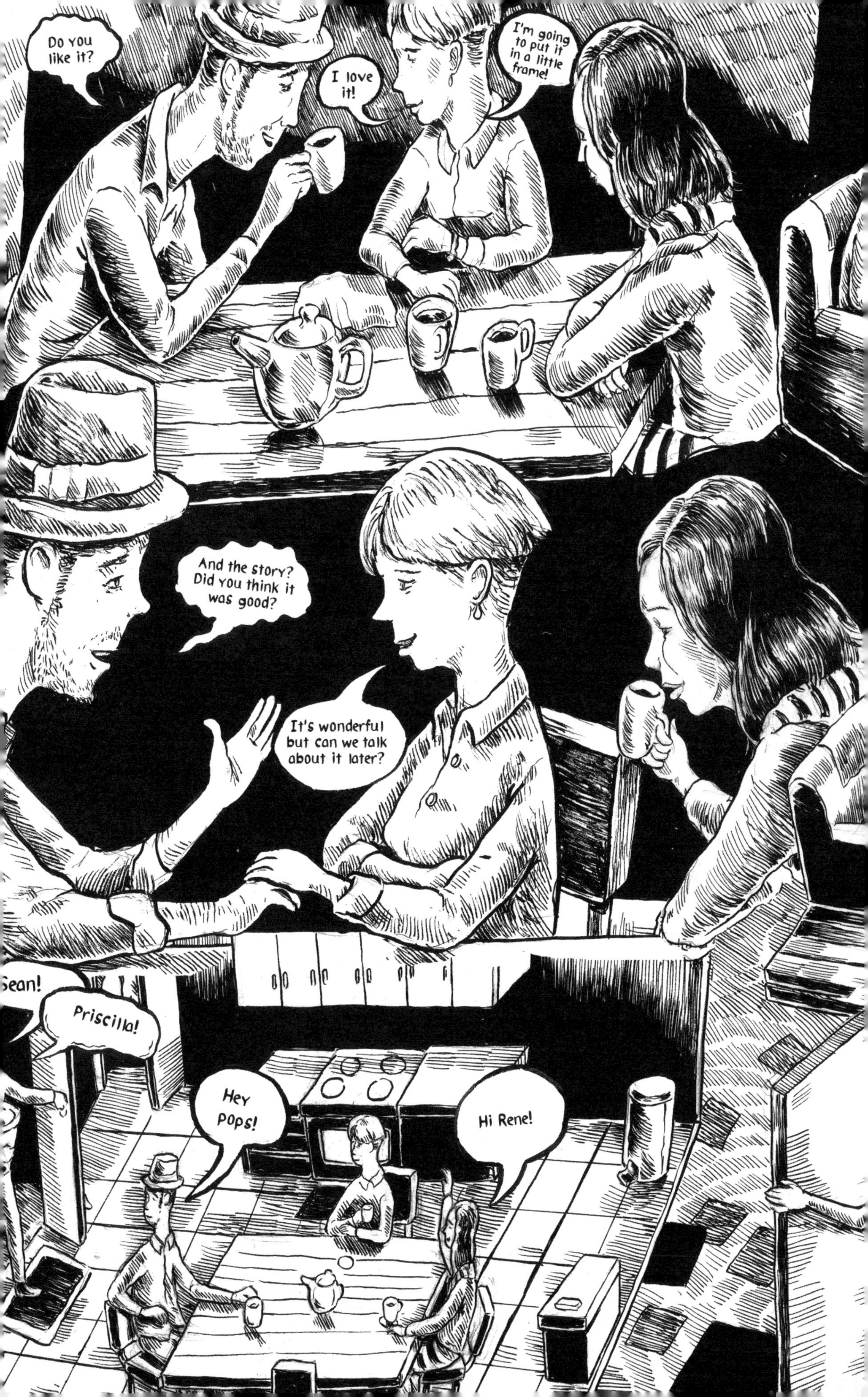
Do you like it?
I love it!
I'm going to put it in a little frame!
And the story? Did you think it was good?
It's wonderful but can we talk about it later?
Sean!
Priscilla!
Hey pops!
Hi Rene!

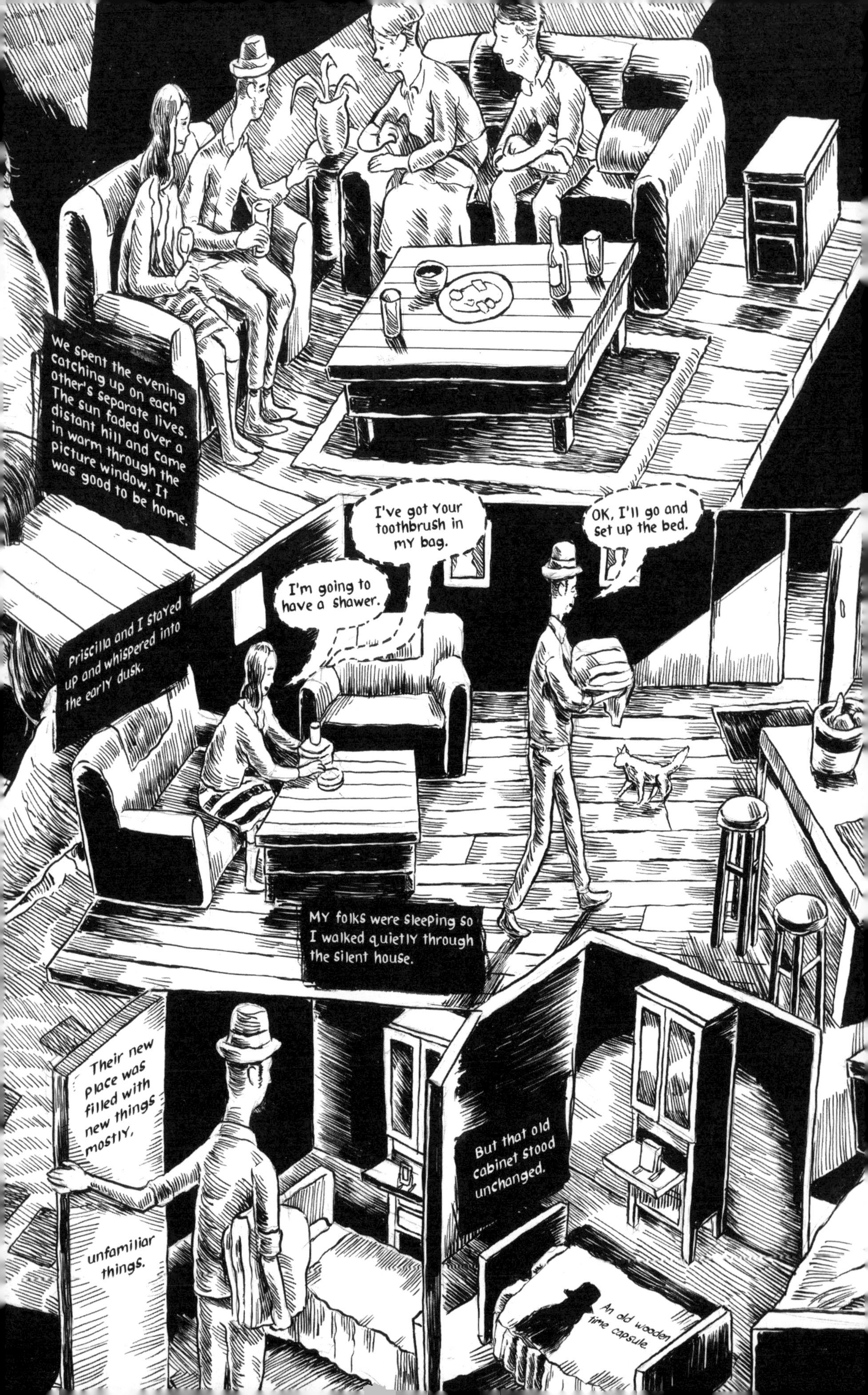
We spent the evening catching up on each other's separate lives. The sun faded over a distant hill and came in warm through the picture window. It was good to be home.
Priscilla and I stayed up and whispered into the early dusk.
I'm going to have a shower.
I've got your toothbrush in my bag.
OK, I'll go and set up the bed.
My folks were sleeping so I walked quietly through the silent house.
Their new place was filled with new things mostly,
unfamiliar things.
But that old cabinet stood unchanged.
An old wooden time capsule.

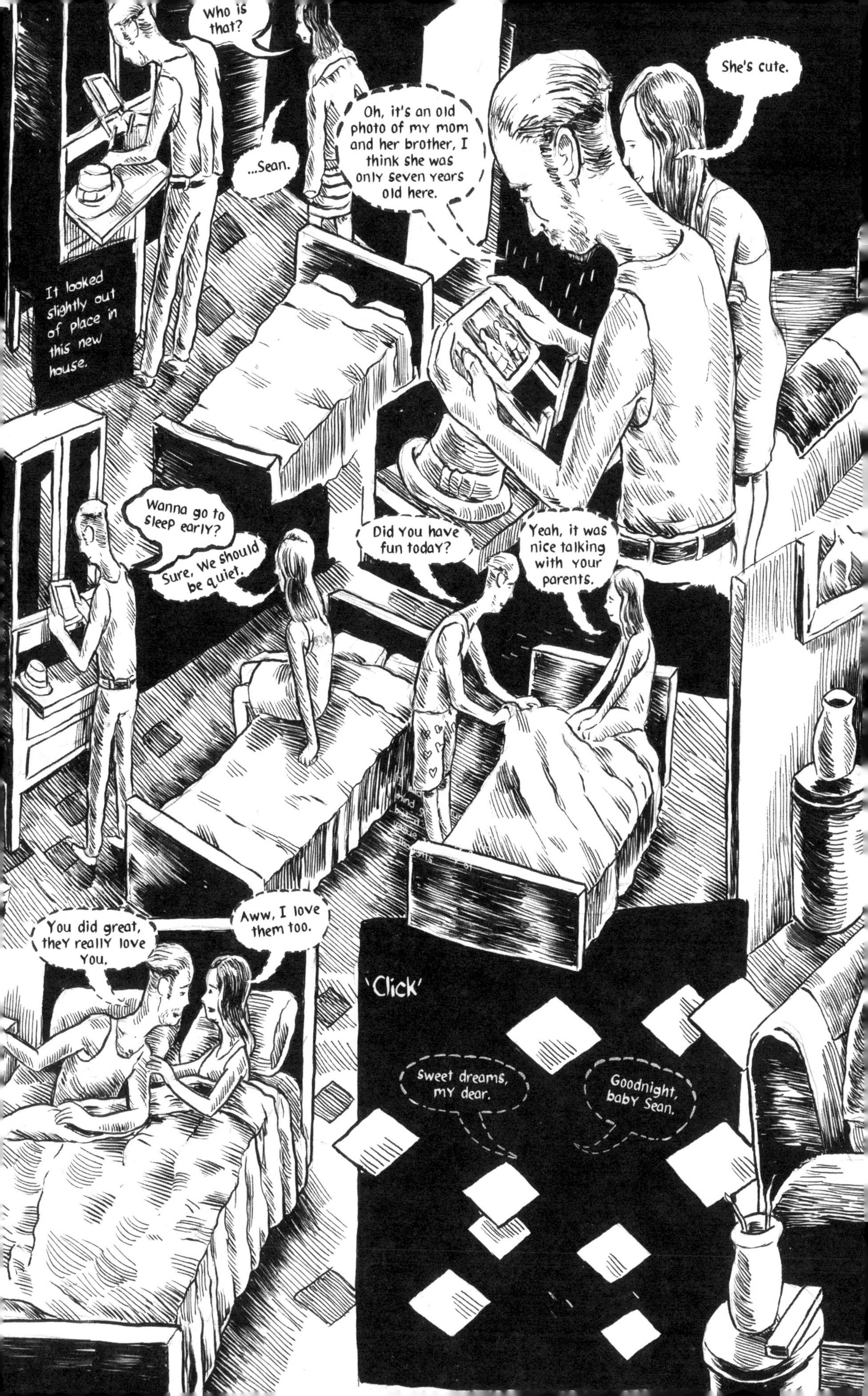
Who is that?
...Sean.
Oh, it's an old photo of my mom and her brother, I think she was only seven years old here.
She's cute.
It looked slightly out of place in this new house.
Wanna go to sleep early?
Sure, we should be quiet.
Did you have fun today?
Yeah, it was nice talking with your parents.
You did great, they really love you.
Aww, I love them too.
'Click'
Sweet dreams, my dear.
Goodnight, baby Sean.

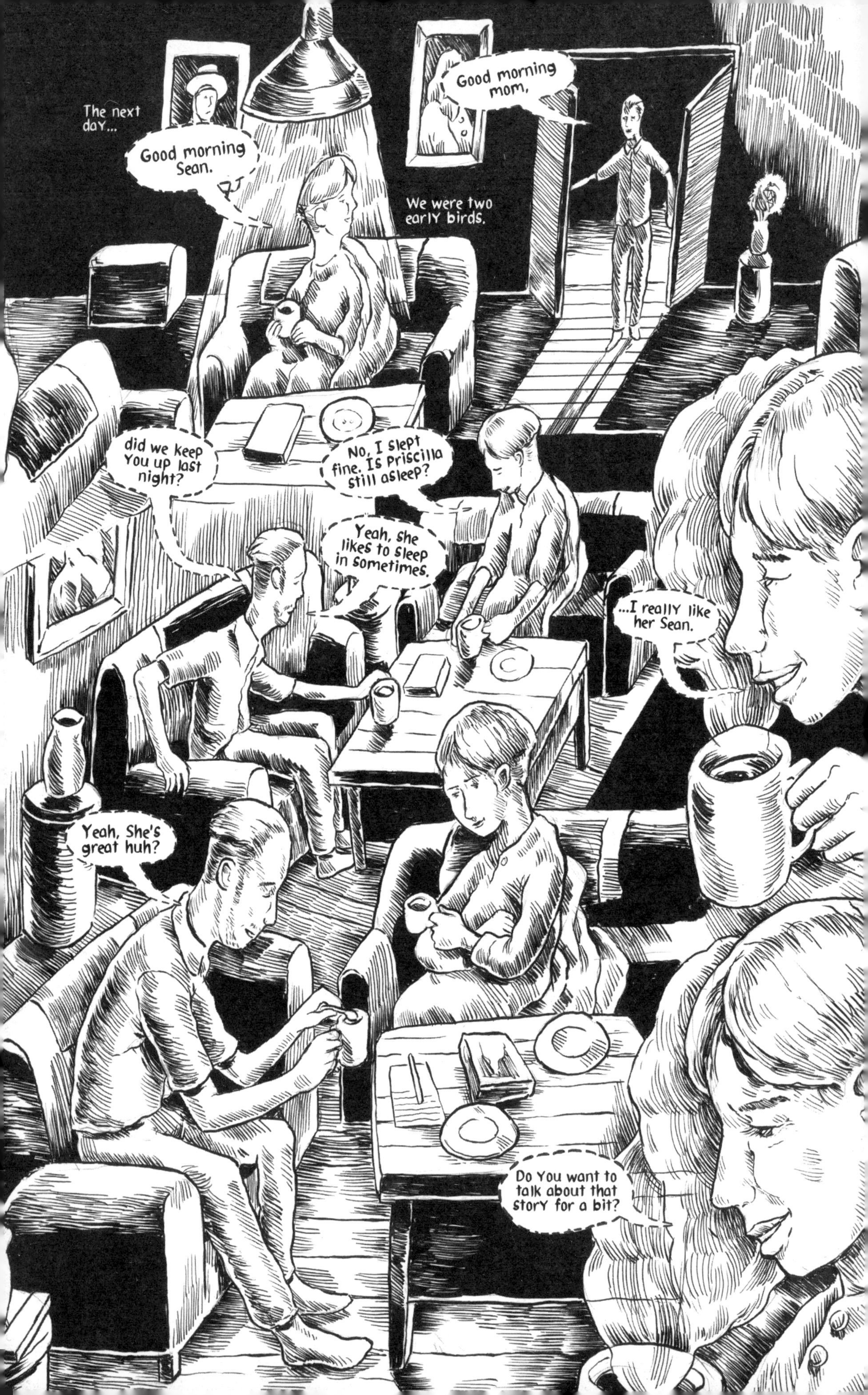
The next day...
Good morning Sean.
We were two early birds.
Good morning mom.
did we keep You up last night?
No, I slept fine. Is Priscilla still asleep?
Yeah, she likes to sleep in sometimes.
...I really like her Sean.
Yeah, She's great huh?
Do You want to talk about that story for a bit?

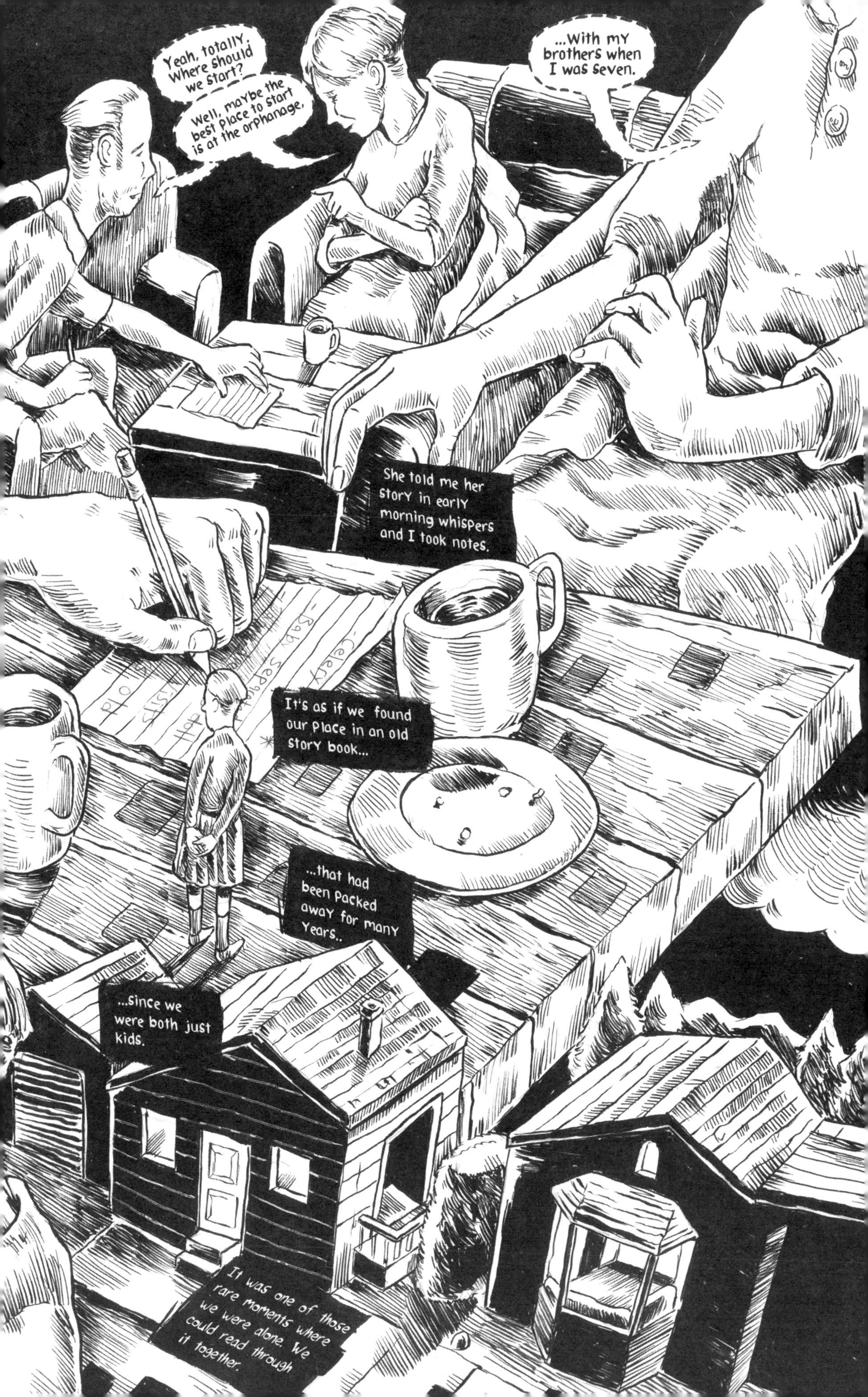

Yeah, totally. Where should we start?
Well, maybe the best place to start is at the orphanage.
...With my brothers when I was seven.
She told me her story in early morning whispers and I took notes.
It's as if we found our place in an old story book...
...that had been packed away for many years..
...since we were both just kids.
It was one of those rare moments where we were alone. We could read through it together.

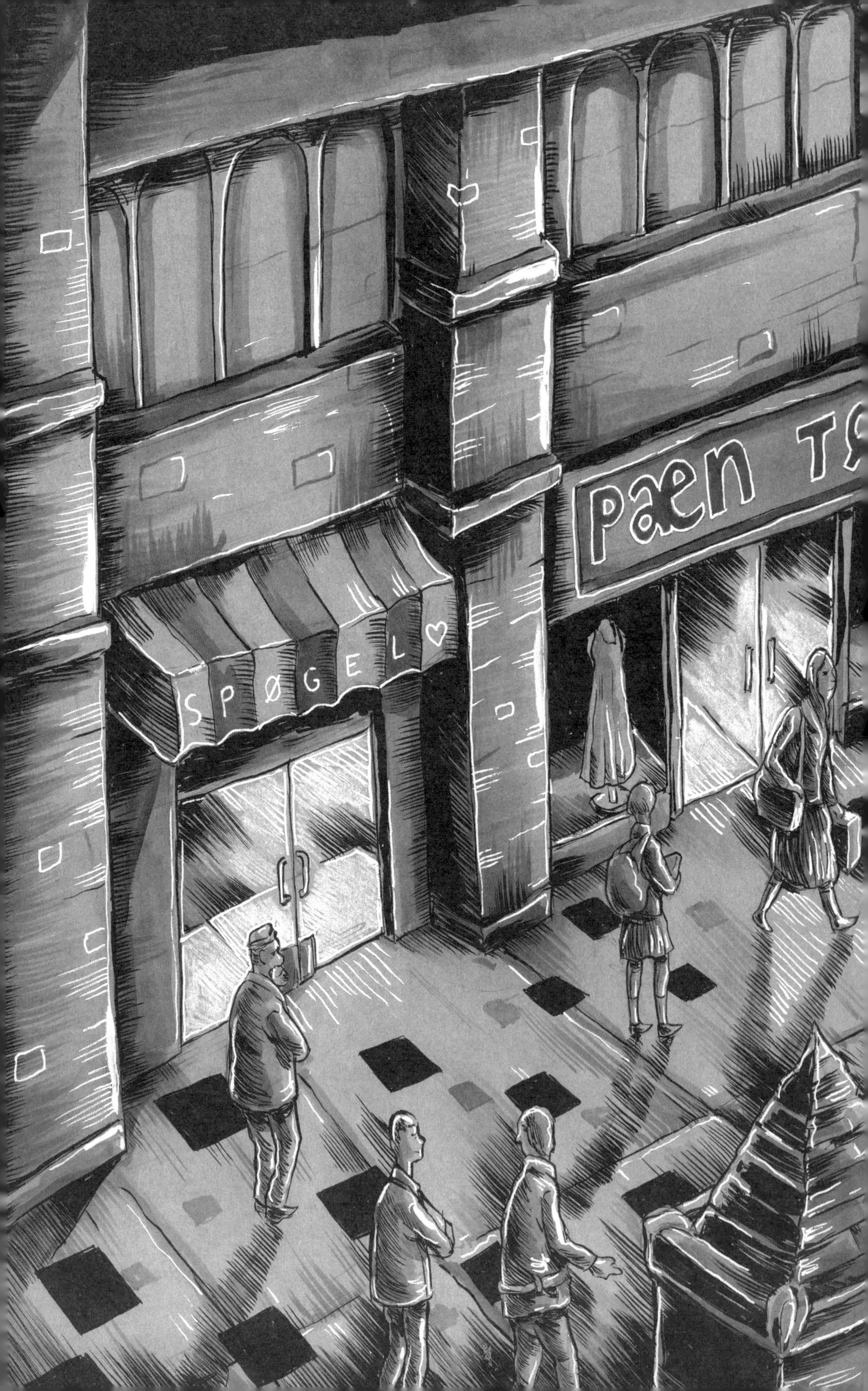
SPØGEL♡
Paen T

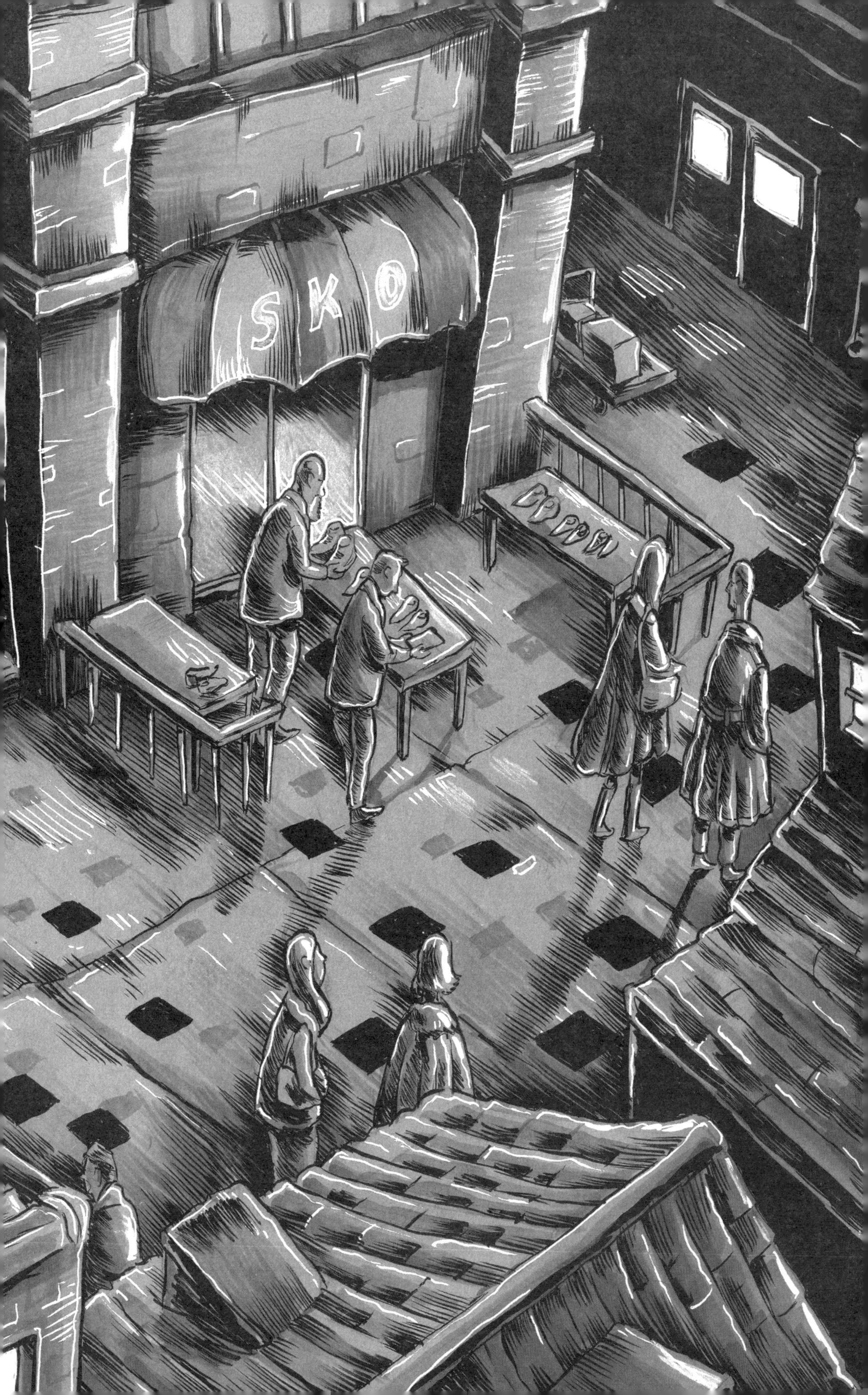
SKO

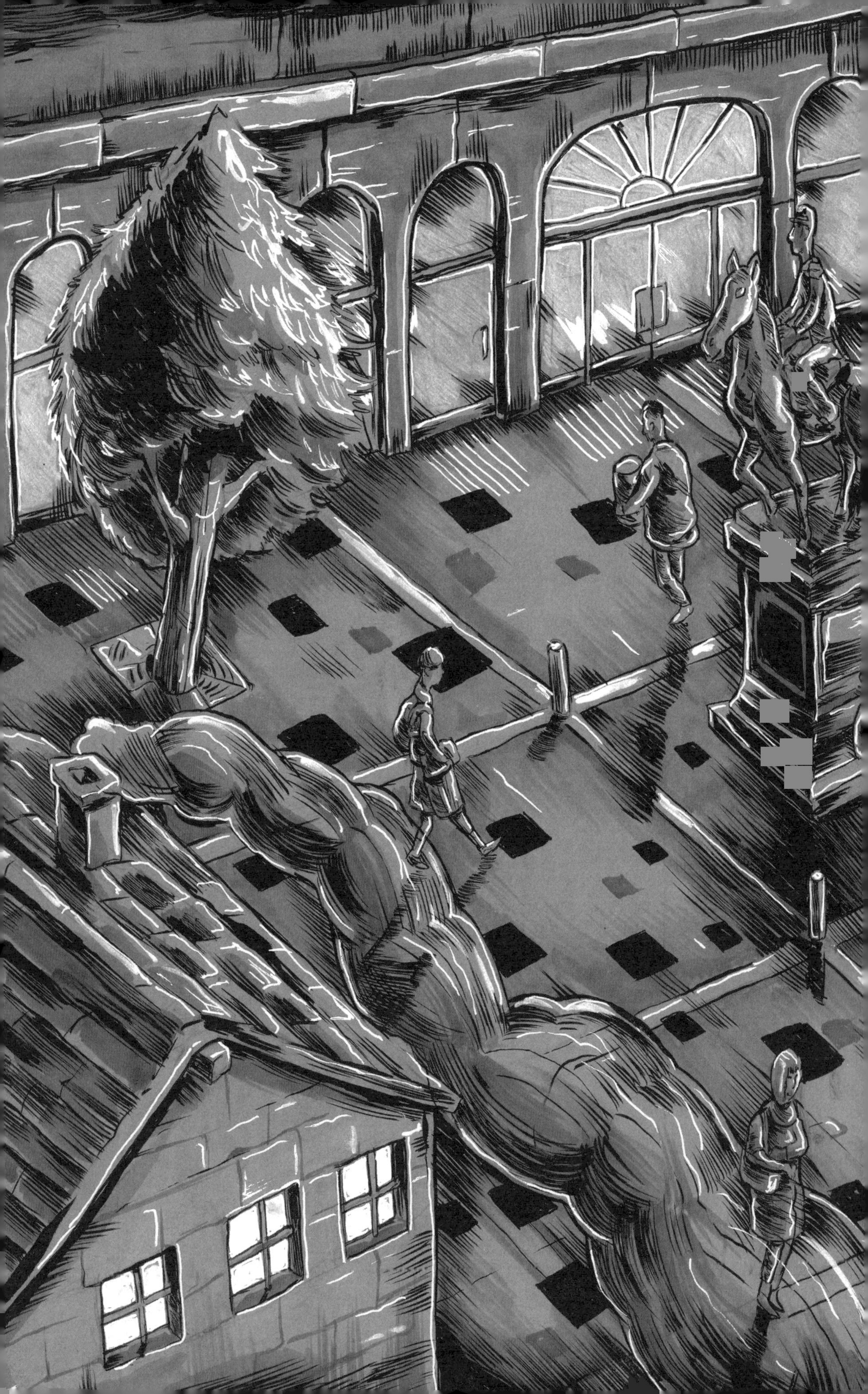

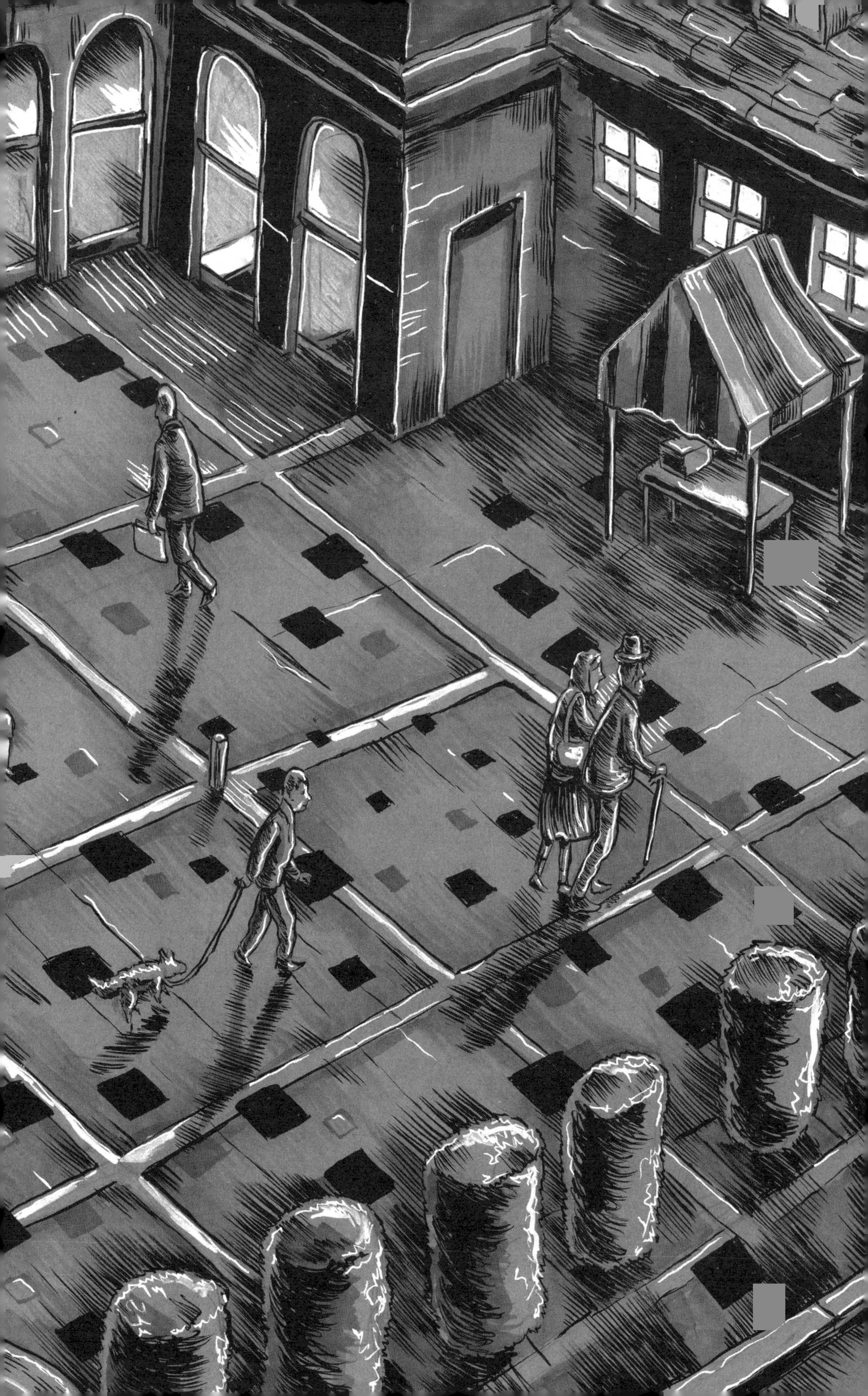

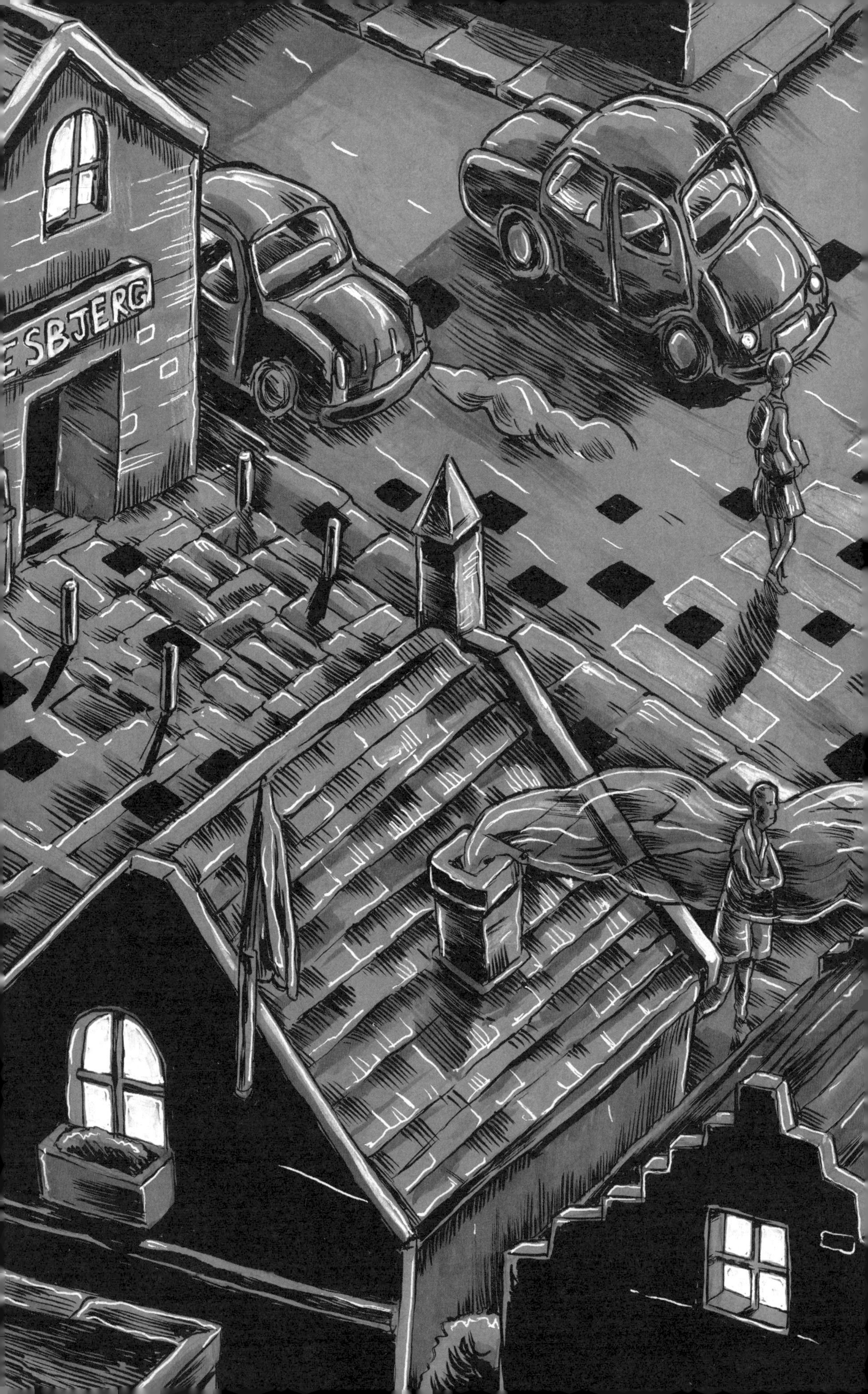
ESBJERG

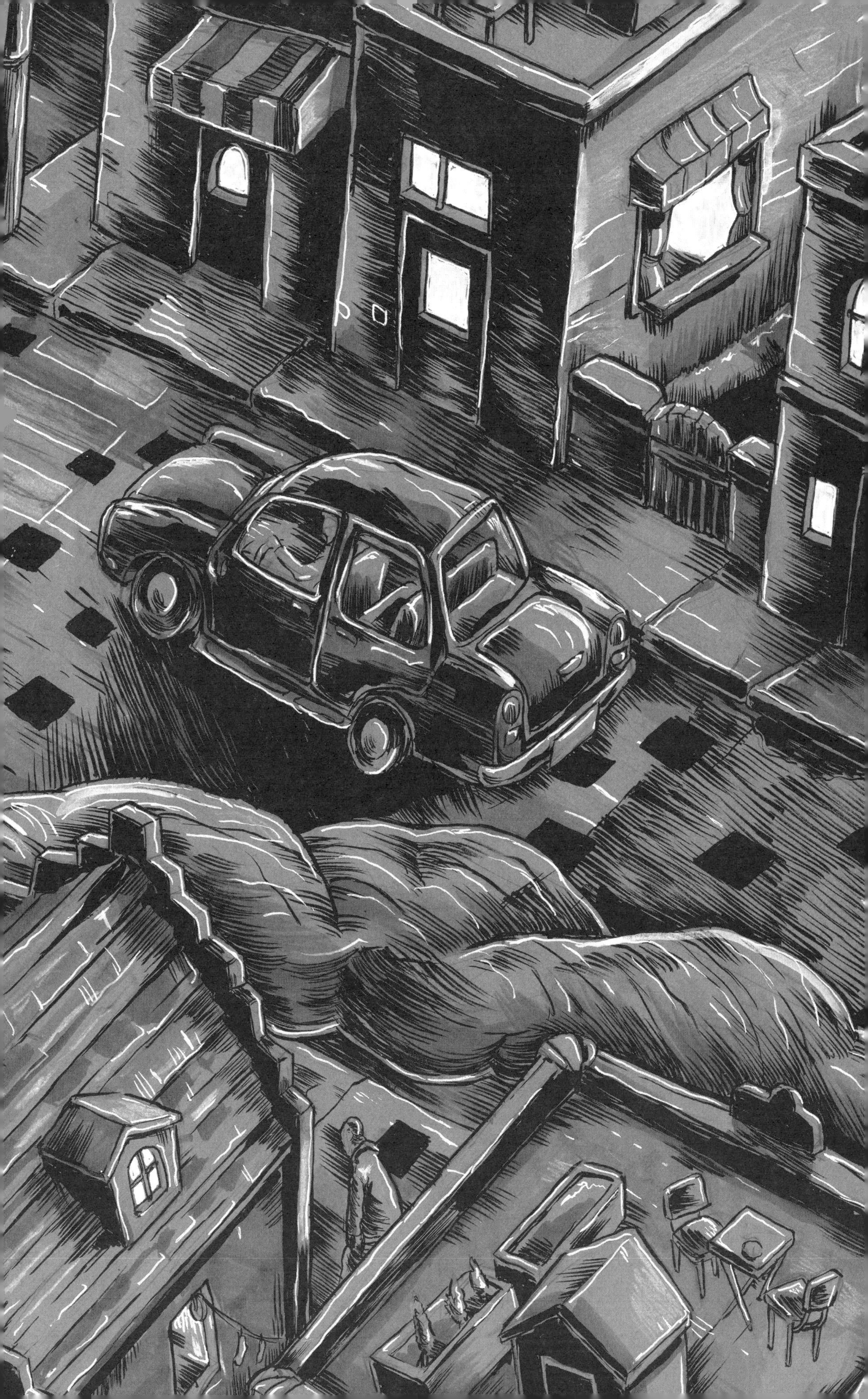

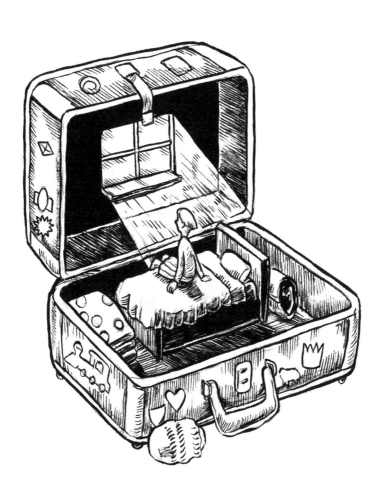

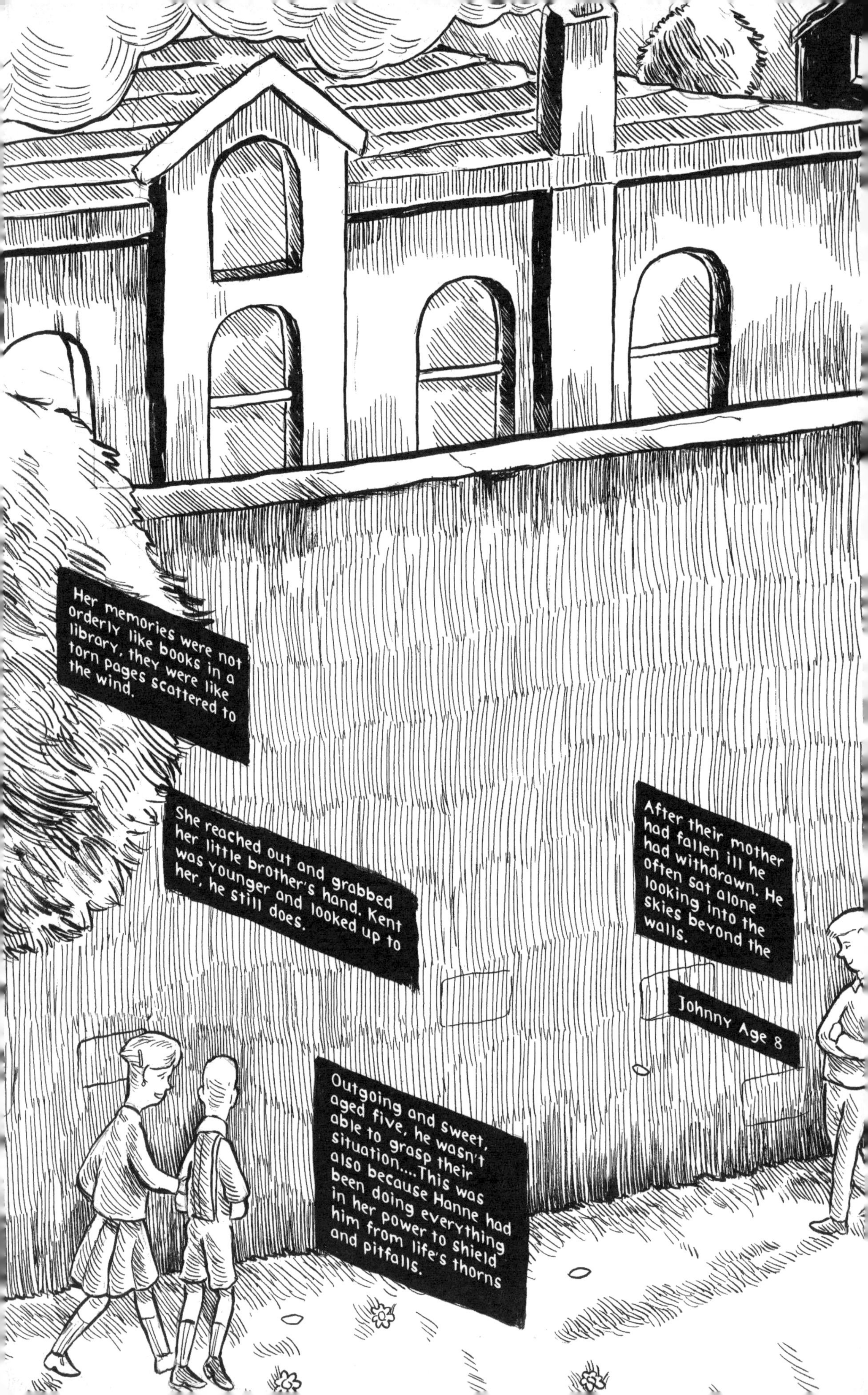
Her memories were not orderly like books in a library, they were like torn pages scattered to the wind.
She reached out and grabbed her little brother's hand. Kent was younger and looked up to her, he still does.
After their mother had fallen ill he had withdrawn. He often sat alone looking into the skies beyond the walls.
Johnny Age 8
Outgoing and sweet, aged five, he wasn't able to grasp their situation....This was also because Hanne had been doing everything in her power to shield him from life's thorns and pitfalls.

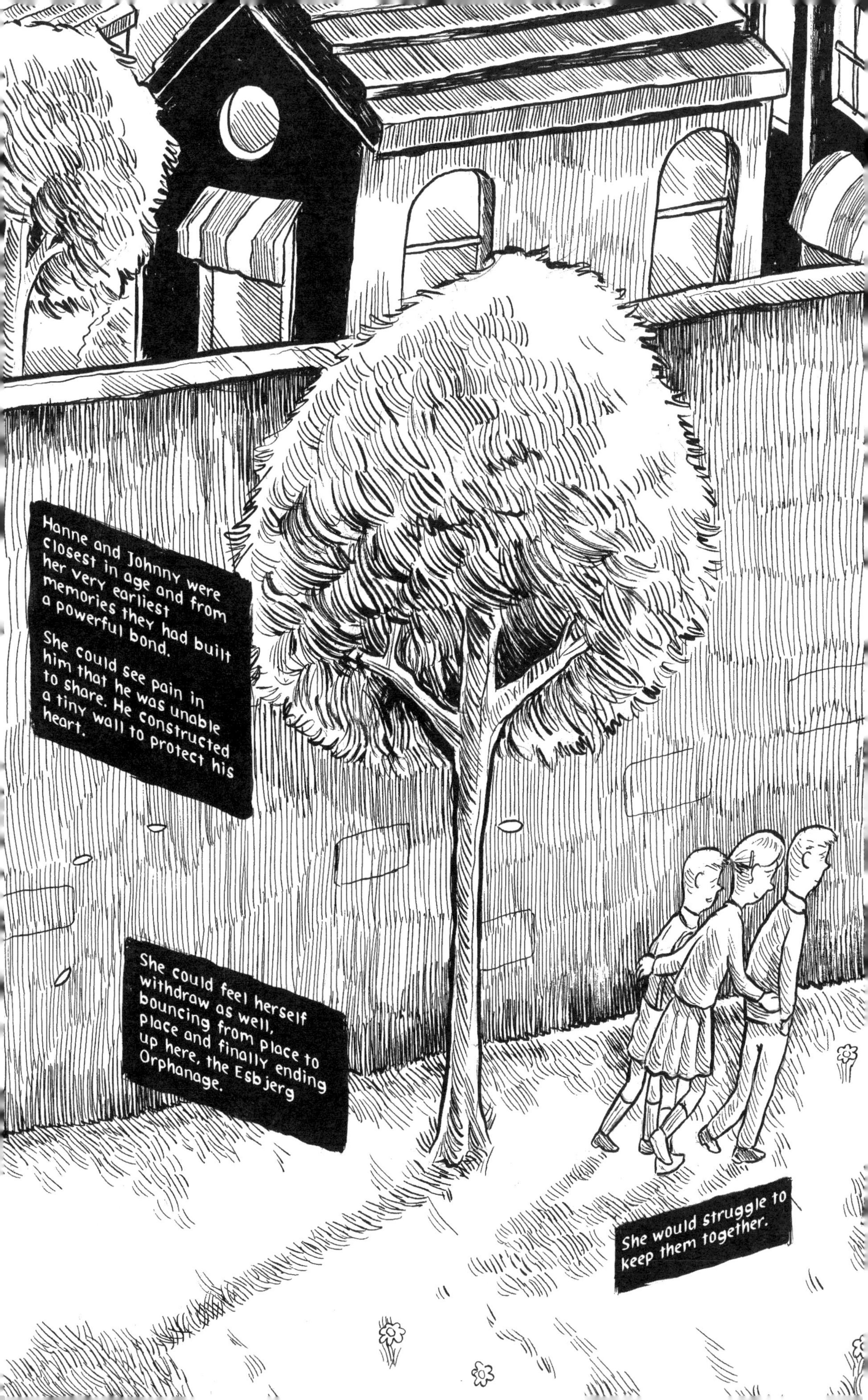
Hanne and Johnny were closest in age and from her very earliest memories they had built a powerful bond.
She could see pain in him that he was unable to share. He constructed a tiny wall to protect his heart.
She could feel herself withdraw as well, bouncing from place to place and finally ending up here, the Esbjerg Orphanage.
She would struggle to keep them together.

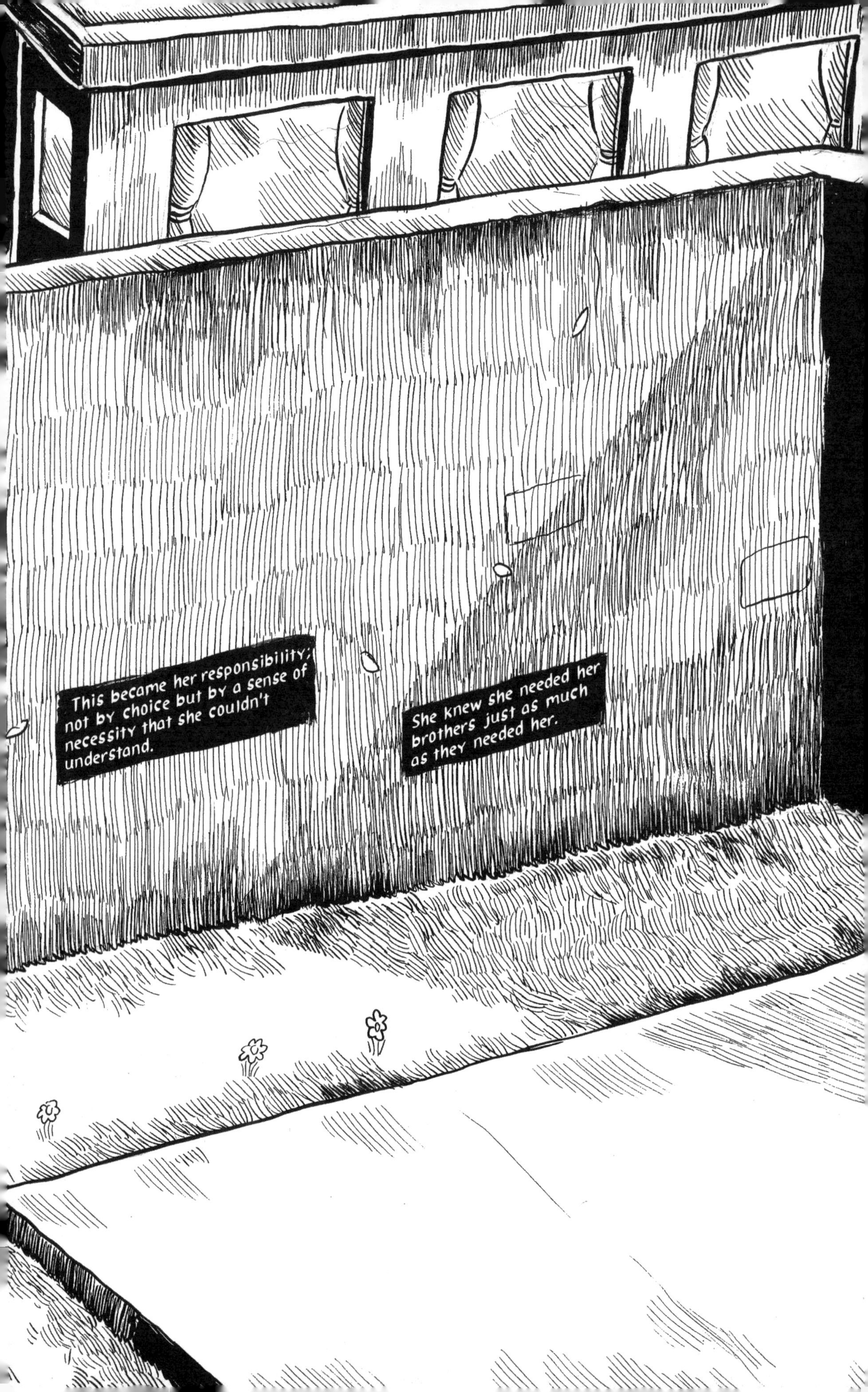
This became her responsibility; not by choice but by a sense of necessity that she couldn't understand.
She knew she needed her brothers just as much as they needed her.

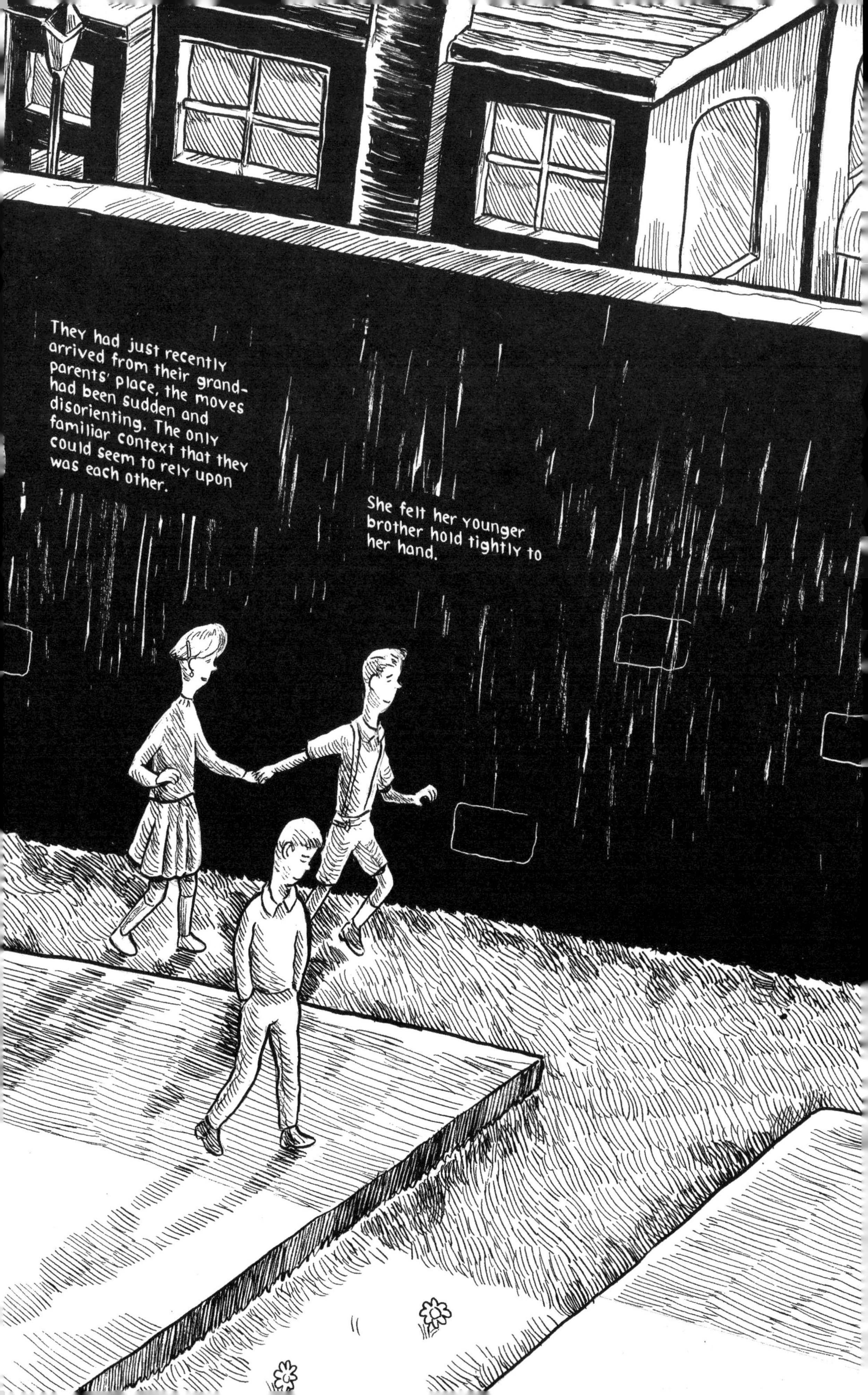
They had just recently arrived from their grand-parents' place, the moves had been sudden and disorienting. The only familiar context that they could seem to rely upon was each other.
She felt her younger brother hold tightly to her hand.

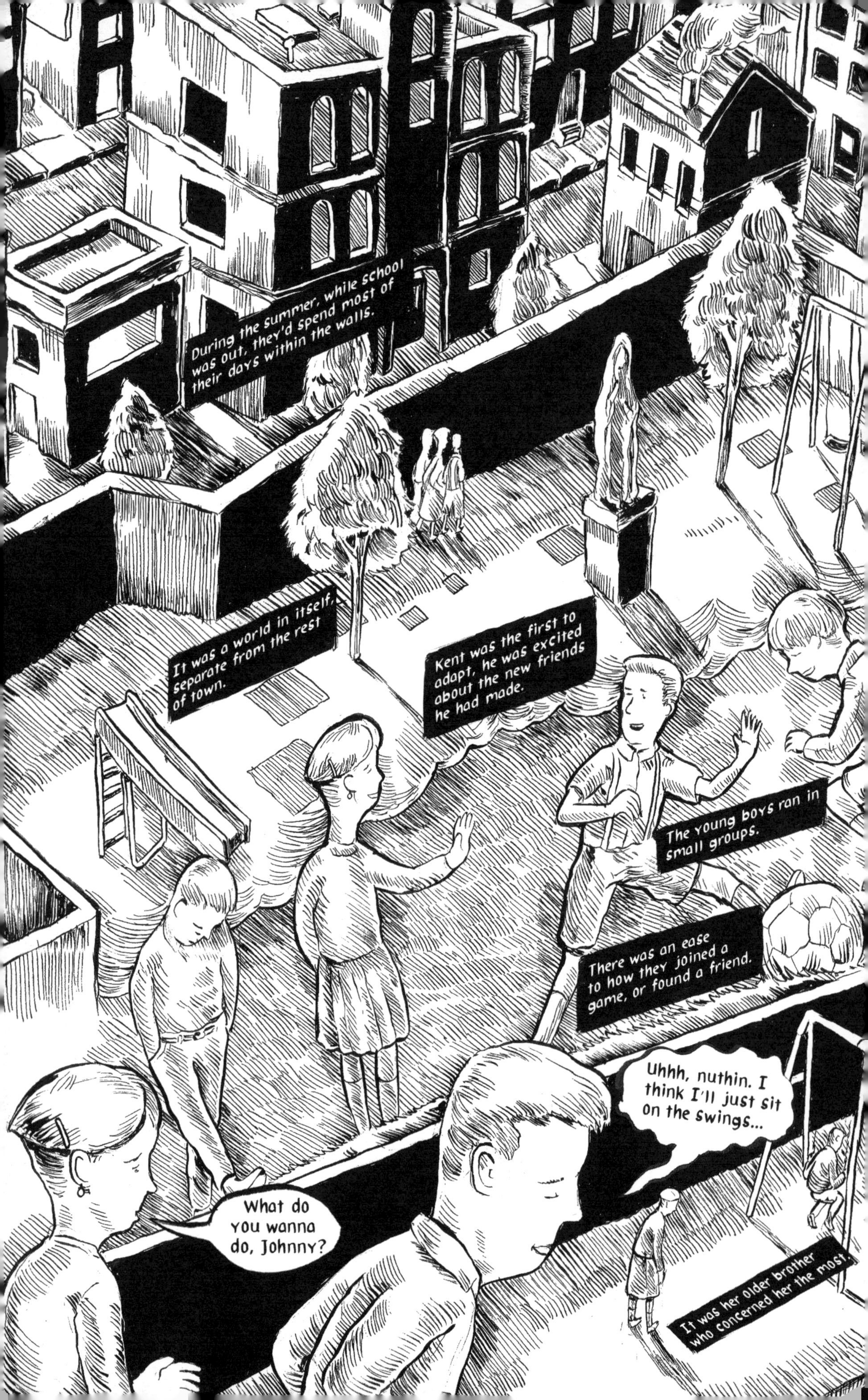
During the summer, while school was out, they'd spend most of their days within the walls.
It was a world in itself, separate from the rest of town.
Kent was the first to adapt, he was excited about the new friends he had made.
The young boys ran in small groups.
There was an ease to how they joined a game, or found a friend.
Uhhh, nuthin. I think I'll just sit on the swings...
What do you wanna do, Johnny?
It was her older brother who concerned her the most.

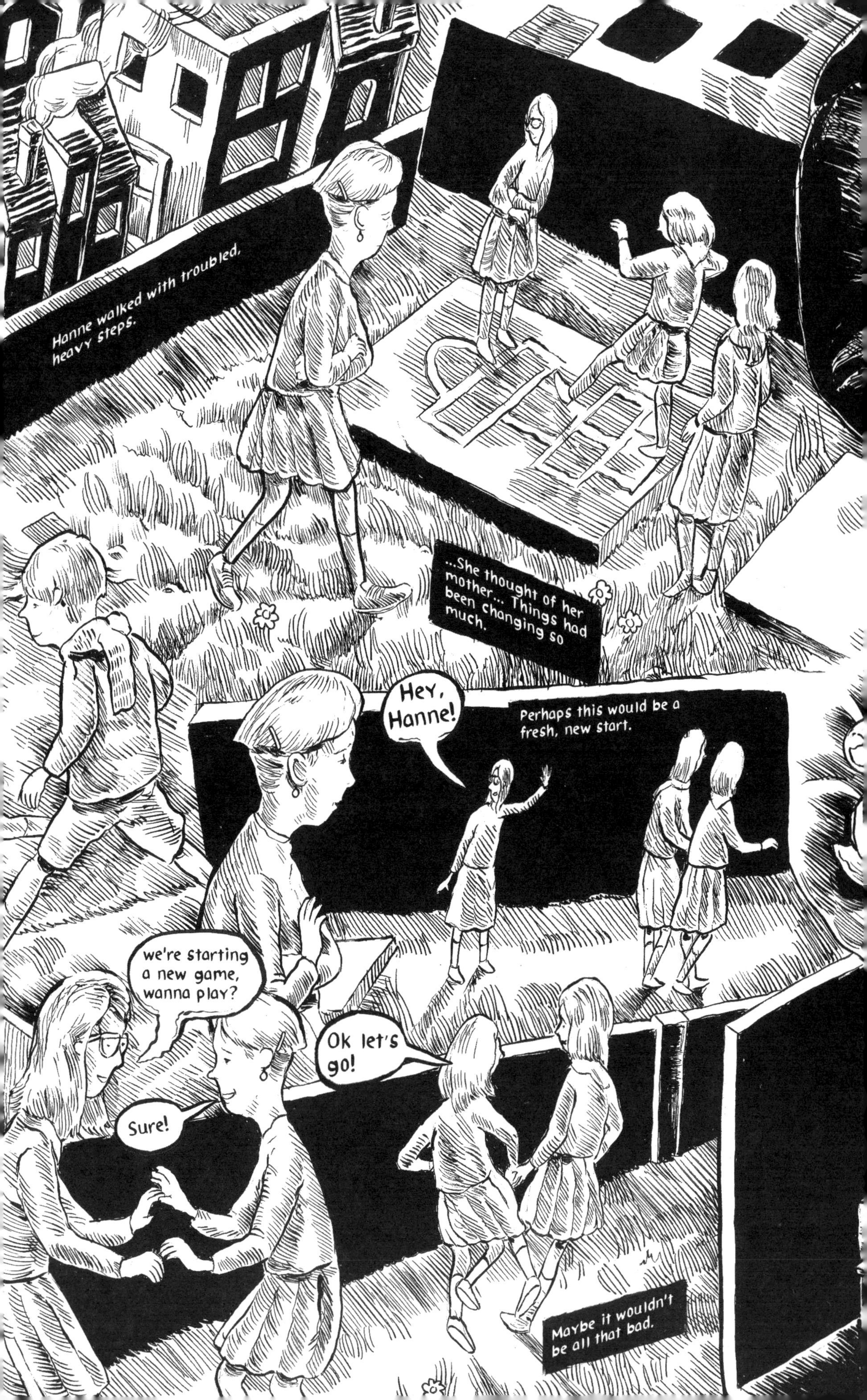
Hanne walked with troubled, heavy steps.
...She thought of her mother... Things had been changing so much.
Hey, Hanne!
Perhaps this would be a fresh, new start.
we're starting a new game, wanna play?
Sure!
Ok let's go!
Maybe it wouldn't be all that bad.

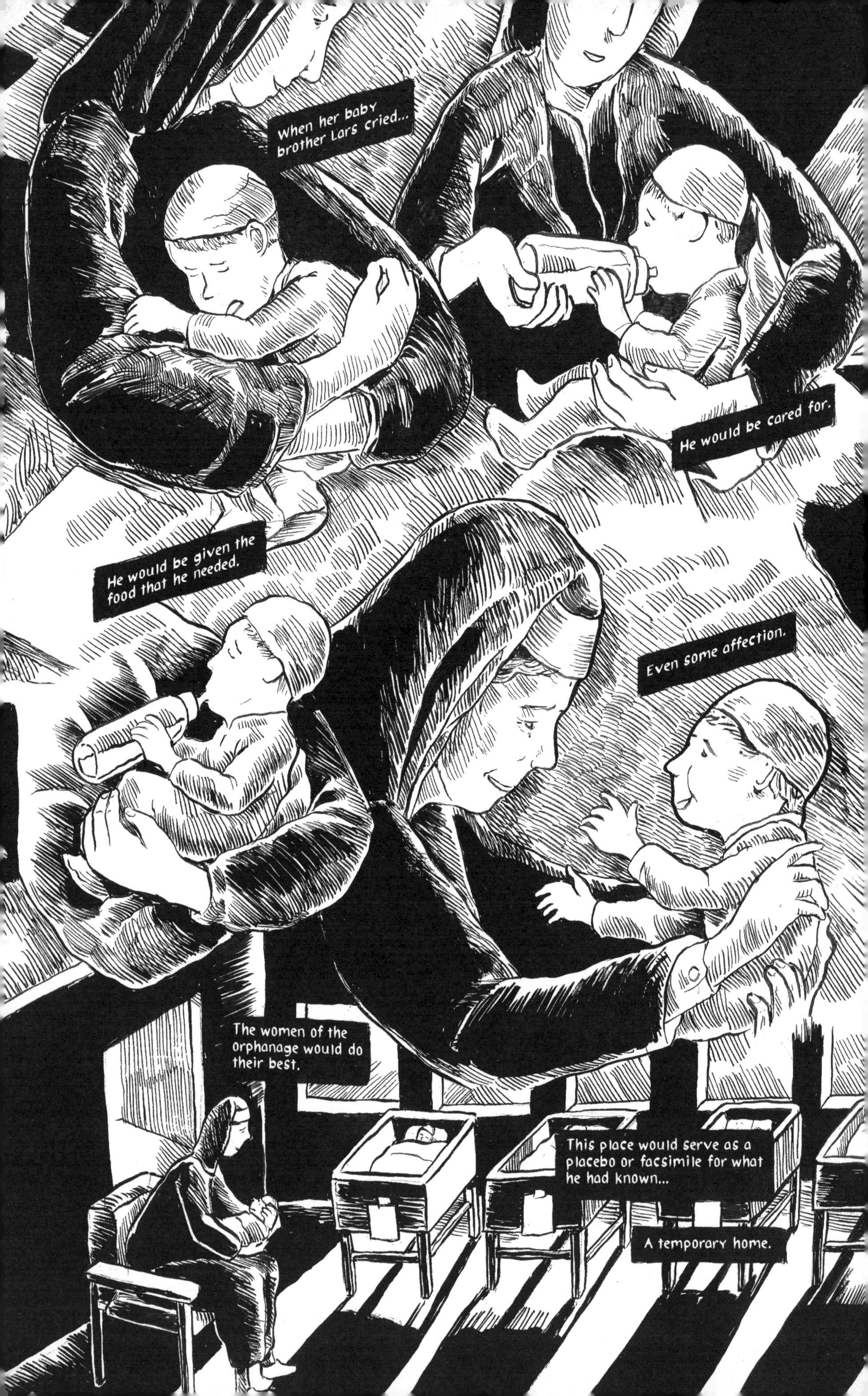
When her baby brother Lars cried...
He would be cared for.
He would be given the food that he needed.
Even some affection.
The women of the orphanage would do their best.
This place would serve as a placebo or facsimile for what he had known...
A temporary home.

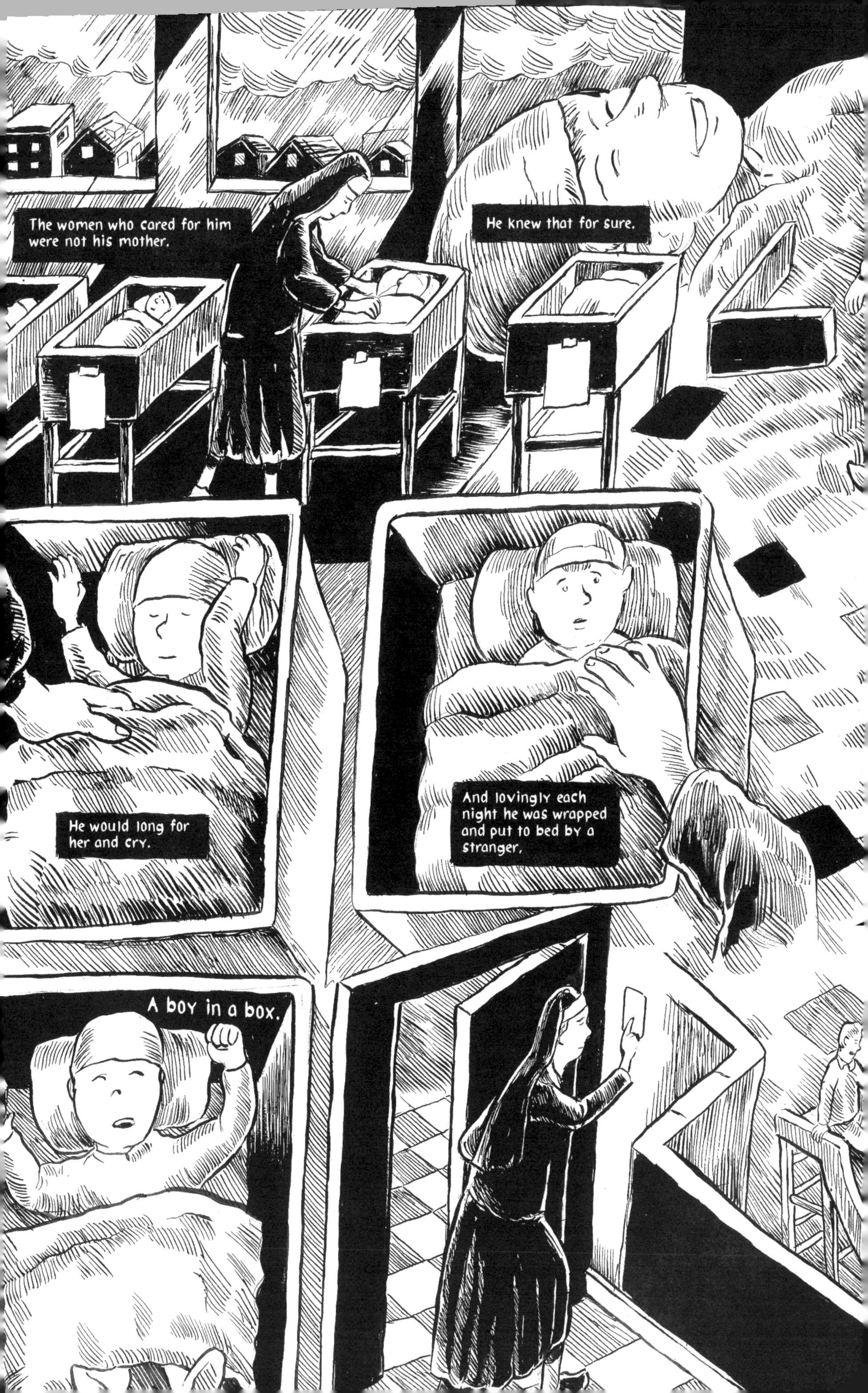
The women who cared for him were not his mother.
He knew that for sure.
He would long for her and cry.
And lovingly each night he was wrapped and put to bed by a stranger.
A boy in a box.

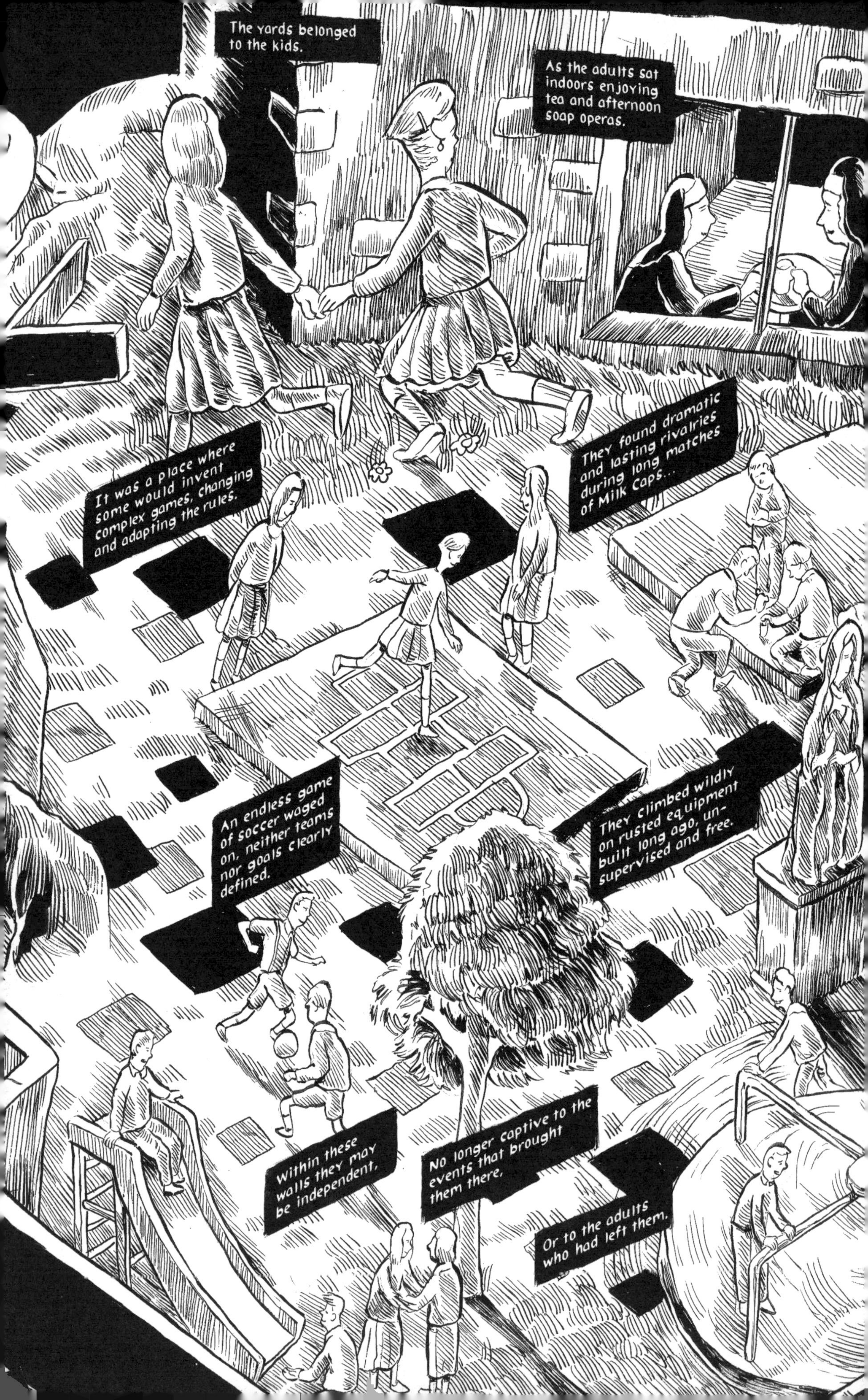
The yards belonged to the kids.
As the adults sat indoors enjoying tea and afternoon soap operas.
It was a place where some would invent complex games, changing and adapting the rules.
They found dramatic and lasting rivalries during long matches of Milk Caps...
An endless game of soccer waged on, neither teams nor goals clearly defined.
They climbed wildly on rusted equipment built long ago, unsupervised and free.
Within these walls they may be independent,
No longer captive to the events that brought them there,
Or to the adults who had left them.

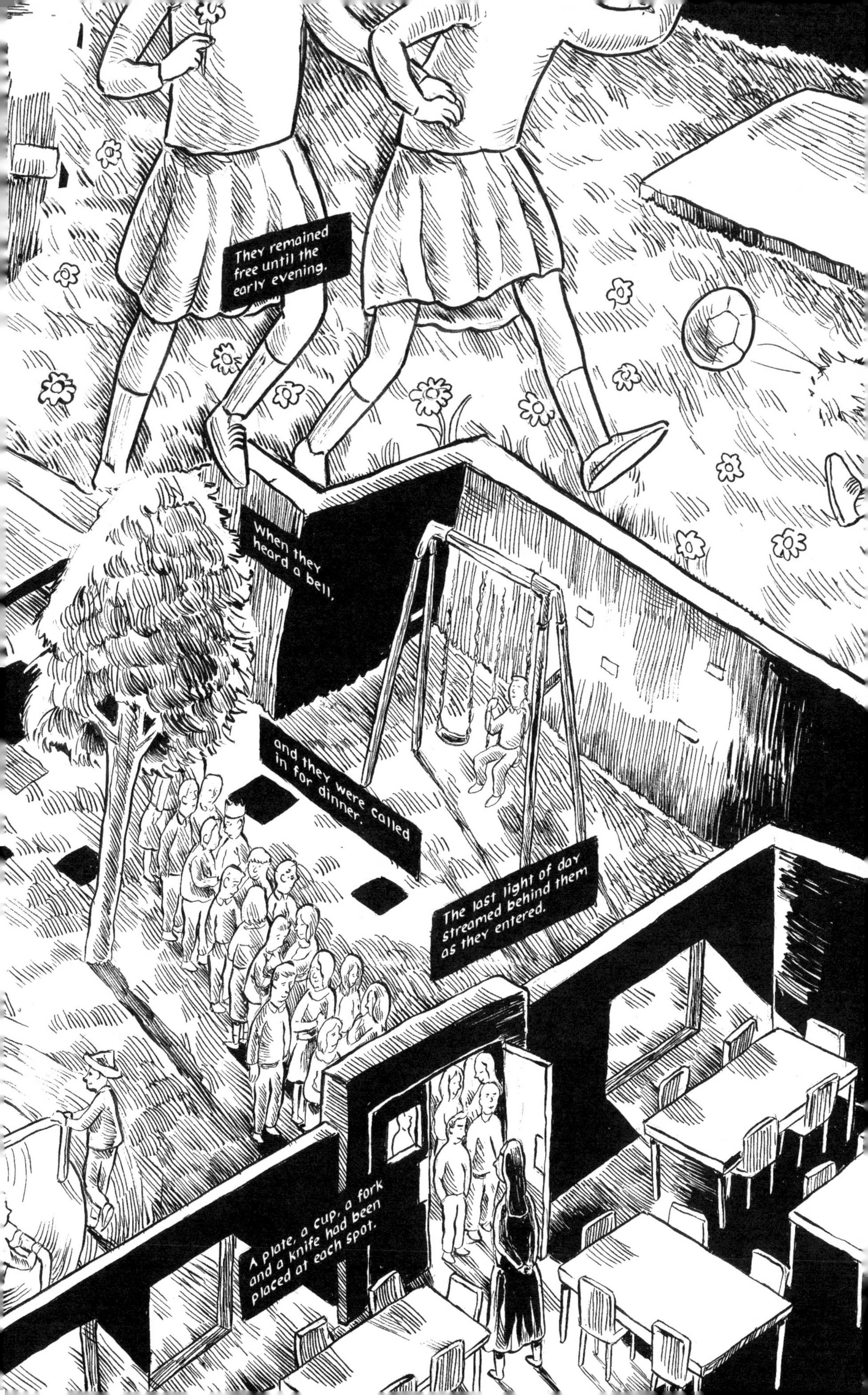
They remained free until the early evening.
When they heard a bell,
and they were called in for dinner.
The last light of day streamed behind them as they entered.
A plate, a cup, a fork and a knife had been placed at each spot.

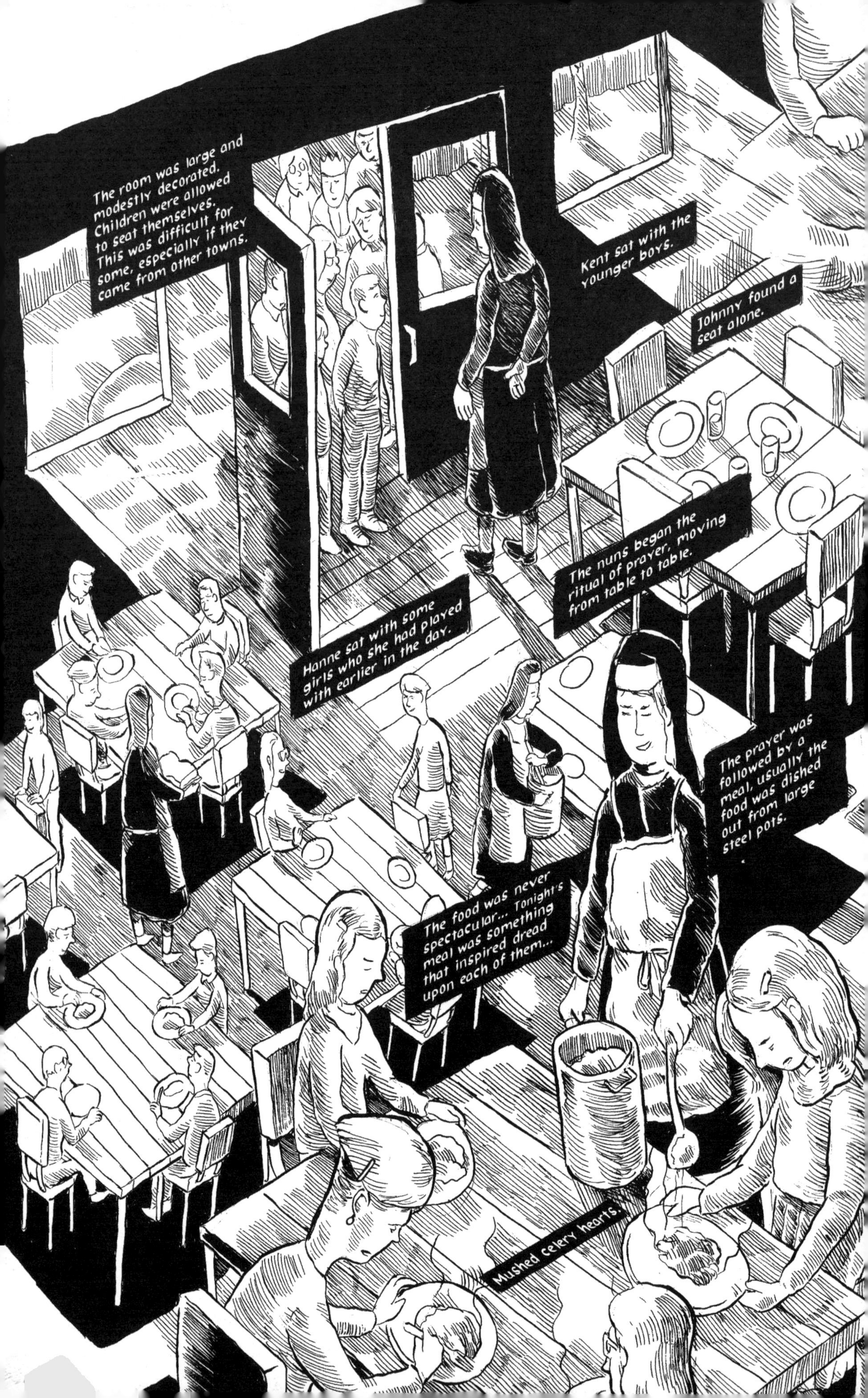
The room was large and modestly decorated. Children were allowed to seat themselves. This was difficult for some, especially if they came from other towns.
Kent sat with the younger boys.
Johnny found a seat alone.
The nuns began the ritual of prayer, moving from table to table.
Hanne sat with some girls who she had played with earlier in the day.
The prayer was followed by a meal, usually the food was dished out from large steel pots.
The food was never spectacular... Tonight's meal was something that inspired dread upon each of them...
Mushed celery hearts.

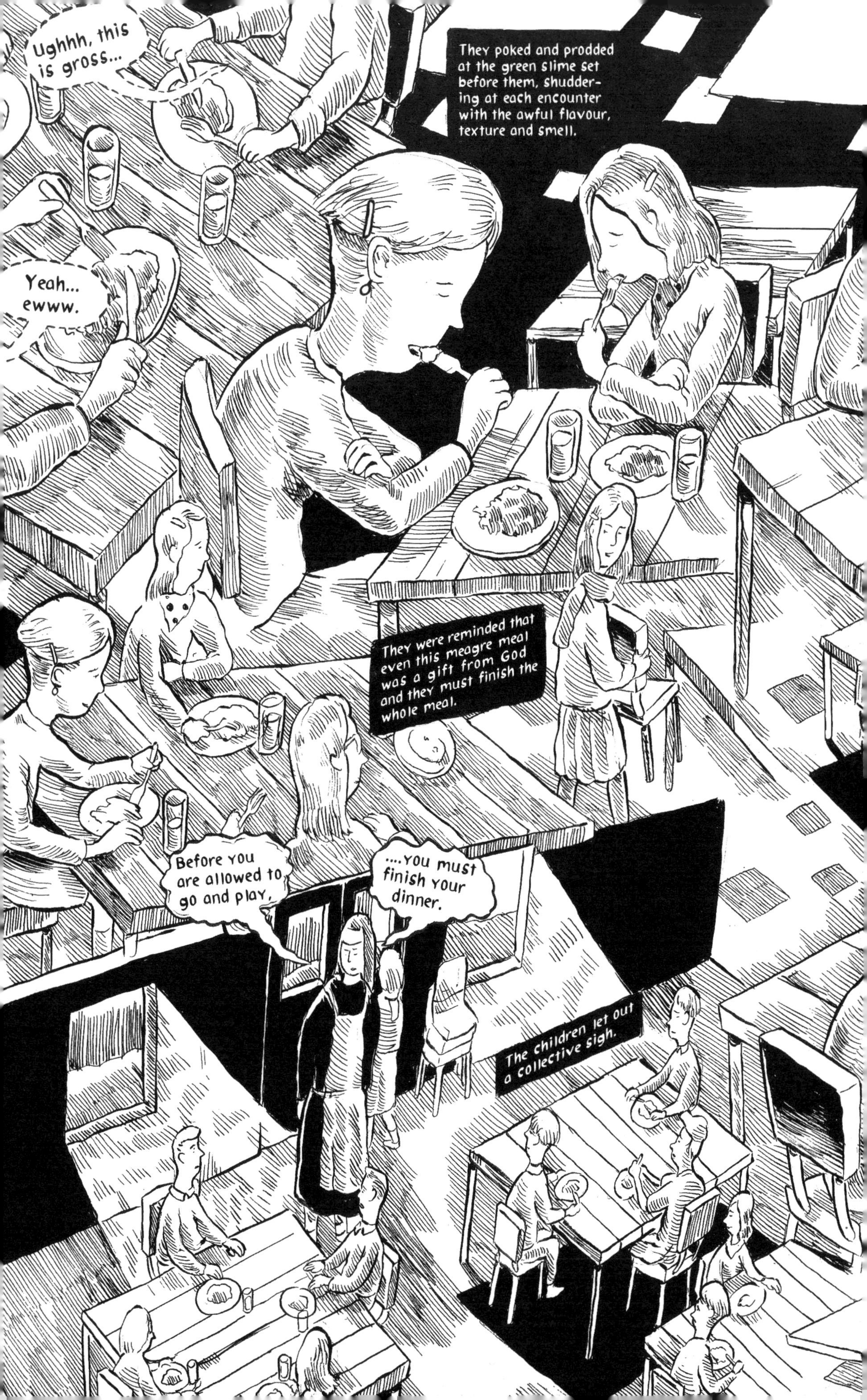
Ughhh, this is gross...
They poked and prodded at the green slime set before them, shuddering at each encounter with the awful flavour, texture and smell.
Yeah... ewww.
They were reminded that even this meagre meal was a gift from God and they must finish the whole meal.
Before you are allowed to go and play,
....You must finish your dinner.
The children let out a collective sigh.

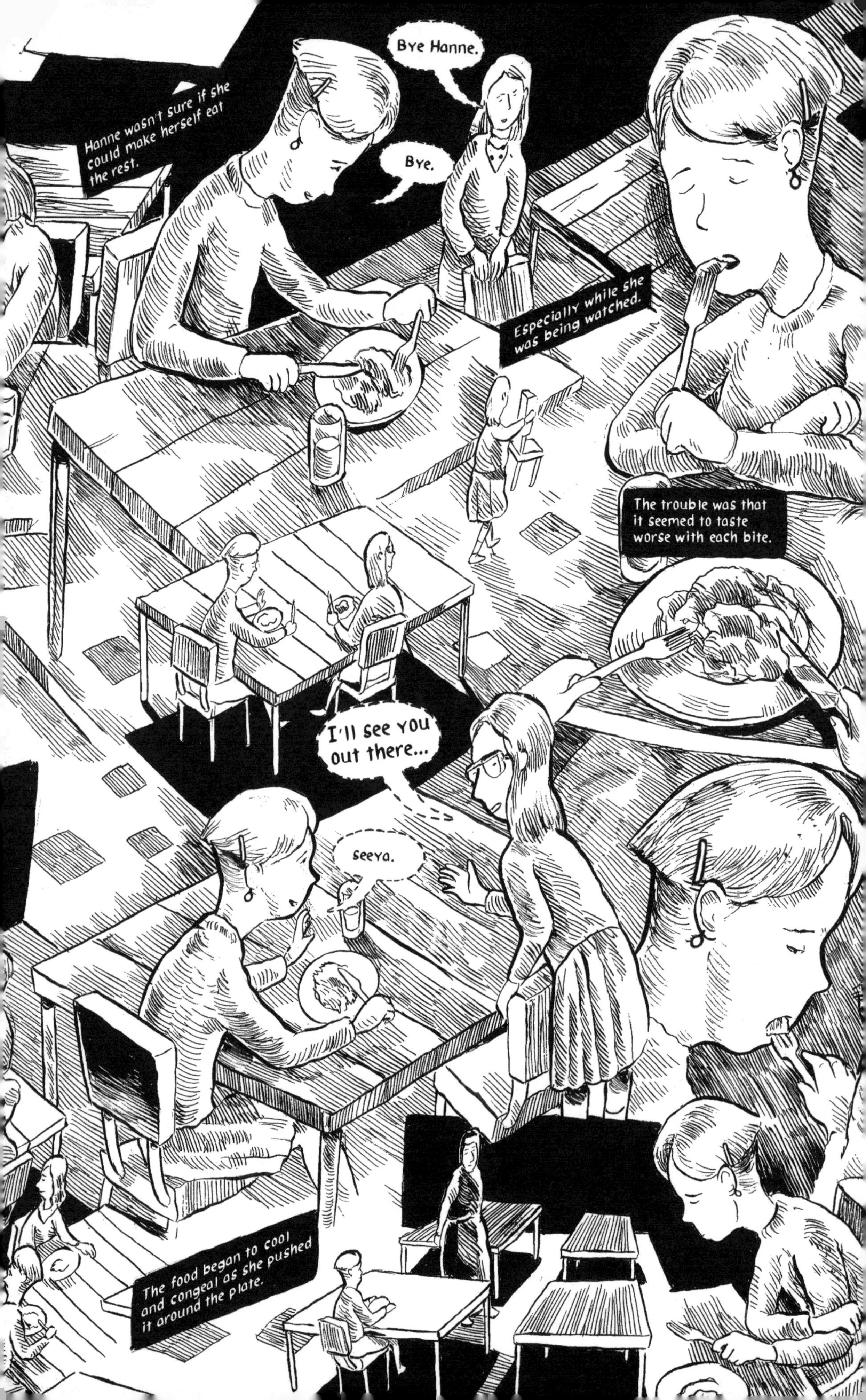
Hanne wasn't sure if she could make herself eat the rest.
Bye Hanne.
Bye.
Especially while she was being watched.
The trouble was that it seemed to taste worse with each bite.
I'll see you out there...
Seeya.
The food began to cool and congeal as she pushed it around the plate.

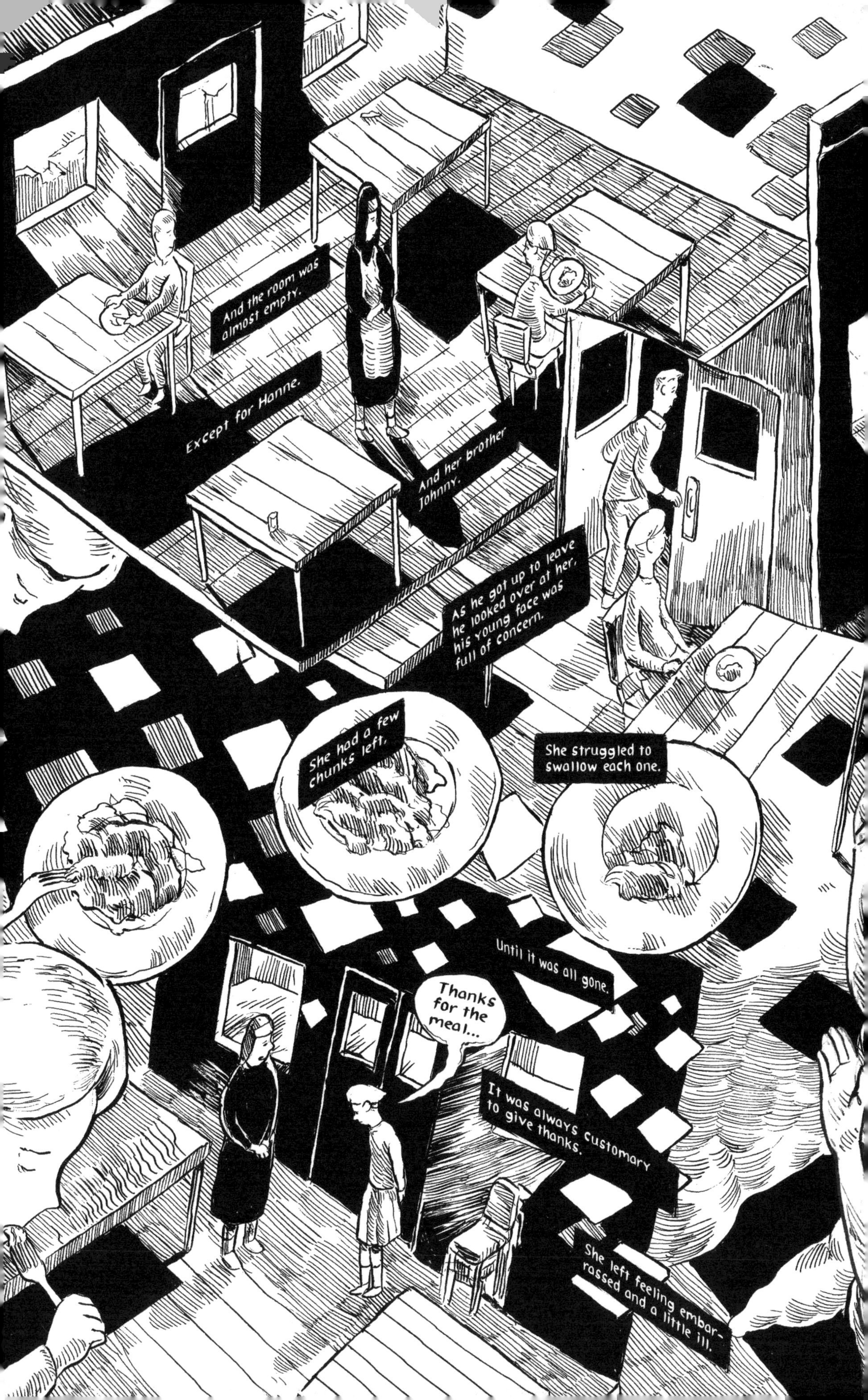
And the room was almost empty.
Except for Hanne.
And her brother Johnny.
As he got up to leave he looked over at her, his young face was full of concern.
She had a few chunks left,
She struggled to swallow each one.
Until it was all gone.
Thanks for the meal...
It was always customary to give thanks.
She left feeling embarrassed and a little ill.

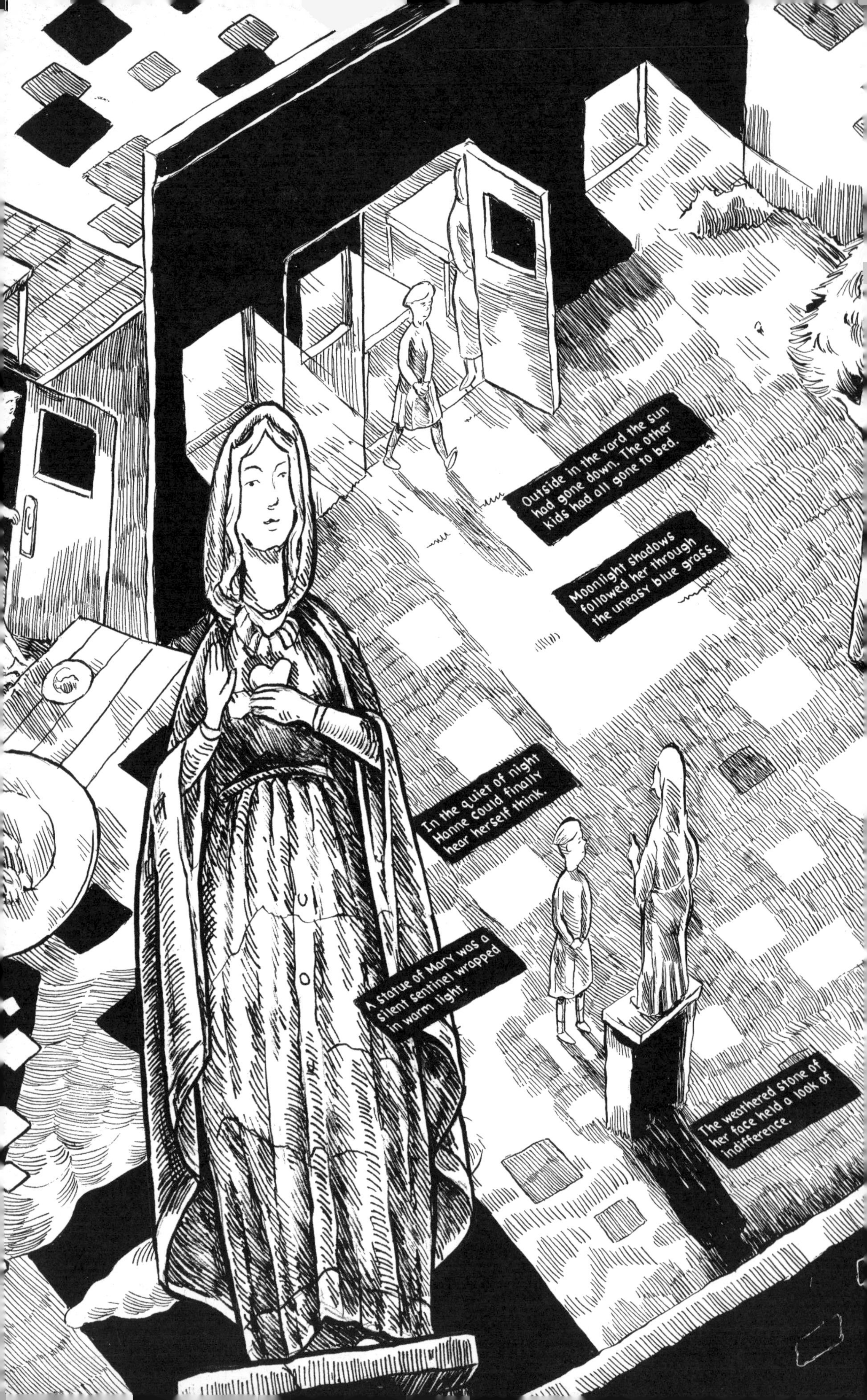
Outside in the yard the sun had gone down. The other kids had all gone to bed.
Moonlight shadows followed her through the uneasy blue grass.
In the quiet of night Hanne could finally hear herself think.
A statue of Mary was a silent sentinel wrapped in warm light.
The weathered stone of her face held a look of indifference.

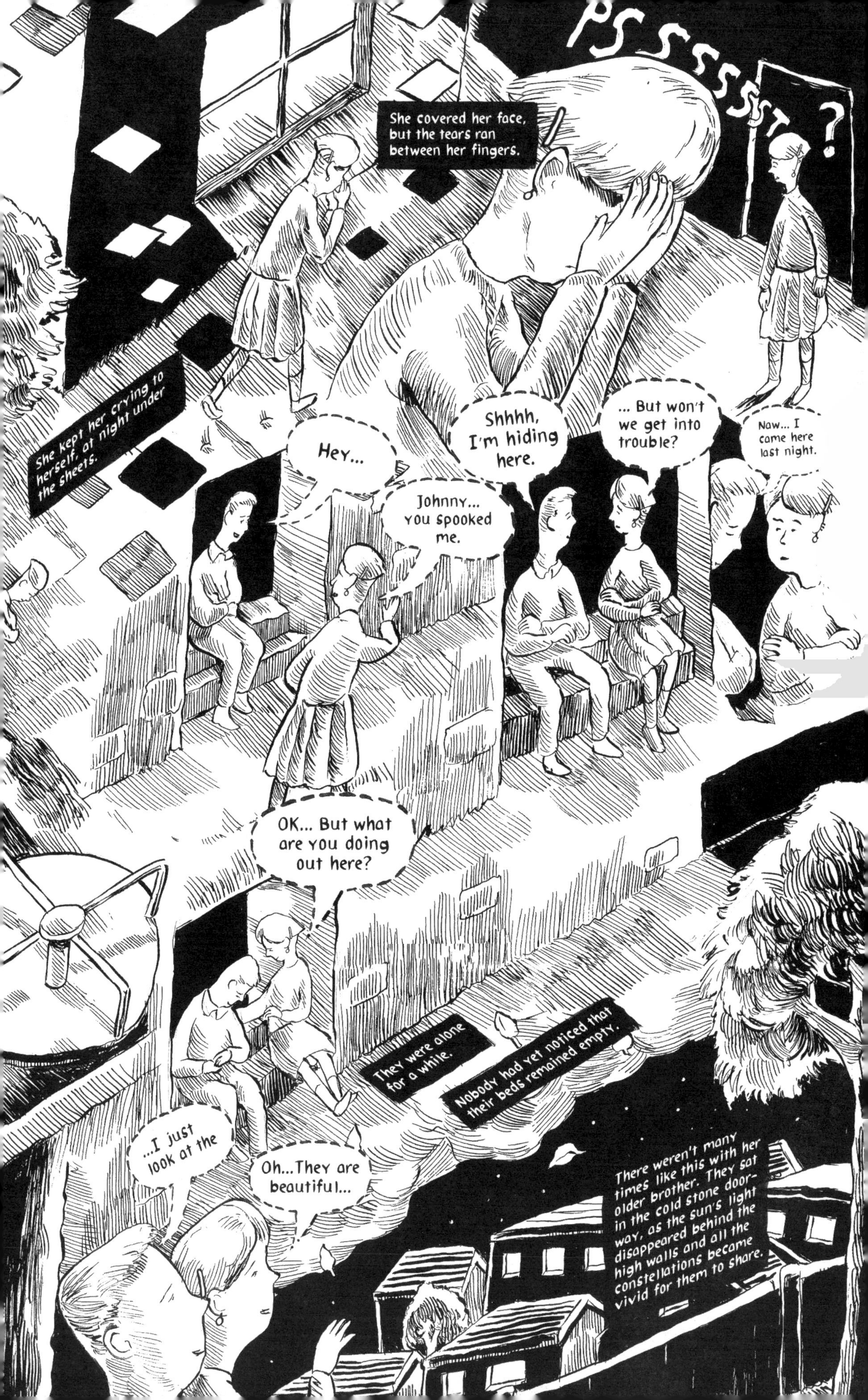
PSSSSSST
?
She covered her face, but the tears ran between her fingers.
She kept her crying to herself, at night under the sheets.
Hey...
Johnny... You spooked me.
Shhhh, I'm hiding here.
... But won't we get into trouble?
Naw... I came here last night.
OK... But what are you doing out here?
They were alone for a while.
Nobody had yet noticed that their beds remained empty.
...I just look at the
Oh...They are beautiful...
There weren't many times like this with her older brother. They sat in the cold stone doorway, as the sun's light disappeared behind the high walls and all the constellations became vivid for them to share.

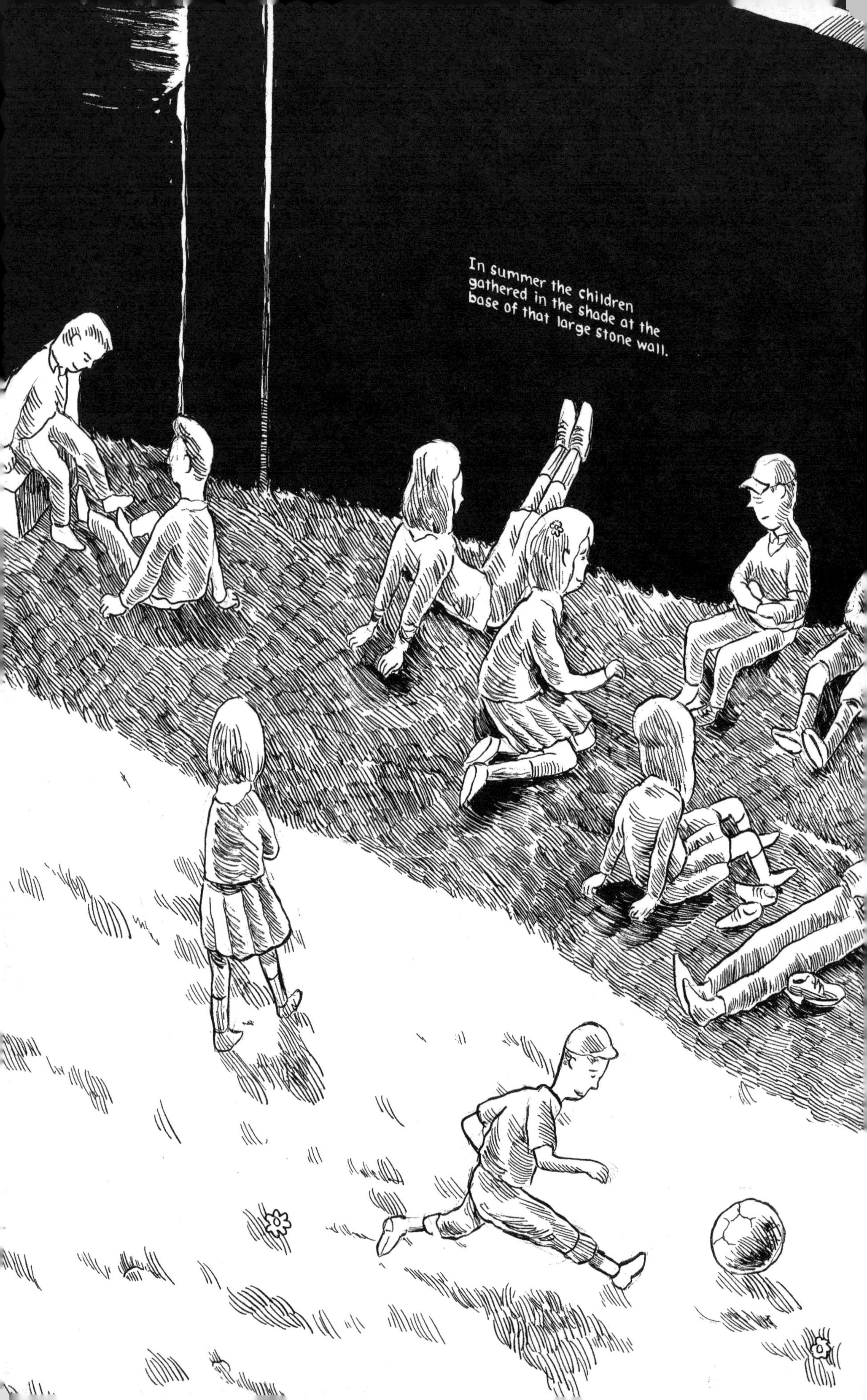
In summer the children gathered in the shade at the base of that large stone wall.

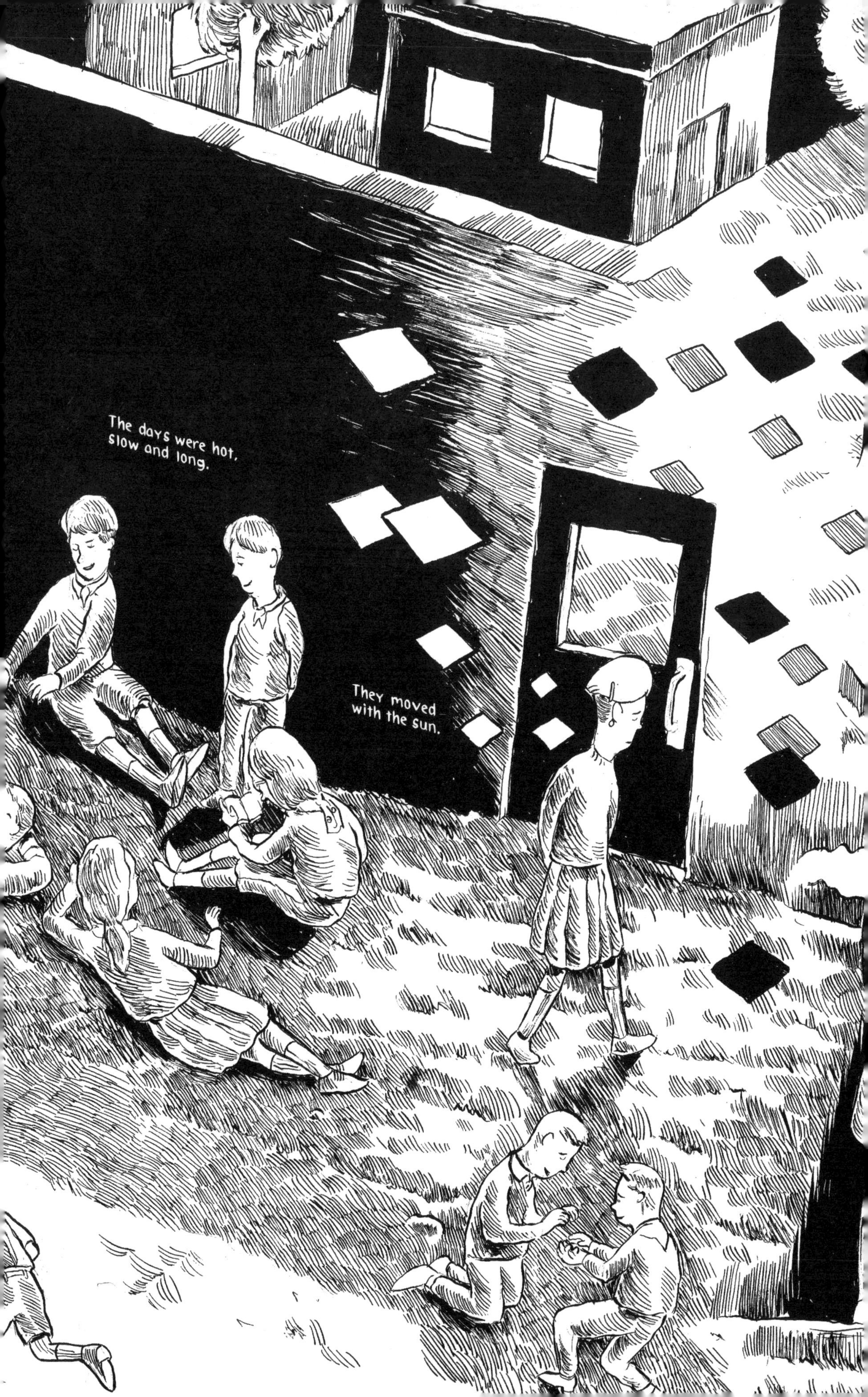
The days were hot,
slow and long.
They moved
with the sun.

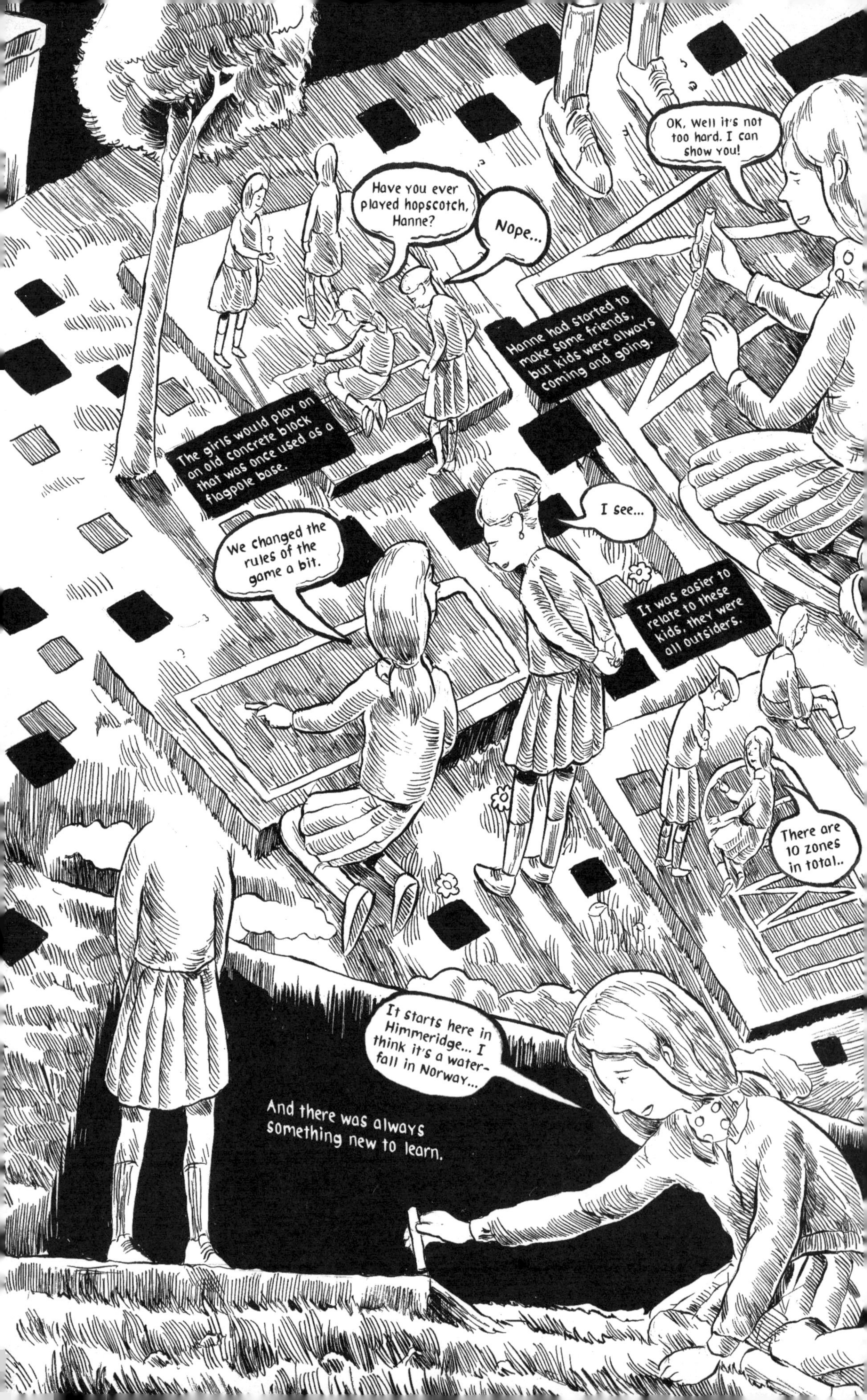
Have you ever played hopscotch, Hanne?
Nope...
OK, Well it's not too hard. I can show you!
Hanne had started to make some friends, but kids were always coming and going.
The girls would play on an old concrete block that was once used as a flagpole base.
We changed the rules of the game a bit.
I see...
It was easier to relate to these kids, they were all outsiders.
There are 10 zones in total..
It starts here in Himmeridge... I think it's a waterfall in Norway...
And there was always something new to learn.

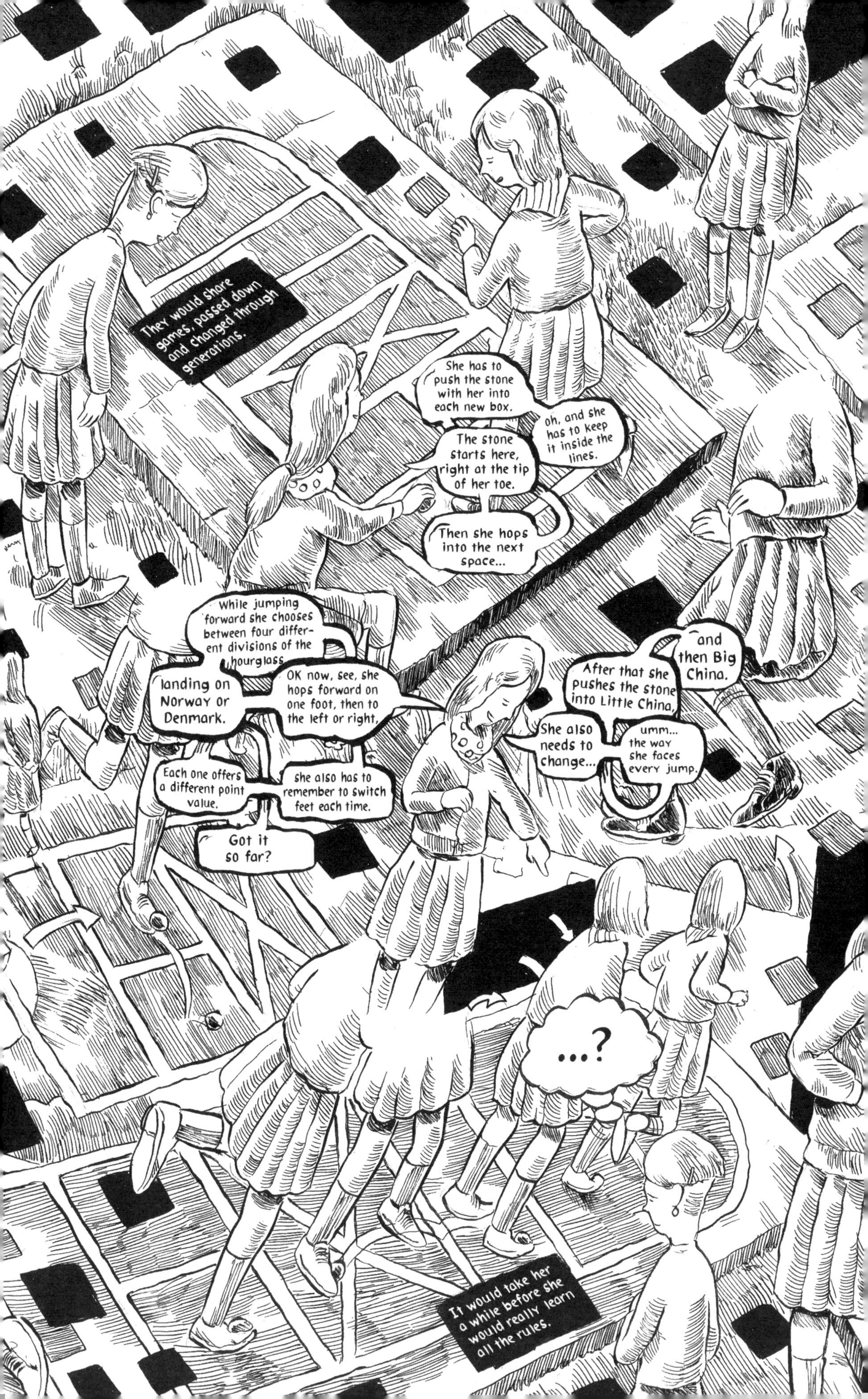
They would share games, passed down and changed through generations.
She has to push the stone with her into each new box.
oh, and she has to keep it inside the lines.
The stone starts here, right at the tip of her toe.
Then she hops into the next space...
While jumping forward she chooses between four different divisions of the hourglass
landing on Norway or Denmark.
OK now, see, she hops forward on one foot, then to the left or right,
Each one offers a different point value.
she also has to remember to switch feet each time.
Got it so far?
and then Big China.
After that she pushes the stone into Little China,
She also needs to change...
umm... the way she faces every jump.
...?
It would take her a while before she would really learn all the rules.

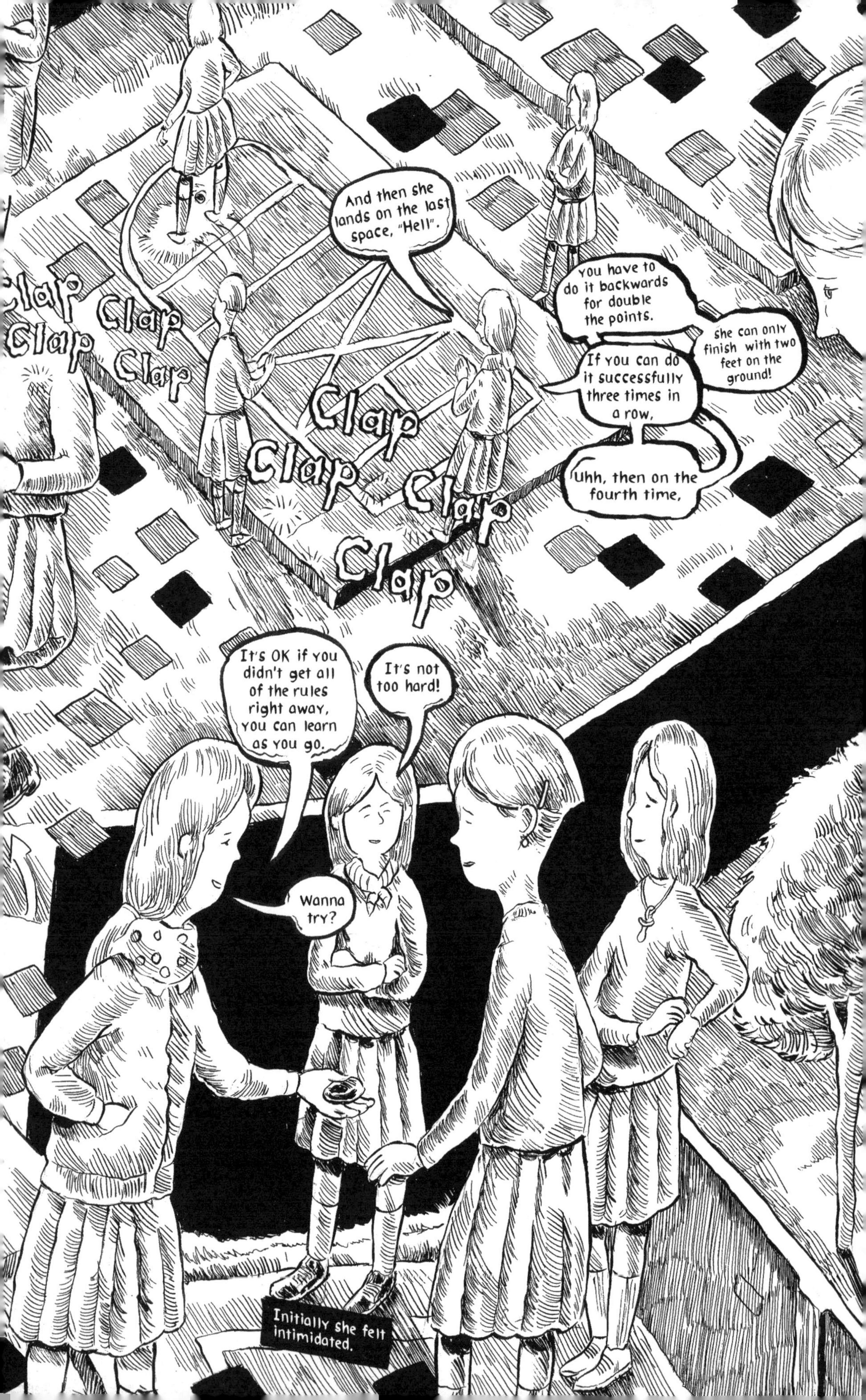
Clap Clap
Clap Clap
And then she lands on the last space, "Hell".
You have to do it backwards for double the points.
If you can do it successfully three times in a row,
Uhh, then on the fourth time,
She can only finish with two feet on the ground!
Clap
Clap Clap
Clap
It's OK if you didn't get all of the rules right away, you can learn as you go.
It's not too hard!
Wanna try?
Initially she felt intimidated.

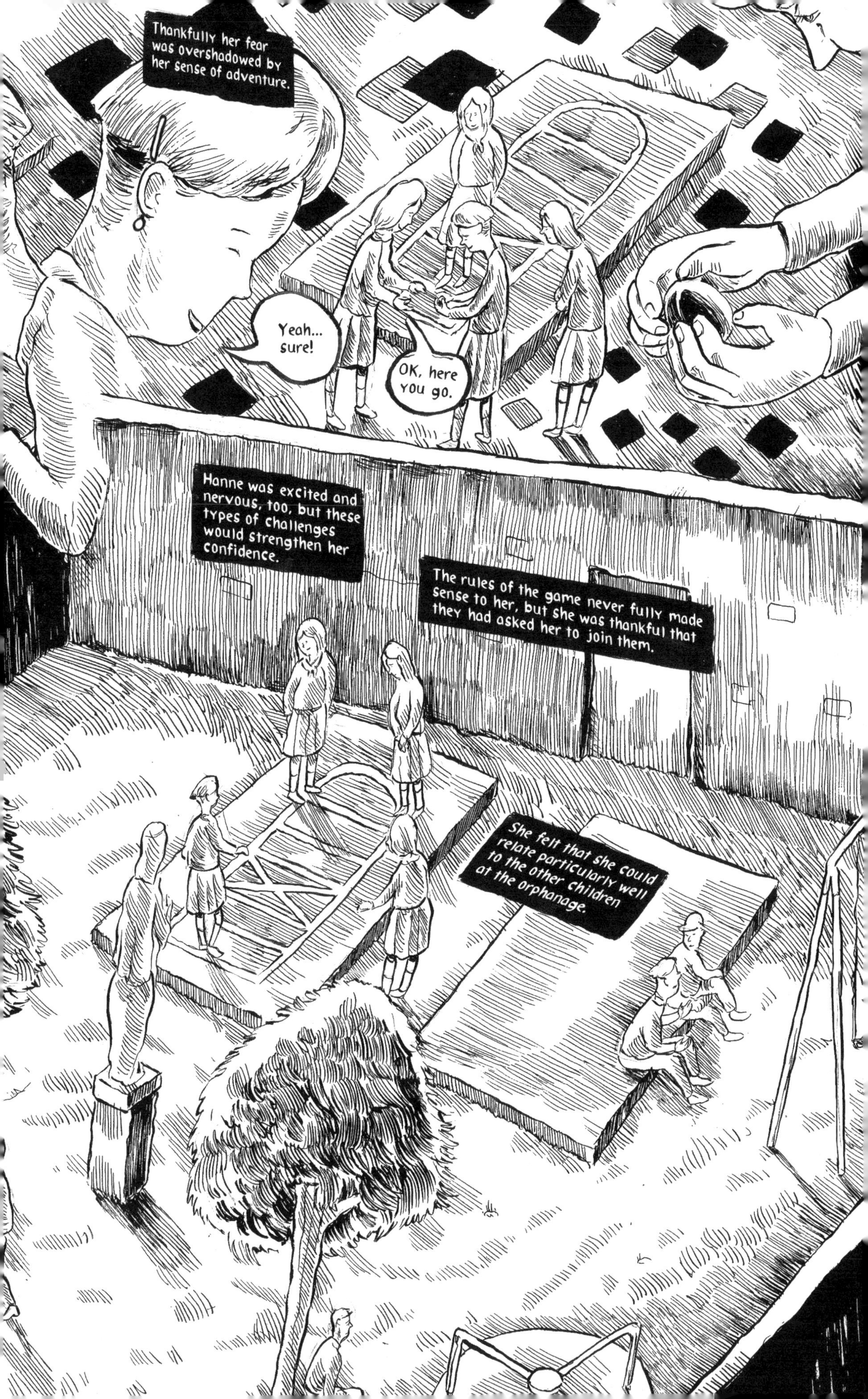
Thankfully her fear was overshadowed by her sense of adventure.
Yeah... sure!
OK, here you go.
Hanne was excited and nervous, too, but these types of challenges would strengthen her confidence.
The rules of the game never fully made sense to her, but she was thankful that they had asked her to join them.
She felt that she could relate particularly well to the other children at the orphanage.

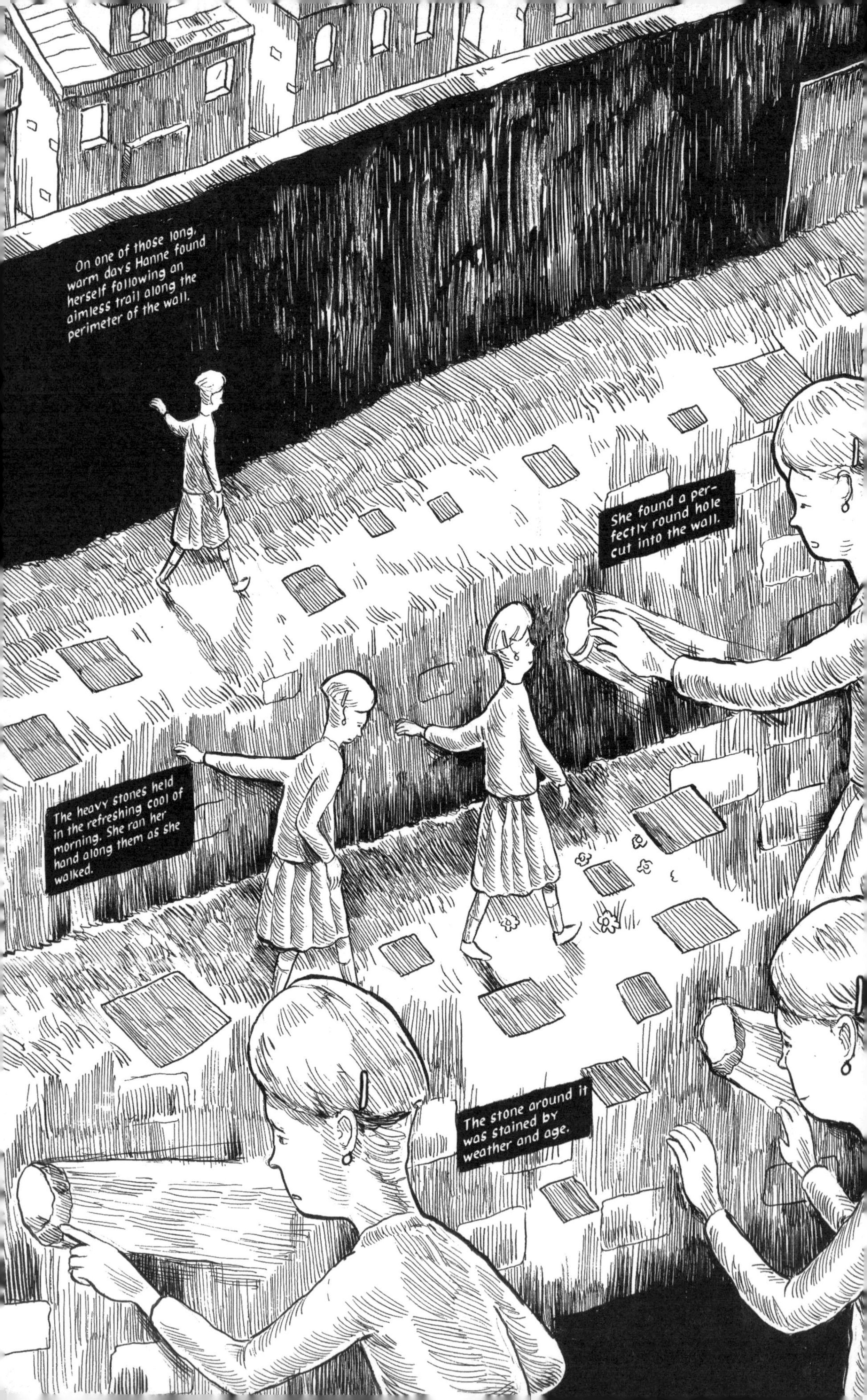
On one of those long, warm days Hanne found herself following an aimless trail along the perimeter of the wall.
She found a perfectly round hole cut into the wall.
The heavy stones held in the refreshing cool of morning. She ran her hand along them as she walked.
The stone around it was stained by weather and age.

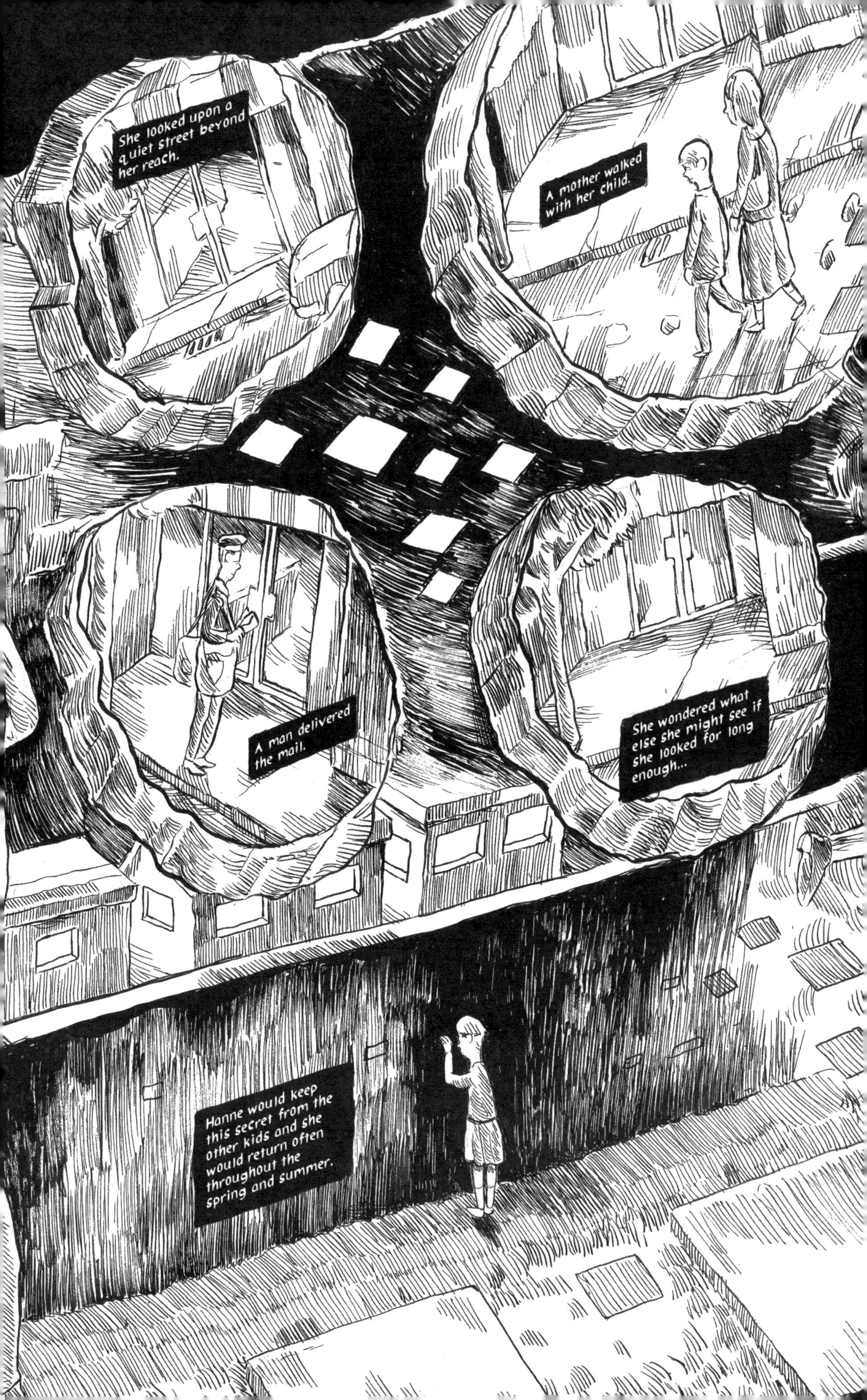
She looked upon a quiet street beyond her reach.
A mother walked with her child.
A man delivered the mail.
She wondered what else she might see if she looked for long enough...
Hanne would keep this secret from the other kids and she would return often throughout the spring and summer.

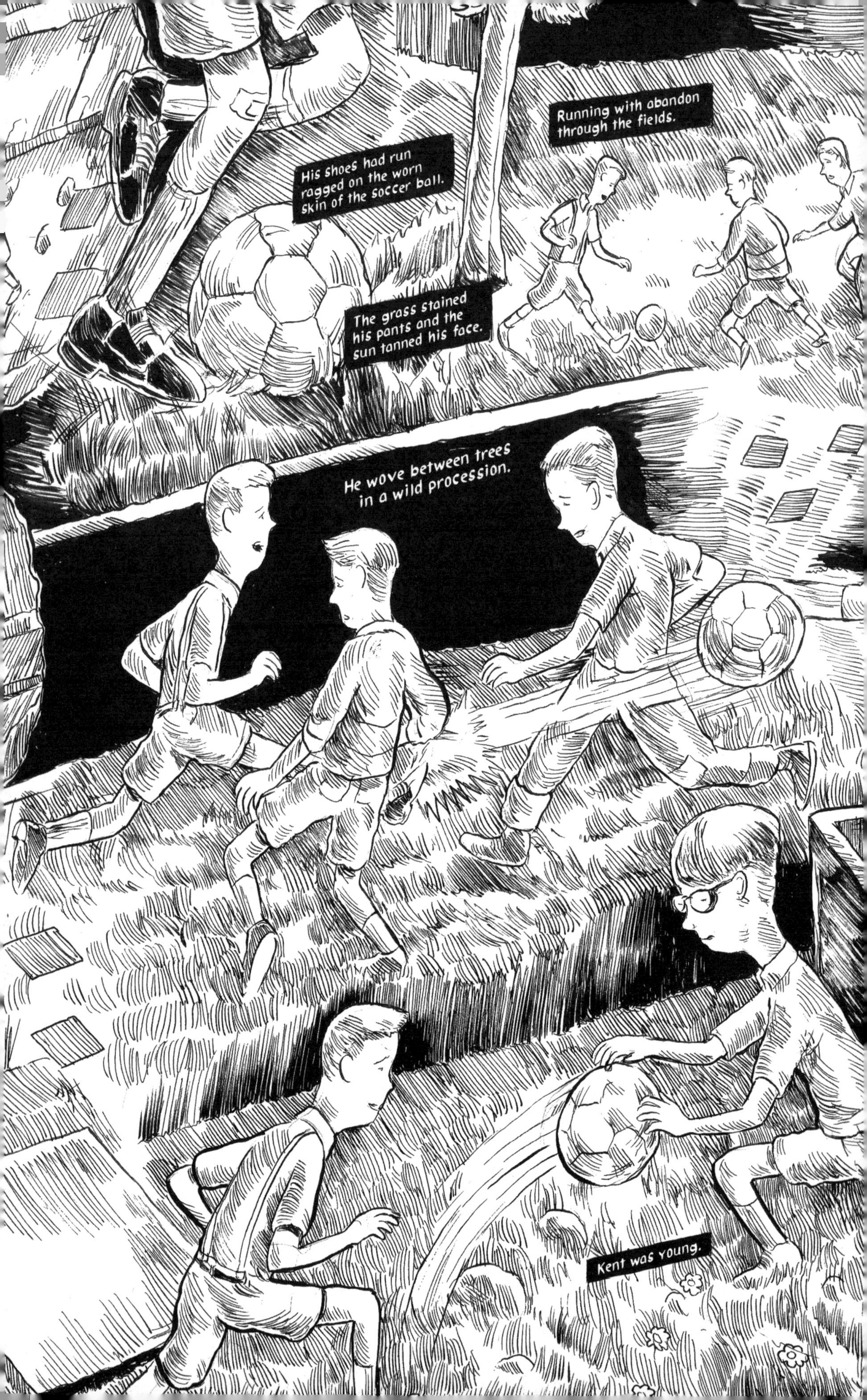
His shoes had run ragged on the worn skin of the soccer ball.
Running with abandon through the fields.
The grass stained his pants and the sun tanned his face.
He wove between trees in a wild procession.
Kent was young.

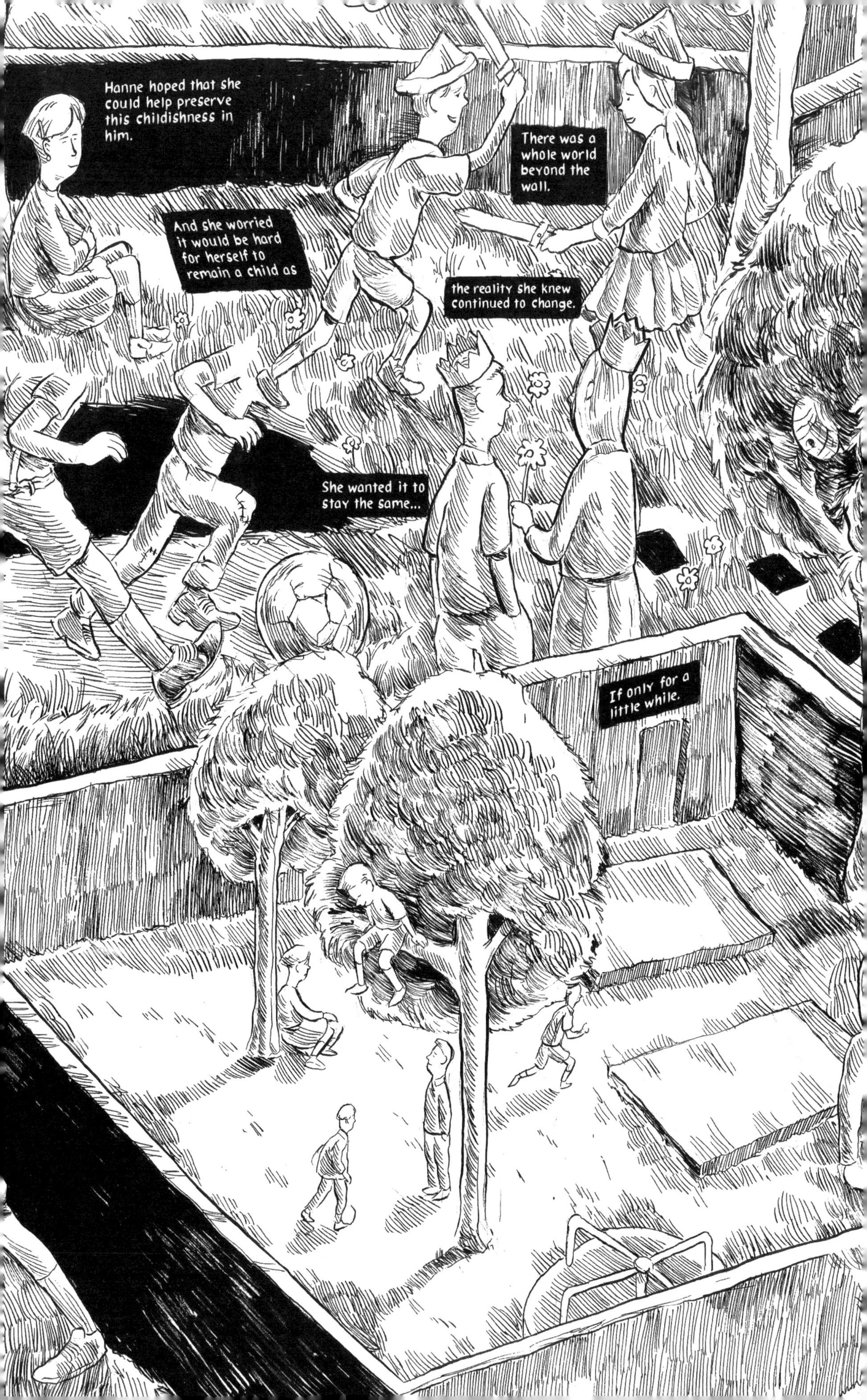
Hanne hoped that she could help preserve this childishness in him.
There was a whole world beyond the wall.
And she worried it would be hard for herself to remain a child as
the reality she knew continued to change.
She wanted it to stay the same...
If only for a little while.

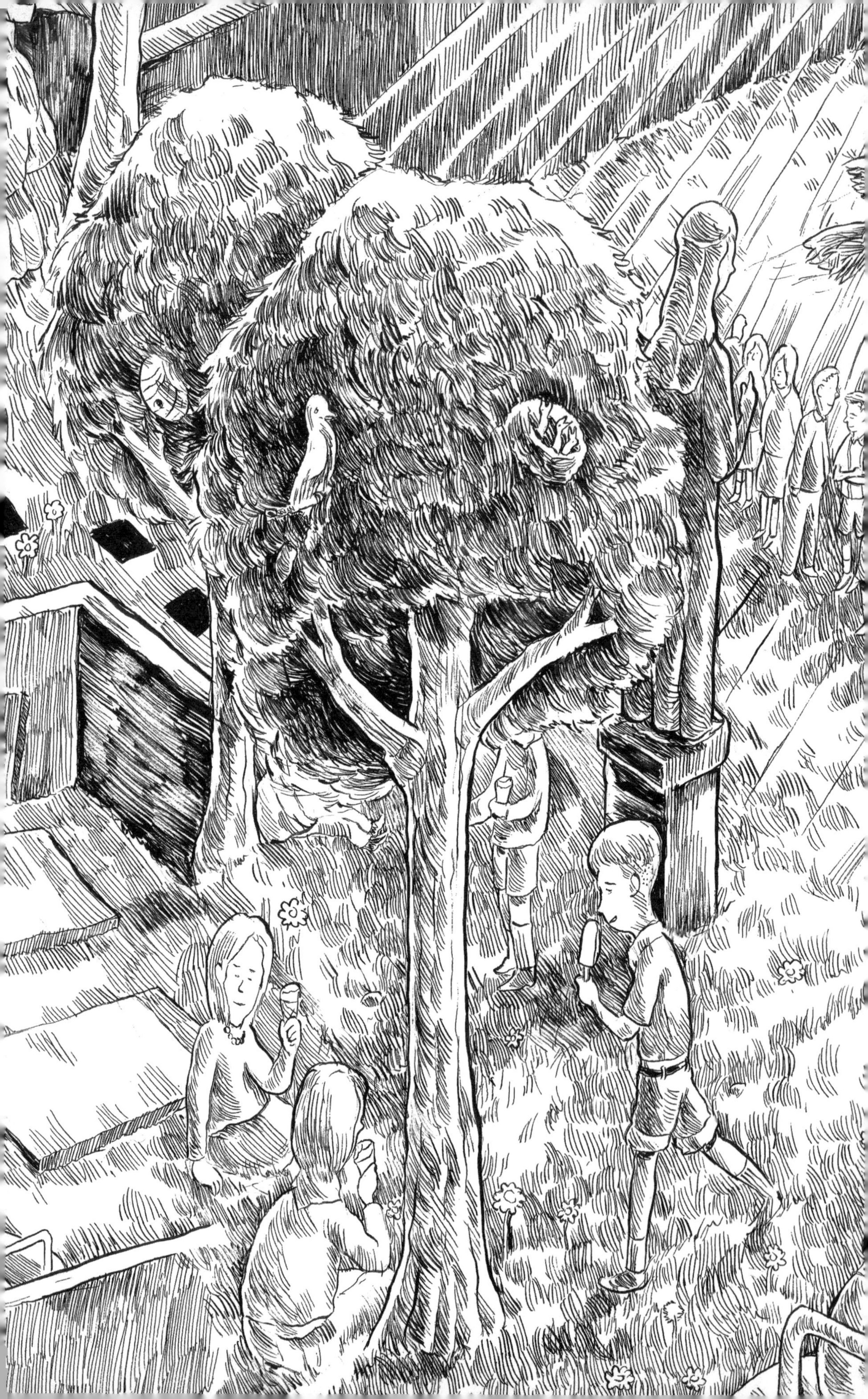

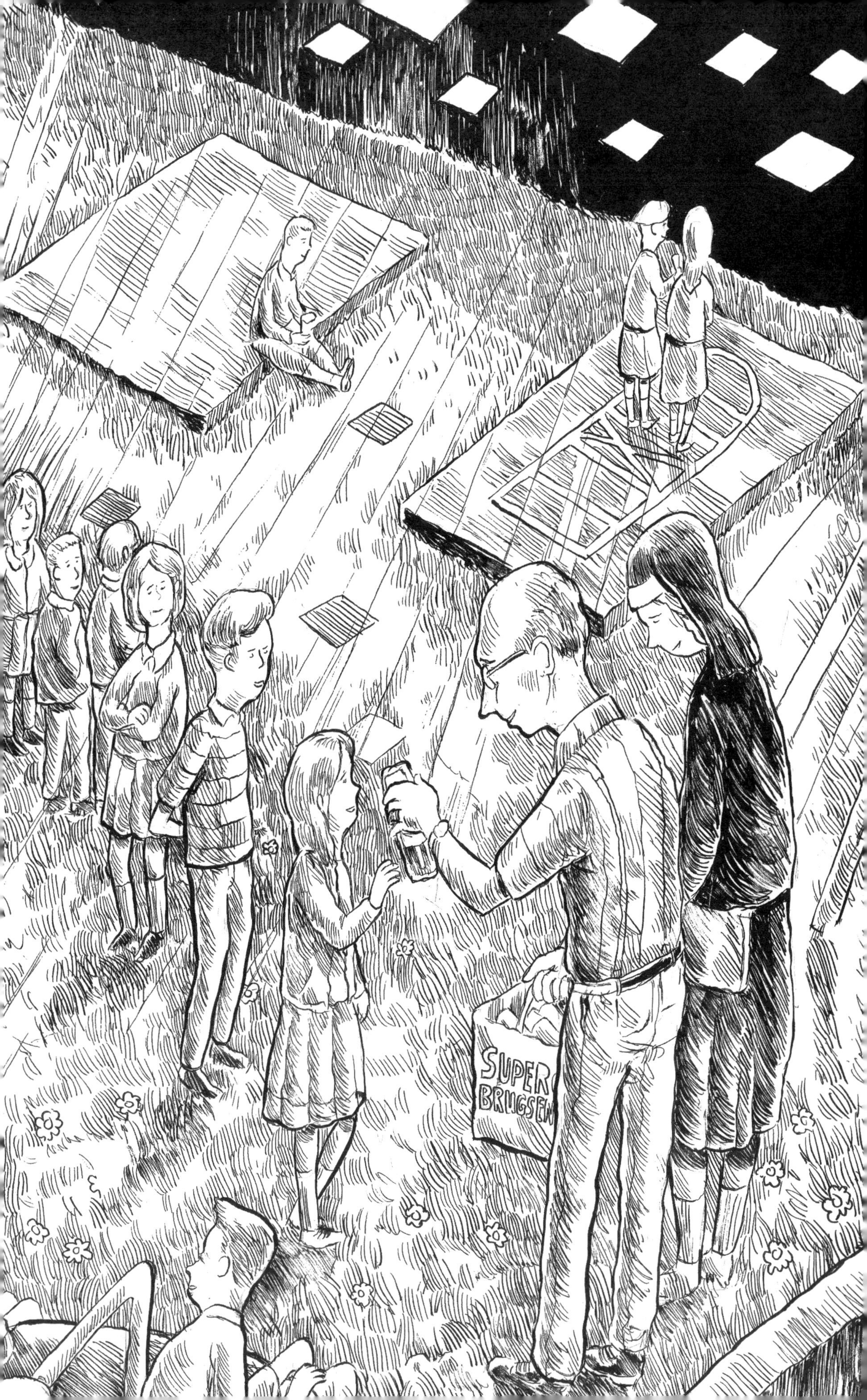
SUPER
BRUGSEN

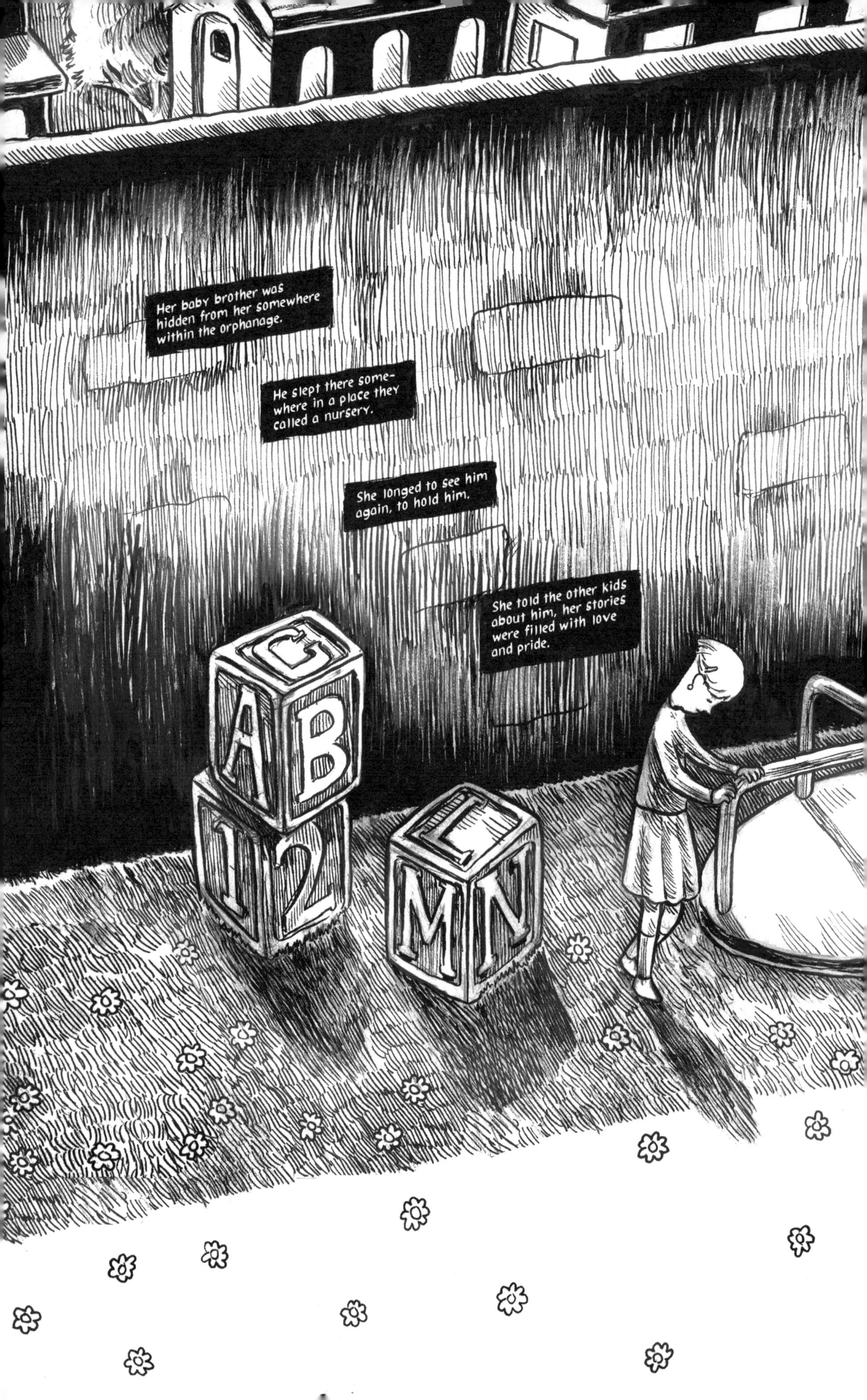
Her baby brother was hidden from her somewhere within the orphanage.
He slept there some-where in a place they called a nursery.
She longed to see him again, to hold him.
She told the other kids about him, her stories were filled with love and pride.
A B
1 2
M N

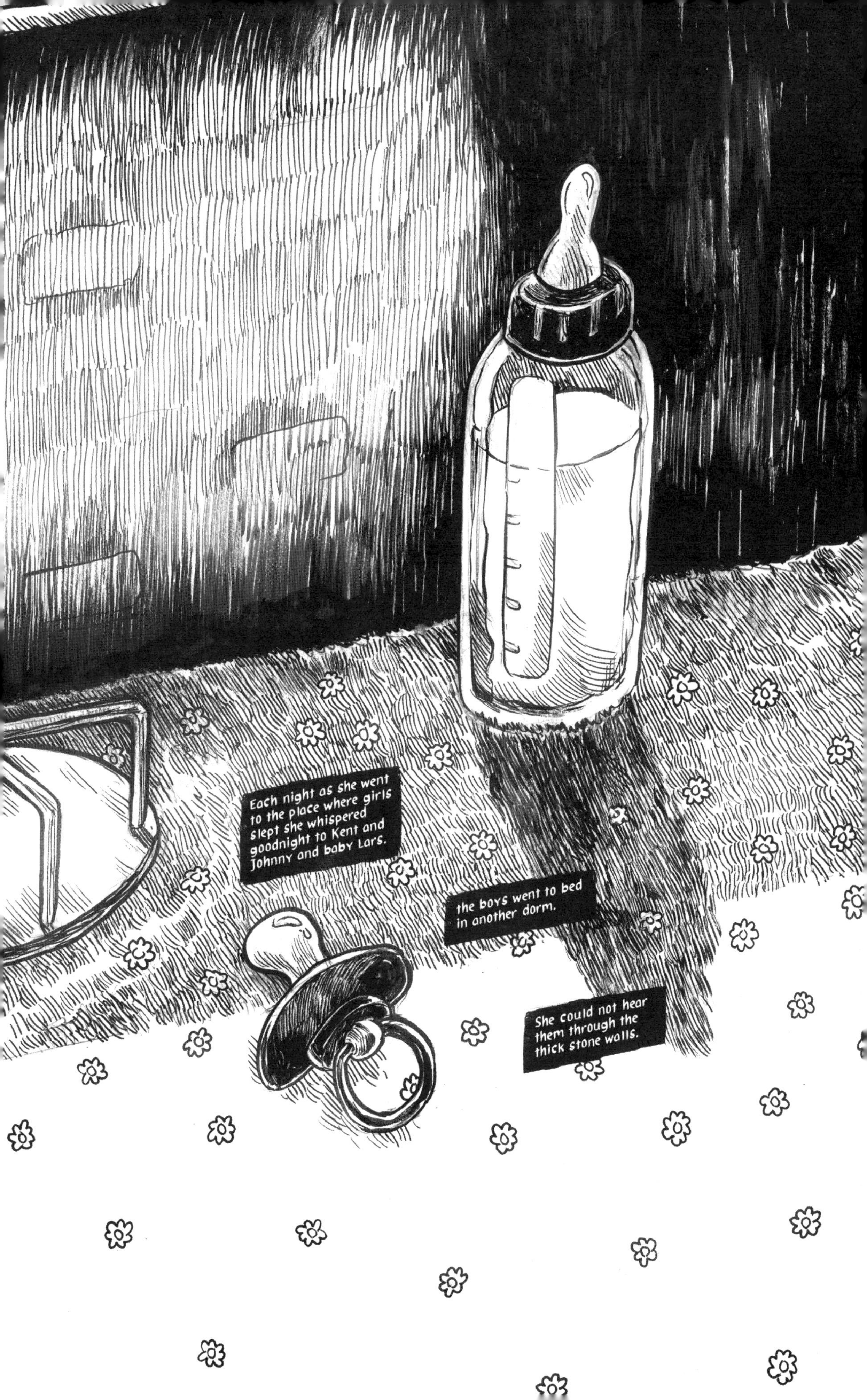
Each night as she went to the place where girls slept she whispered goodnight to Kent and Johnny and baby Lars.
the boys went to bed in another dorm.
She could not hear them through the thick stone walls.

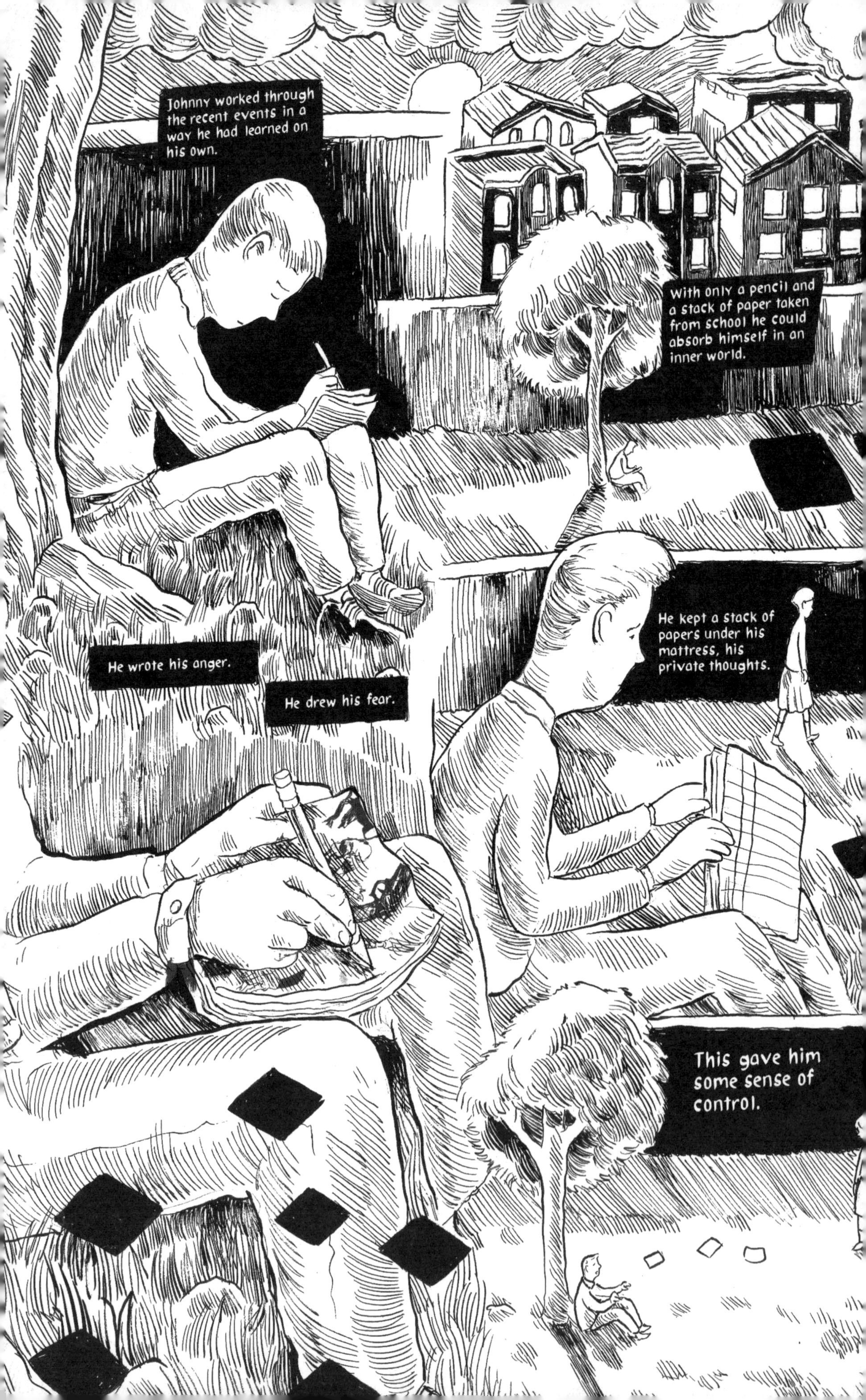
Johnny worked through the recent events in a way he had learned on his own.
With only a pencil and a stack of paper taken from school he could absorb himself in an inner world.
He wrote his anger.
He drew his fear.
He kept a stack of papers under his mattress, his private thoughts.
This gave him some sense of control.

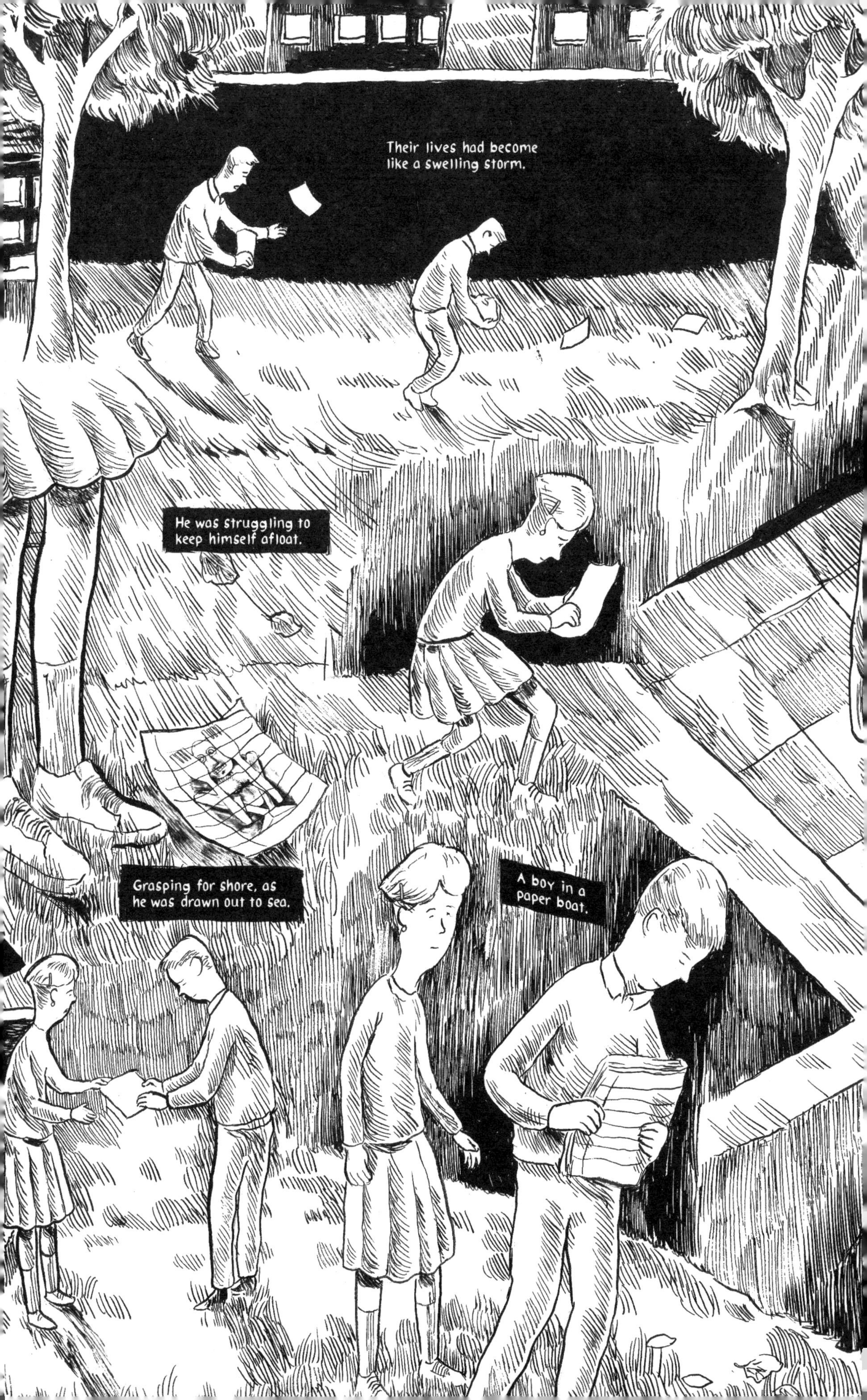
Their lives had become like a swelling storm.
He was struggling to keep himself afloat.
Grasping for shore, as he was drawn out to sea.
A boy in a paper boat.

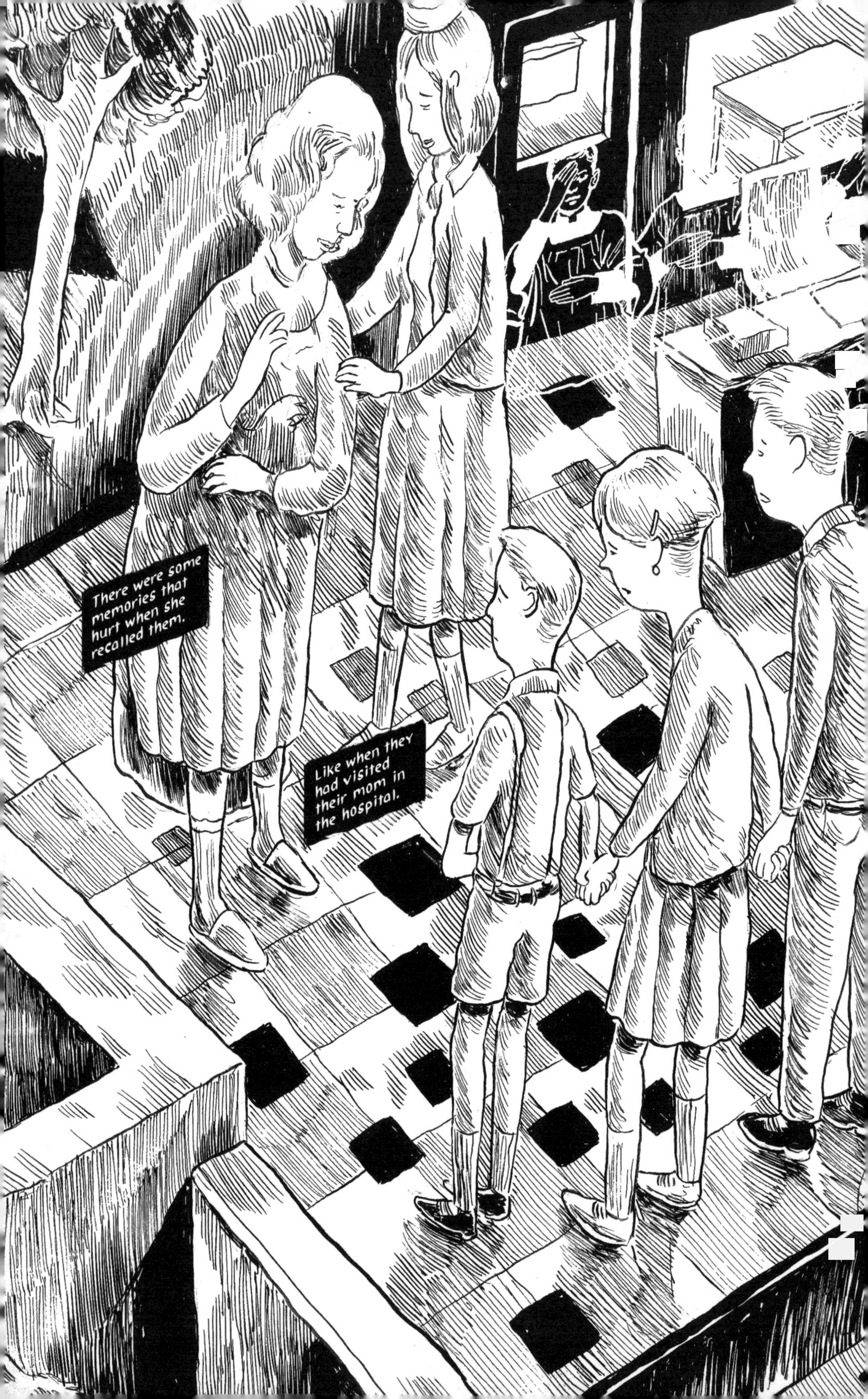
There were some memories that hurt when she recalled them.
Like when they had visited their mom in the hospital.

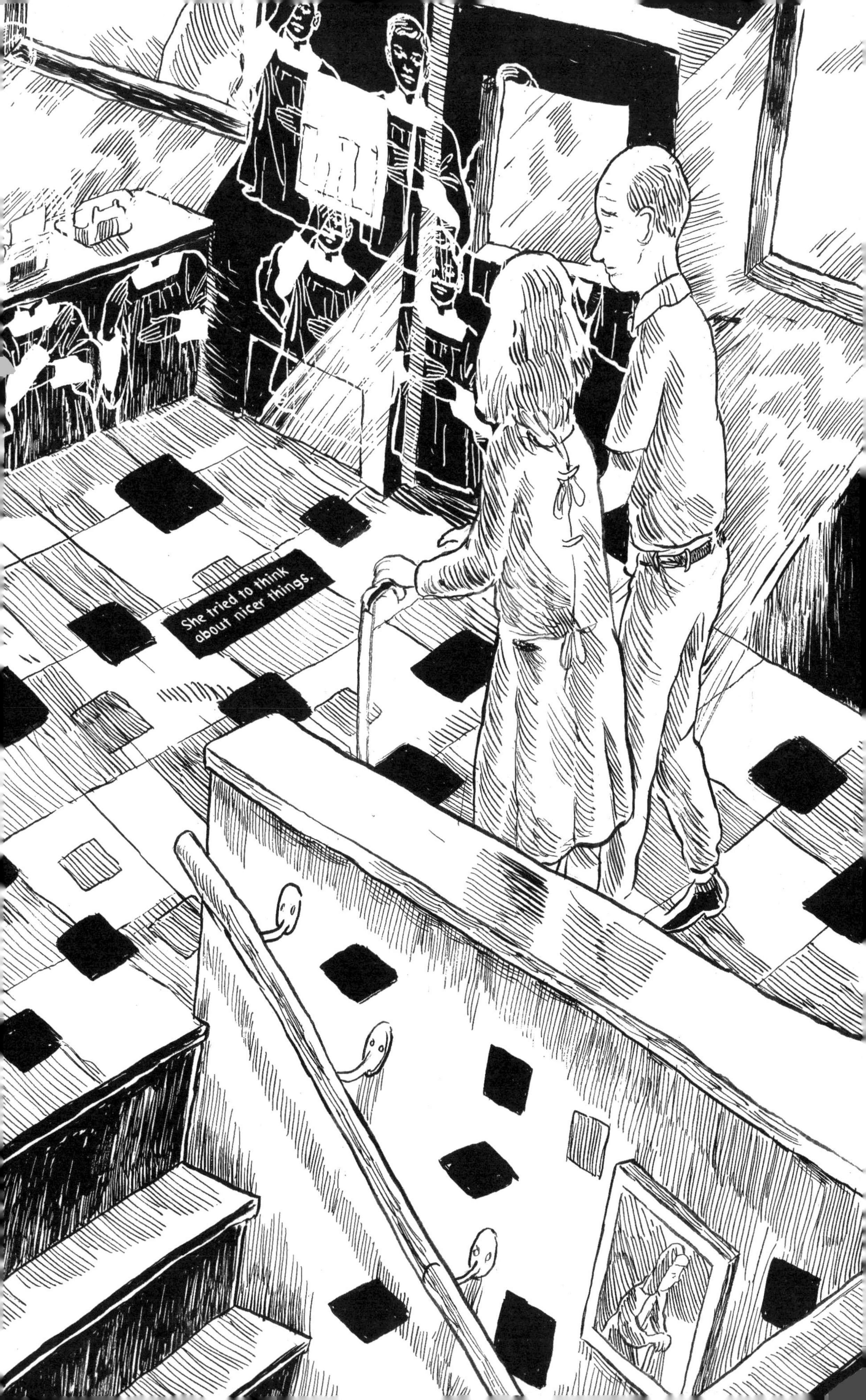
She tried to think
about nicer things.

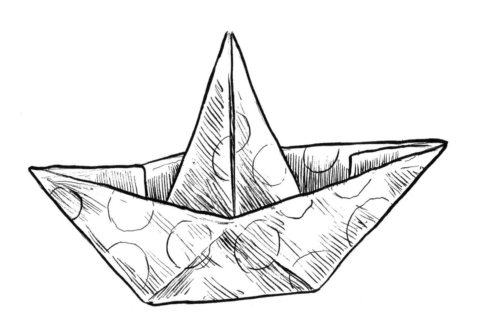

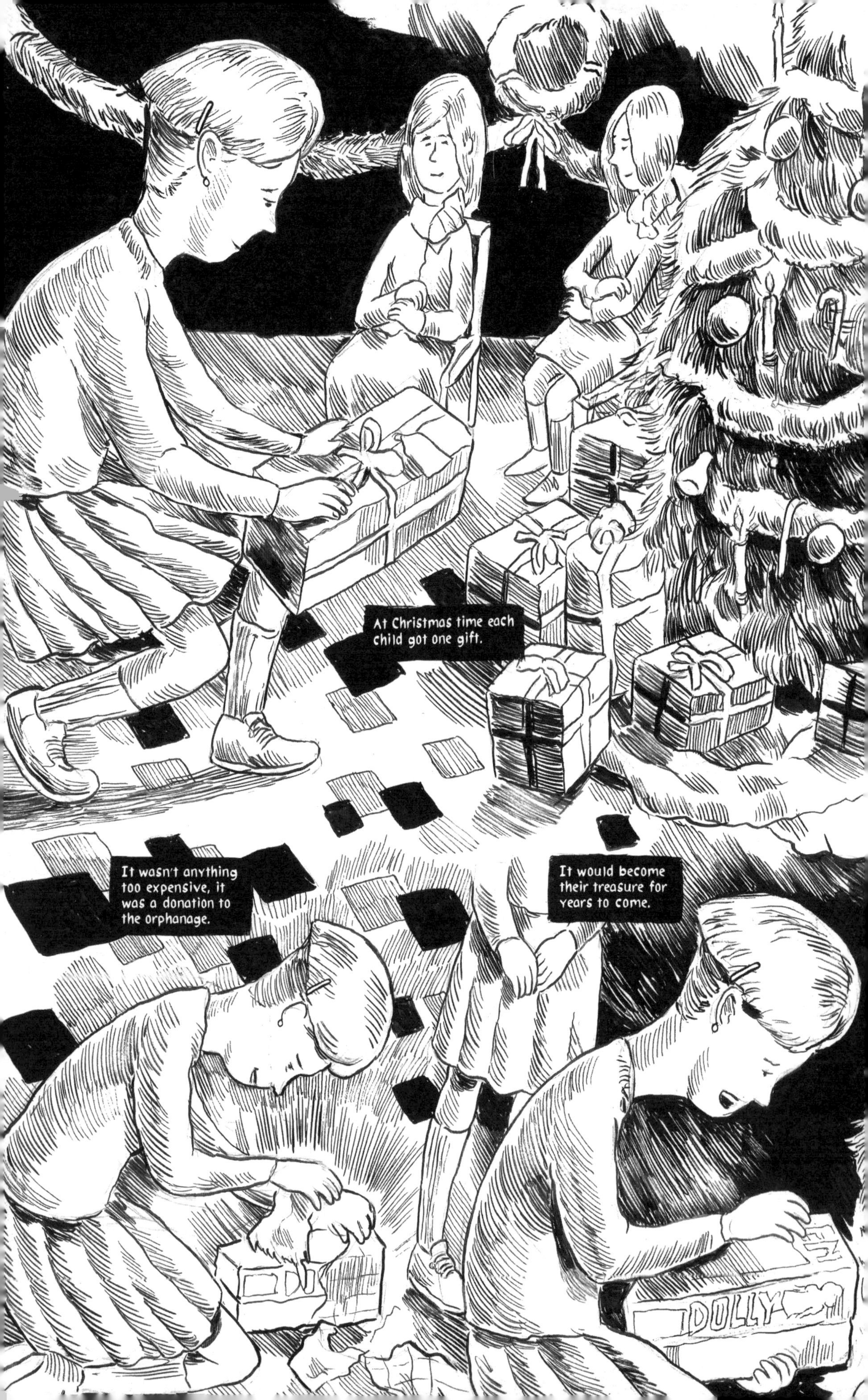
At Christmas time each child got one gift.
It wasn't anything too expensive, it was a donation to the orphanage.
It would become their treasure for years to come.
DOLLY

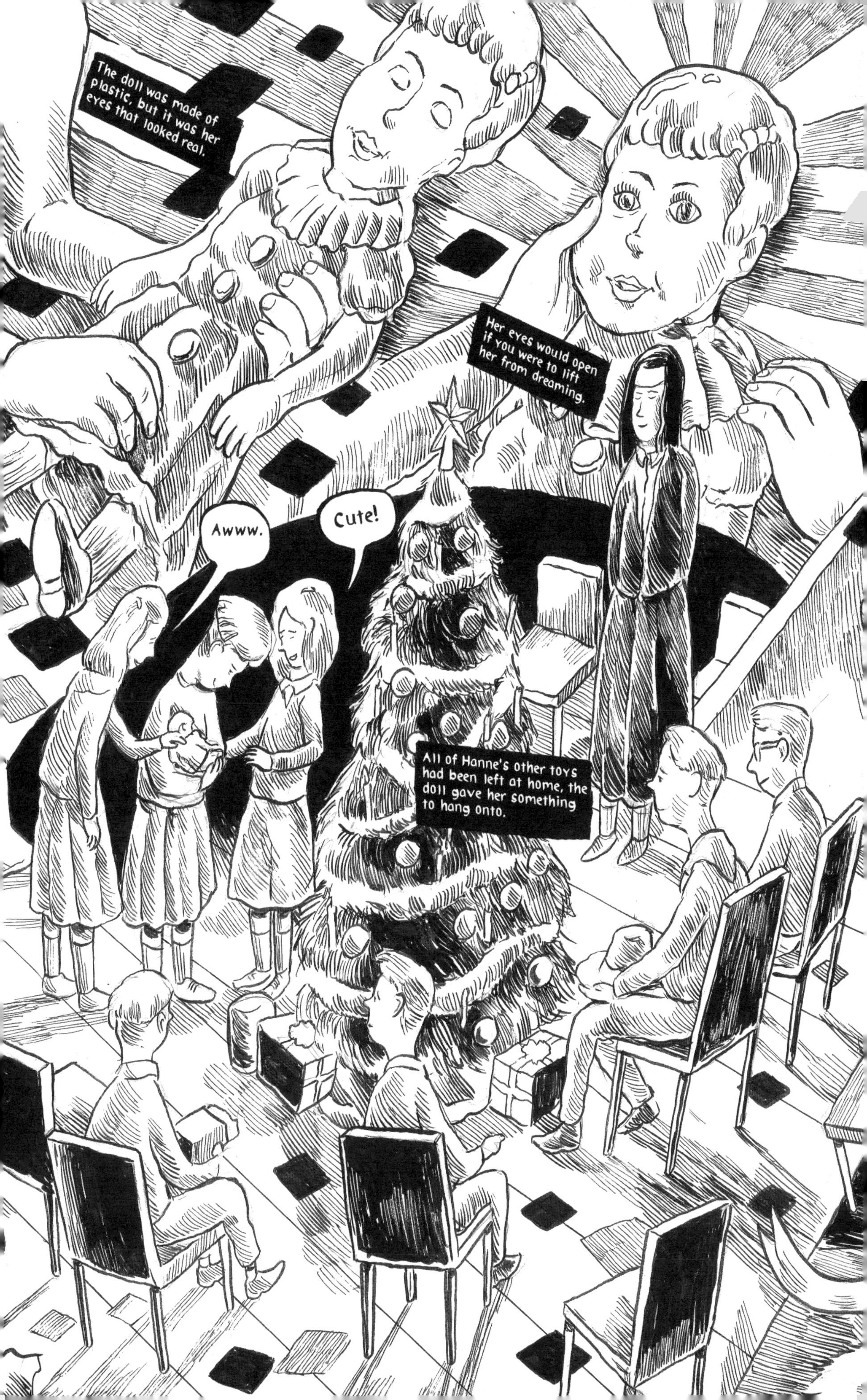
The doll was made of plastic, but it was her eyes that looked real.
Her eyes would open if you were to lift her from dreaming.
Awww.
Cute!
All of Hanne's other toys had been left at home, the doll gave her something to hang onto.

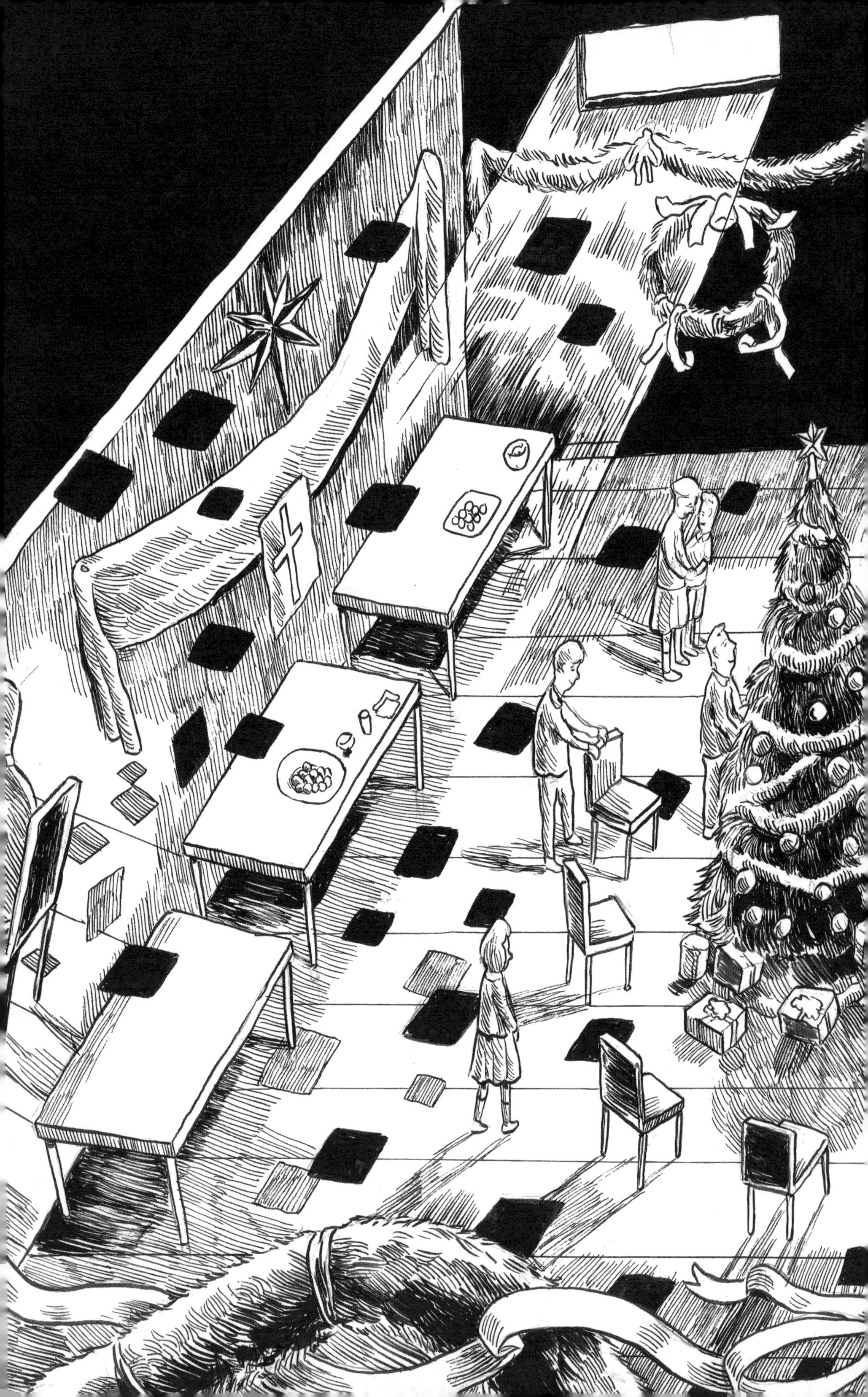

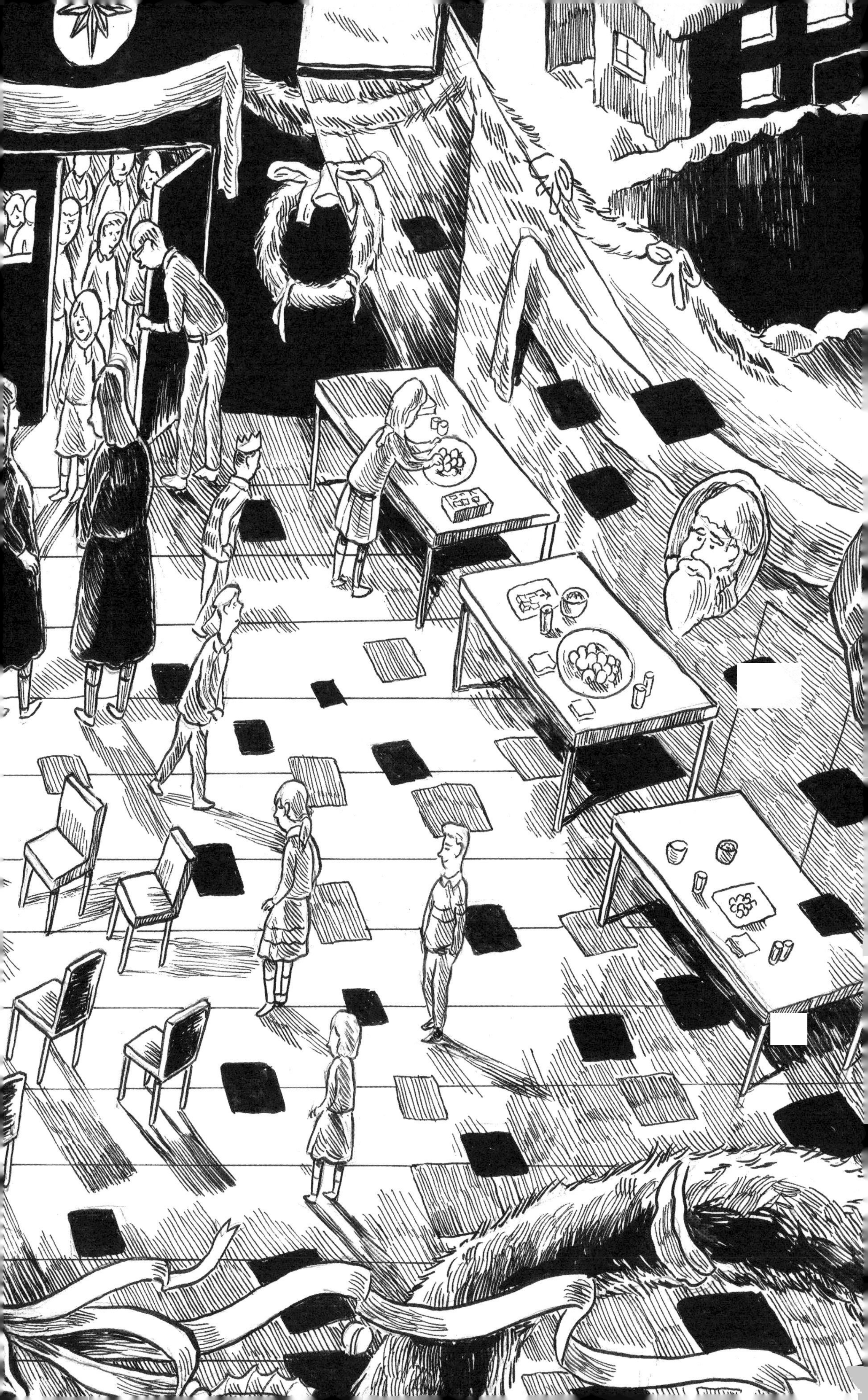

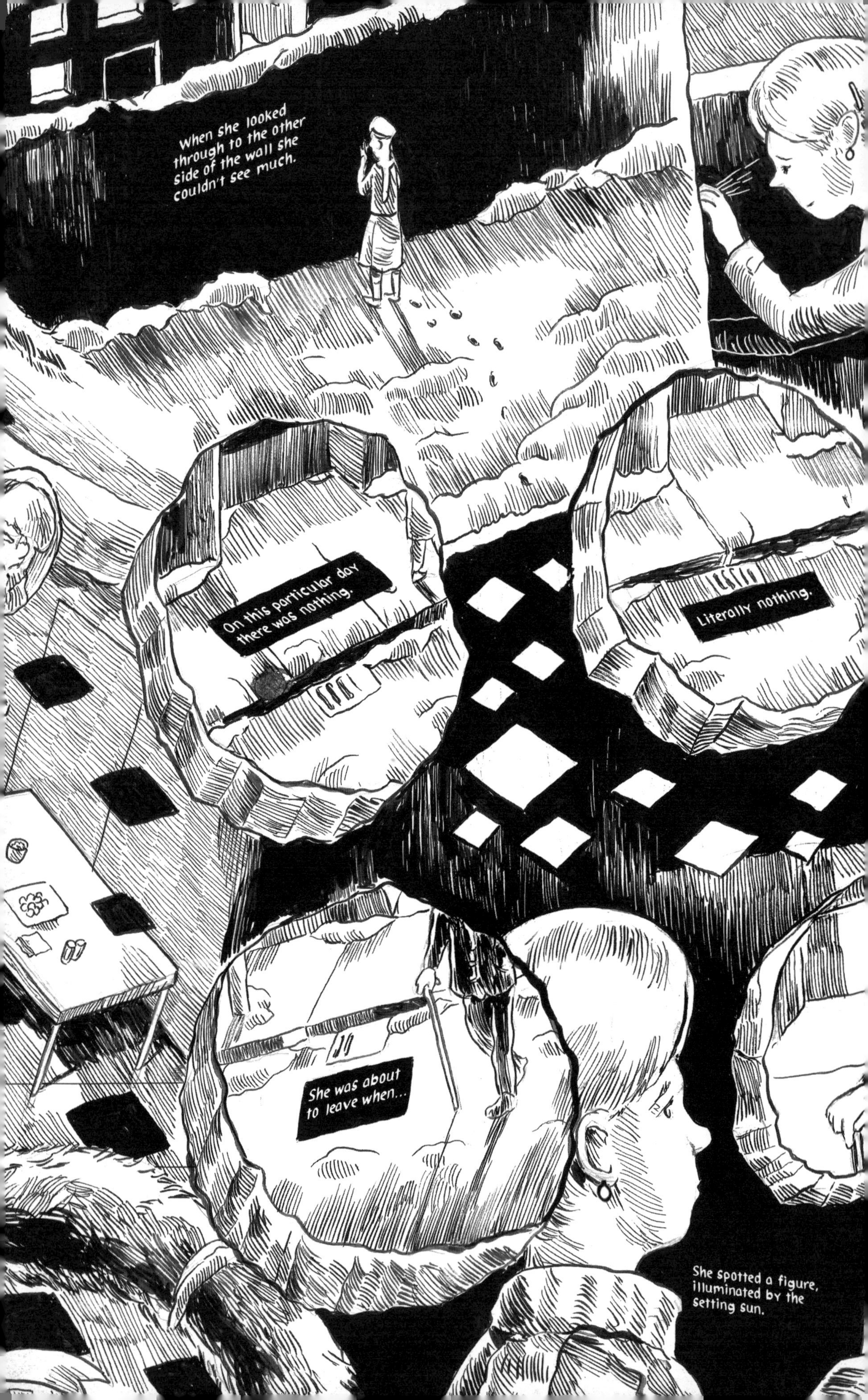
When she looked through to the other side of the wall she couldn't see much.
On this particular day there was nothing.
Literally nothing.
She was about to leave when...
She spotted a figure, illuminated by the setting sun.

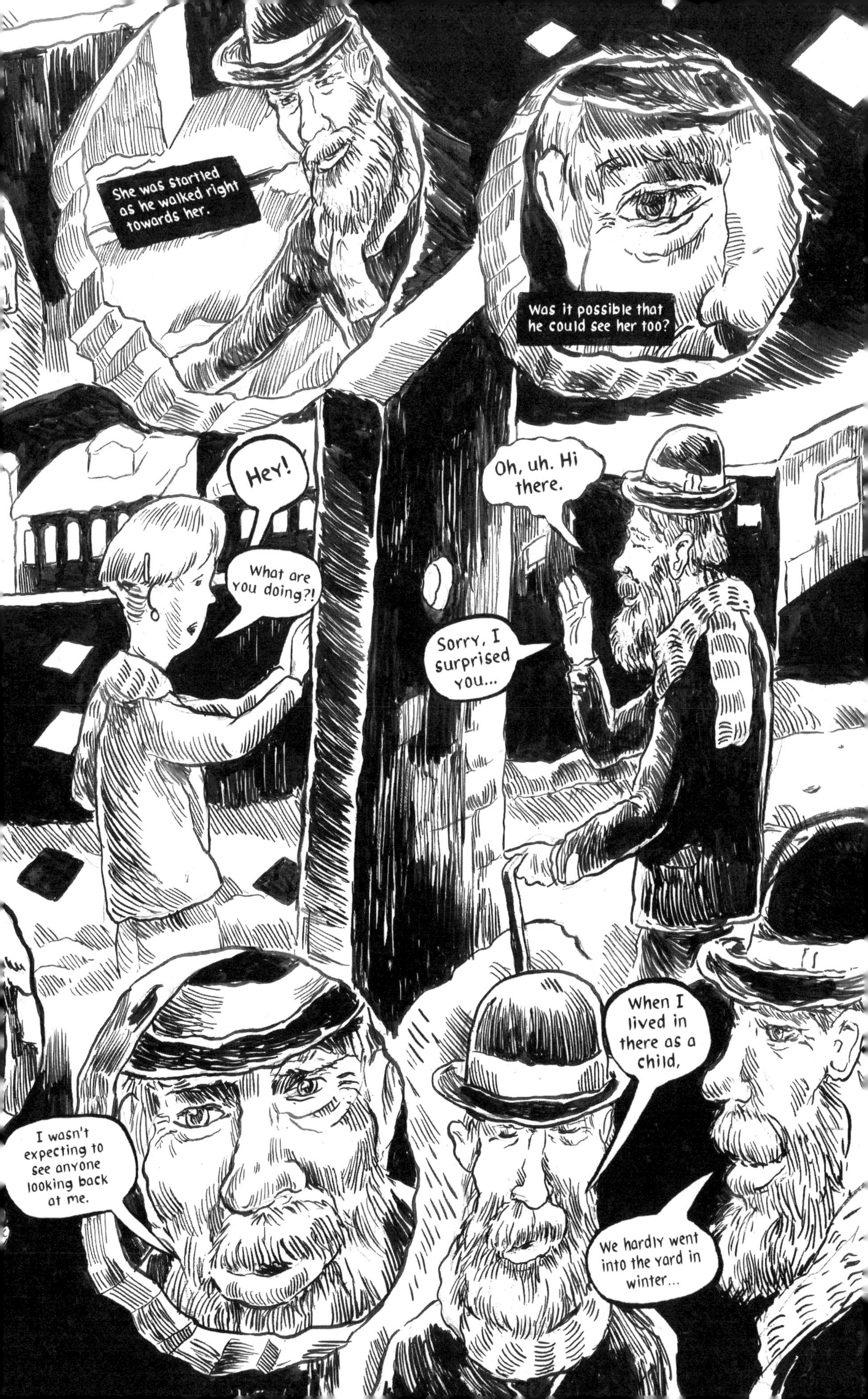
She was startled as he walked right towards her.
Was it possible that he could see her too?
Hey!
What are you doing?!
Oh, uh. Hi there.
Sorry, I surprised you...
I wasn't expecting to see anyone looking back at me.
When I lived in there as a child,
We hardly went into the yard in winter...

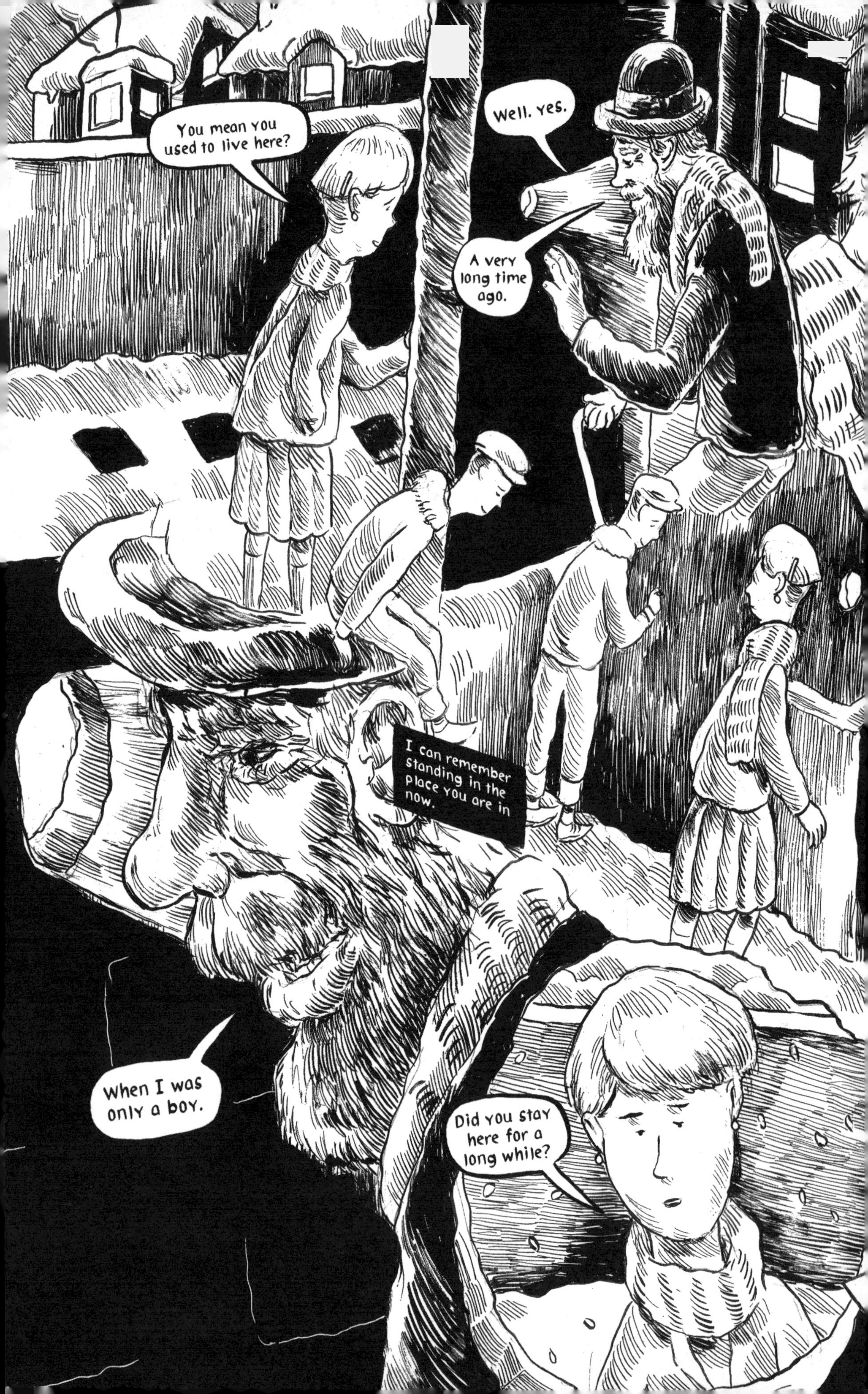
You mean you used to live here?
Well. yes.
A very long time ago.
I can remember standing in the place you are in now.
When I was only a boy.
Did you stay here for a long while?

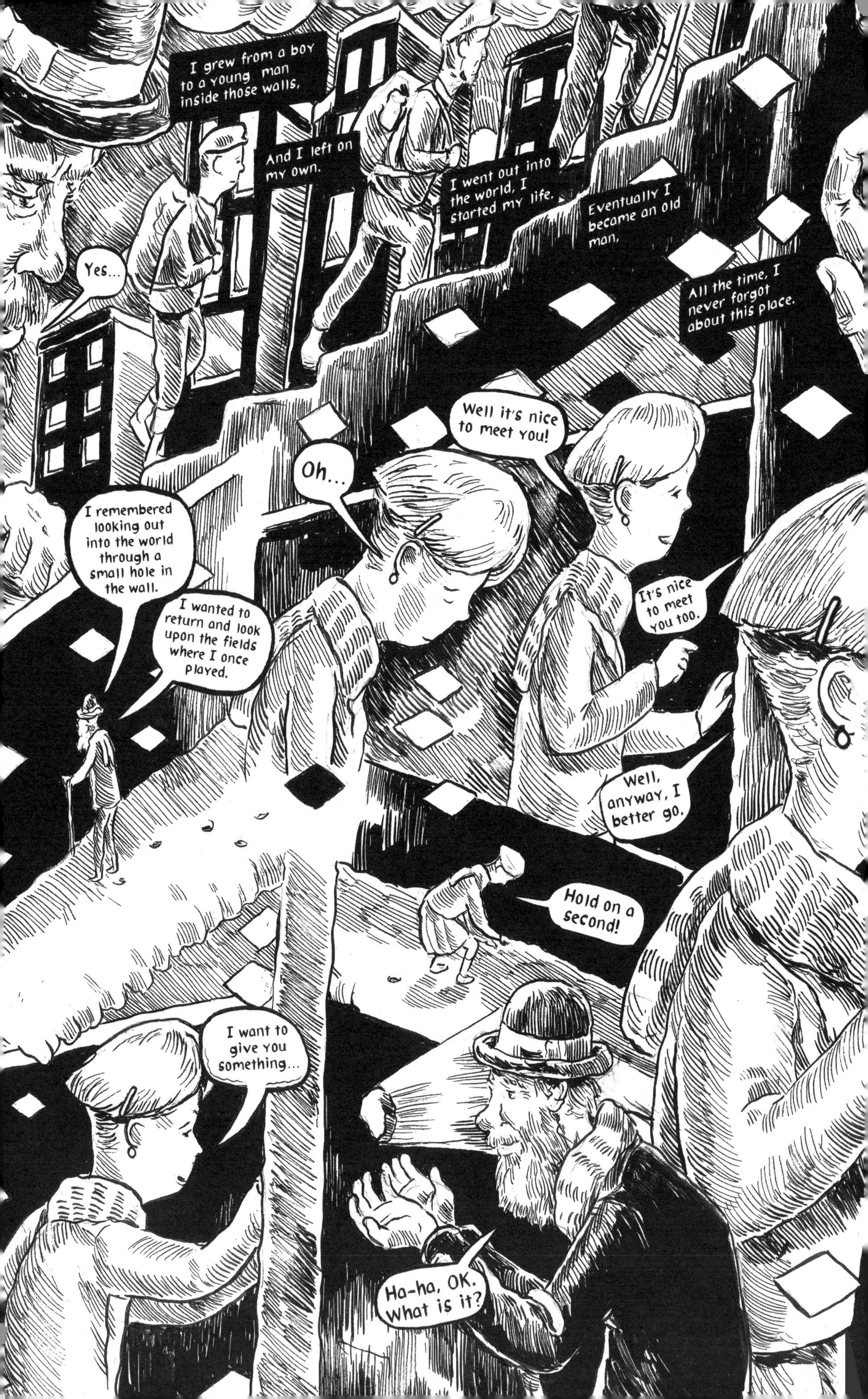
I grew from a boy to a young man inside those walls,
And I left on my own.
I went out into the world, I started my life.
Eventually I became an old man,
All the time, I never forgot about this place.
Yes...
Well it's nice to meet you!
Oh...
I remembered looking out into the world through a small hole in the wall.
I wanted to return and look upon the fields where I once played.
It's nice to meet you too.
Well, anyway, I better go.
Hold on a second!
I want to give you something...
Ha-ha, OK. What is it?

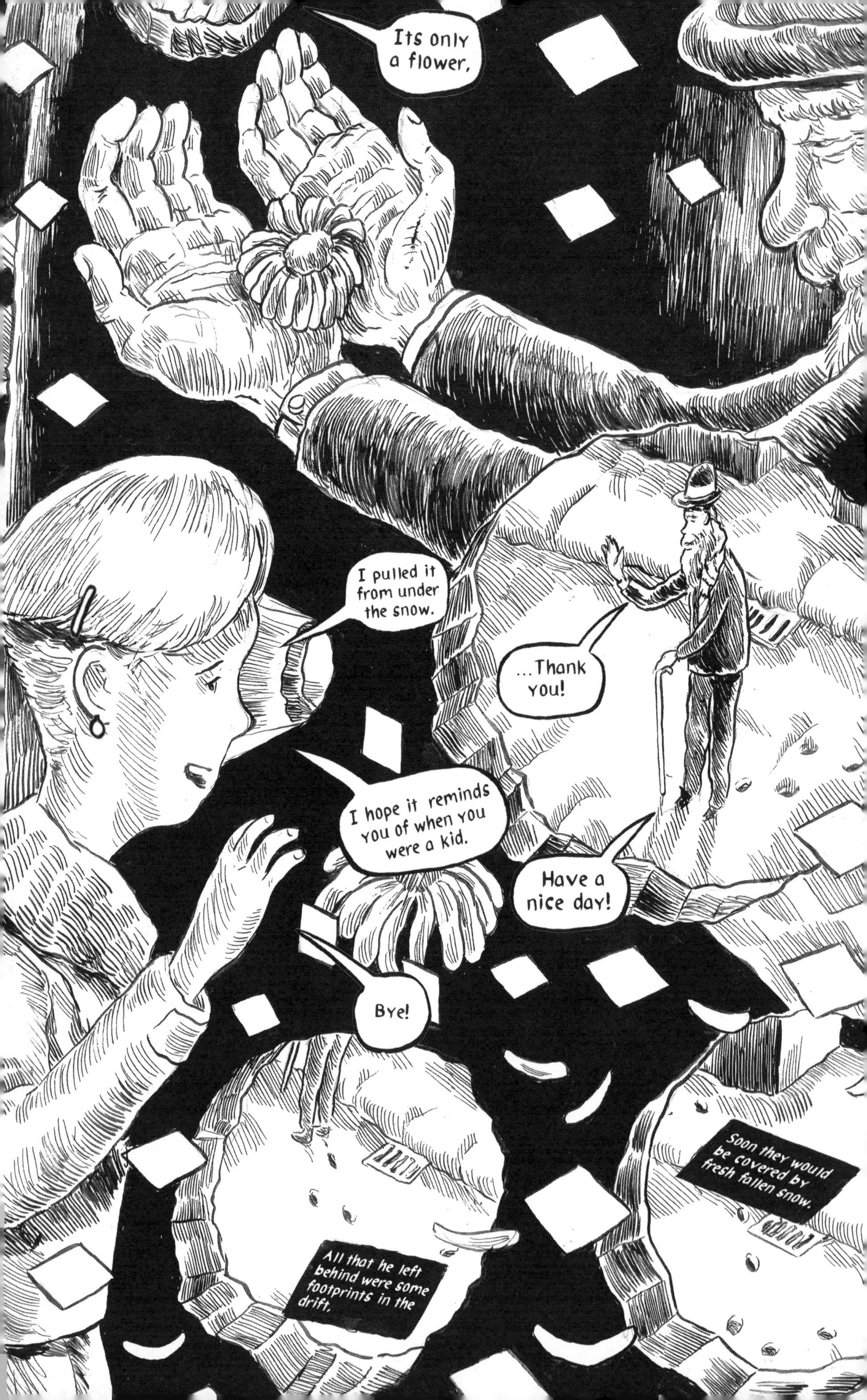
Its only a flower,
I pulled it from under the snow.
...Thank you!
I hope it reminds you of when you were a kid.
Have a nice day!
Bye!
All that he left behind were some footprints in the drift,
Soon they would be covered by fresh fallen snow.

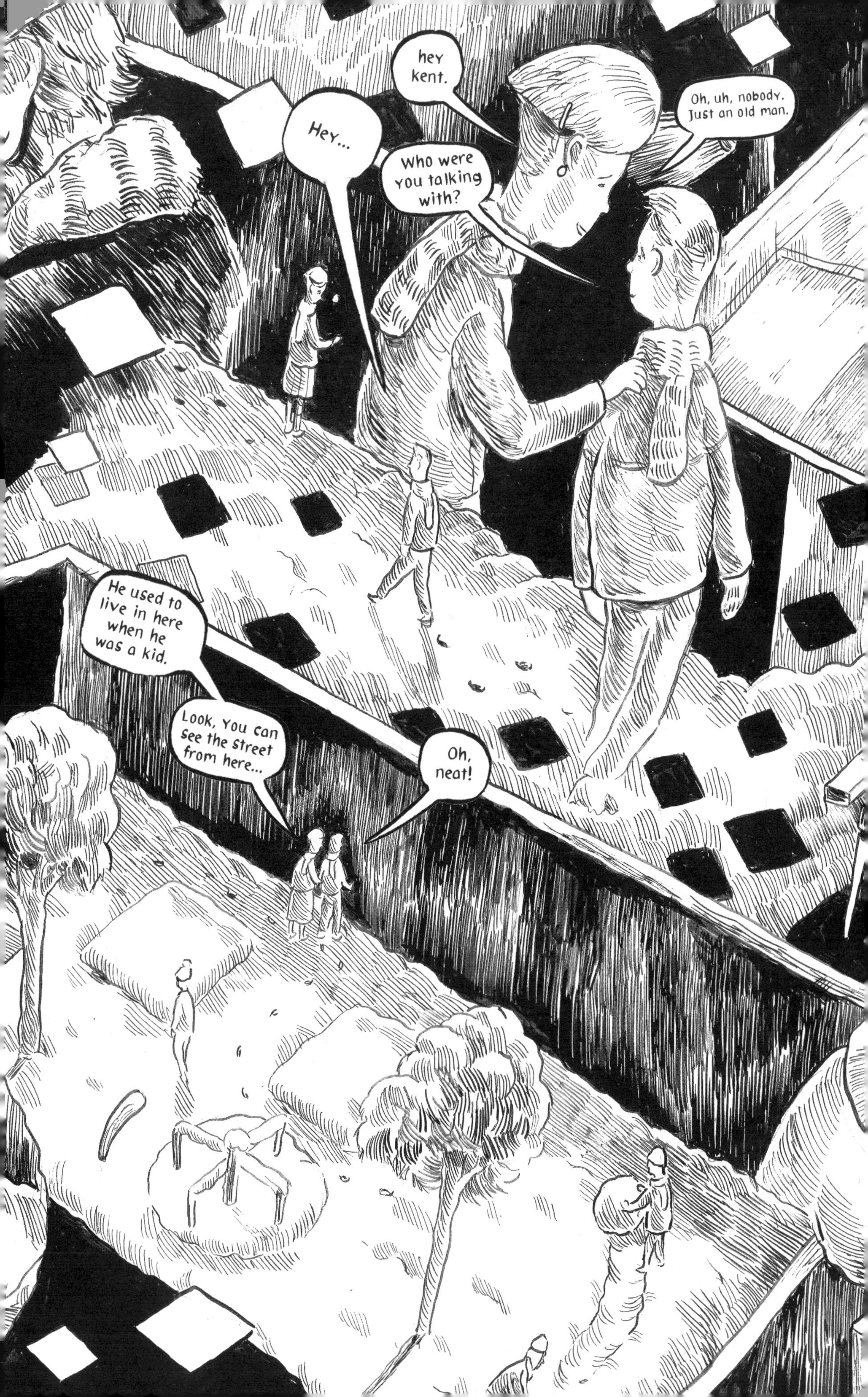
hey kent.
Hey...
Who were you talking with?
Oh, uh, nobody. Just an old man.
He used to live in here when he was a kid.
Look, You can see the street from here...
Oh, neat!

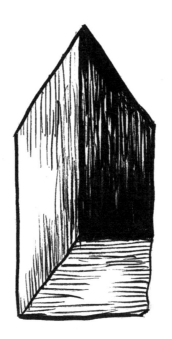

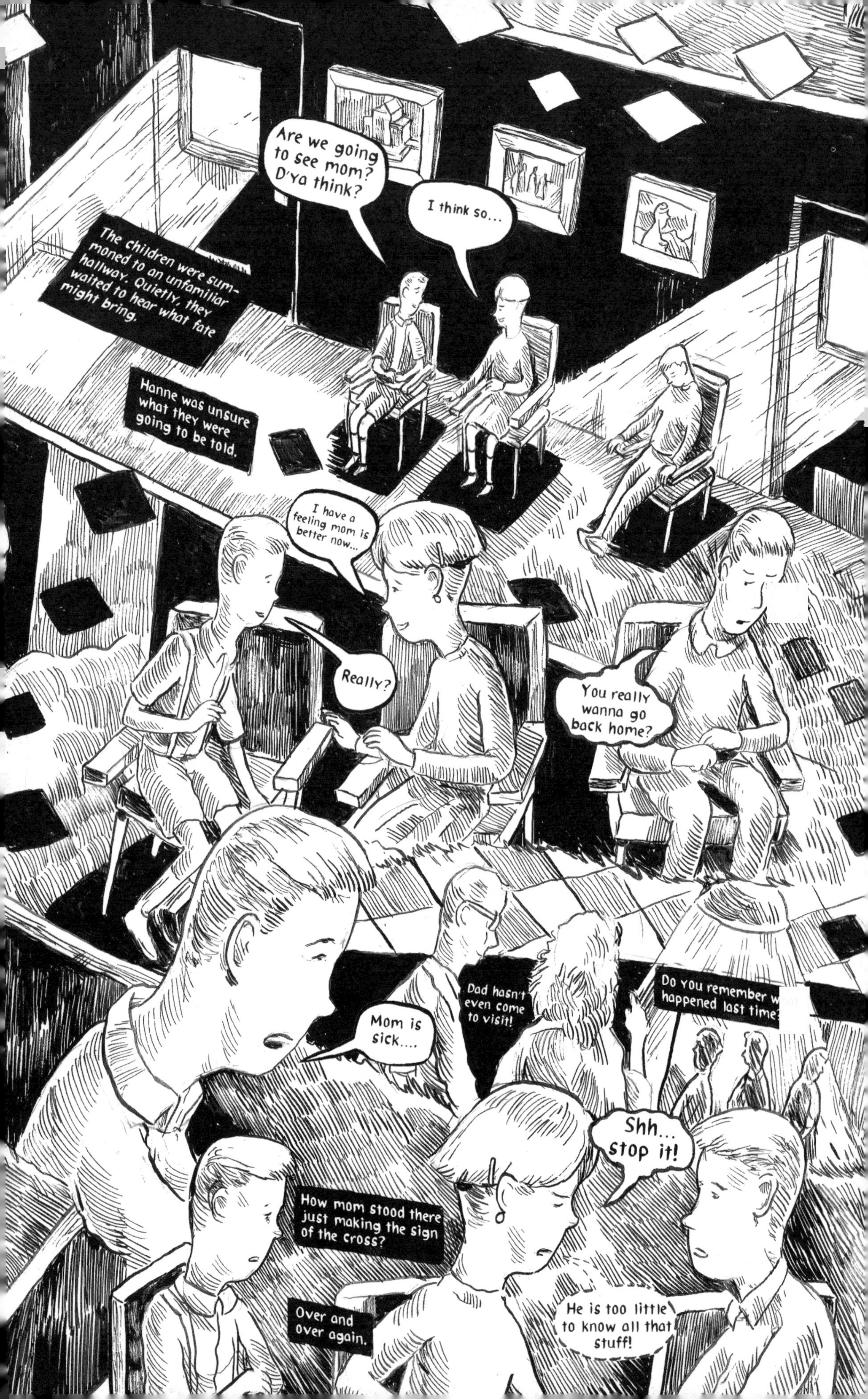
The children were summoned to an unfamiliar hallway. Quietly, they waited to hear what fate might bring.
Are we going to see mom? D'ya think?
I think so...
Hanne was unsure what they were going to be told.
I have a feeling mom is better now...
Really?
You really wanna go back home?
Mom is sick....
Dad hasn't even come to visit!
Do you remember what happened last time?
Shh... stop it!
How mom stood there just making the sign of the cross?
Over and over again.
He is too little to know all that stuff!

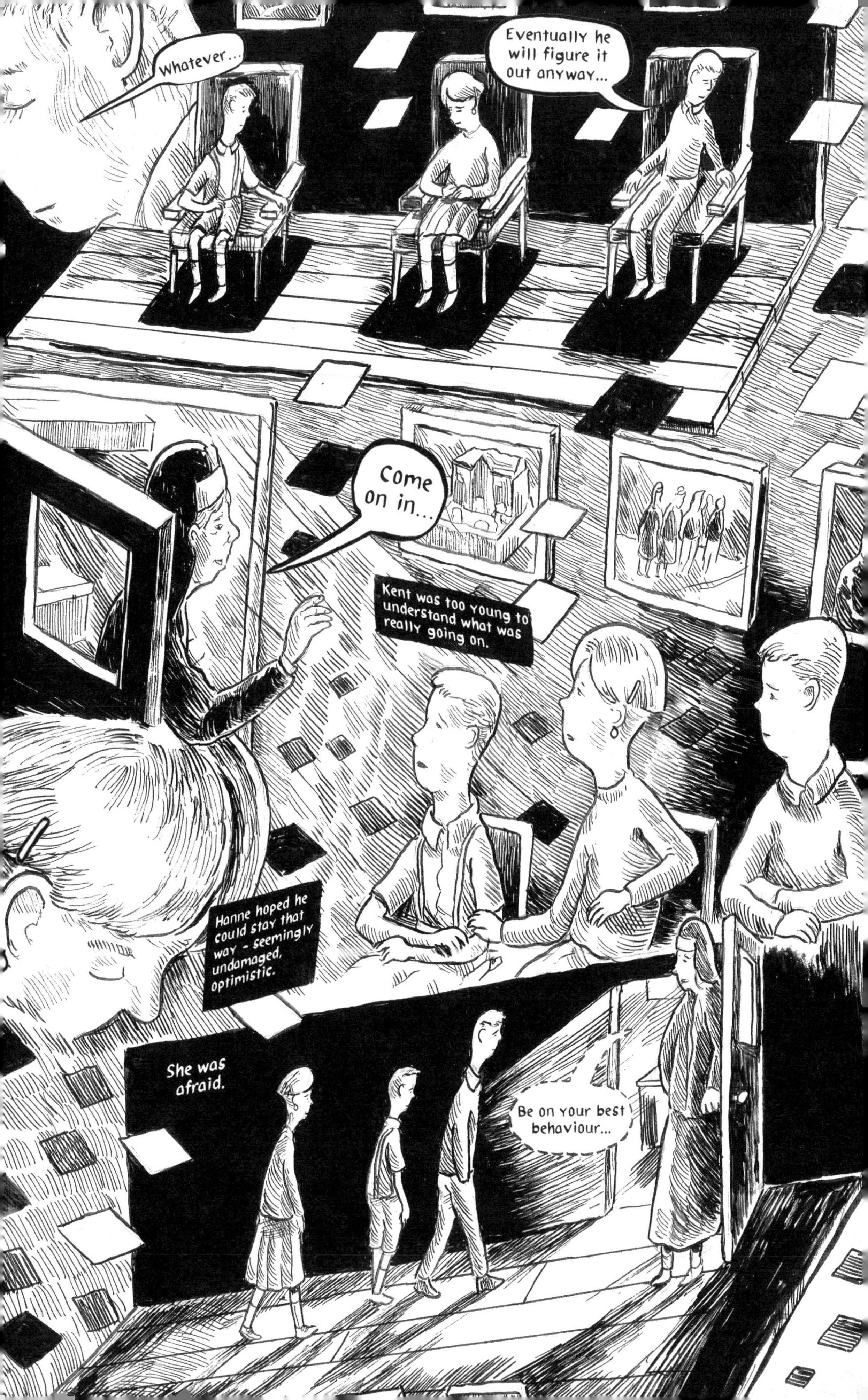
Whatever...
Eventually he will figure it out anyway...
Come on in...
Kent was too young to understand what was really going on.
Hanne hoped he could stay that way – seemingly undamaged, optimistic.
She was afraid.
Be on your best behaviour...

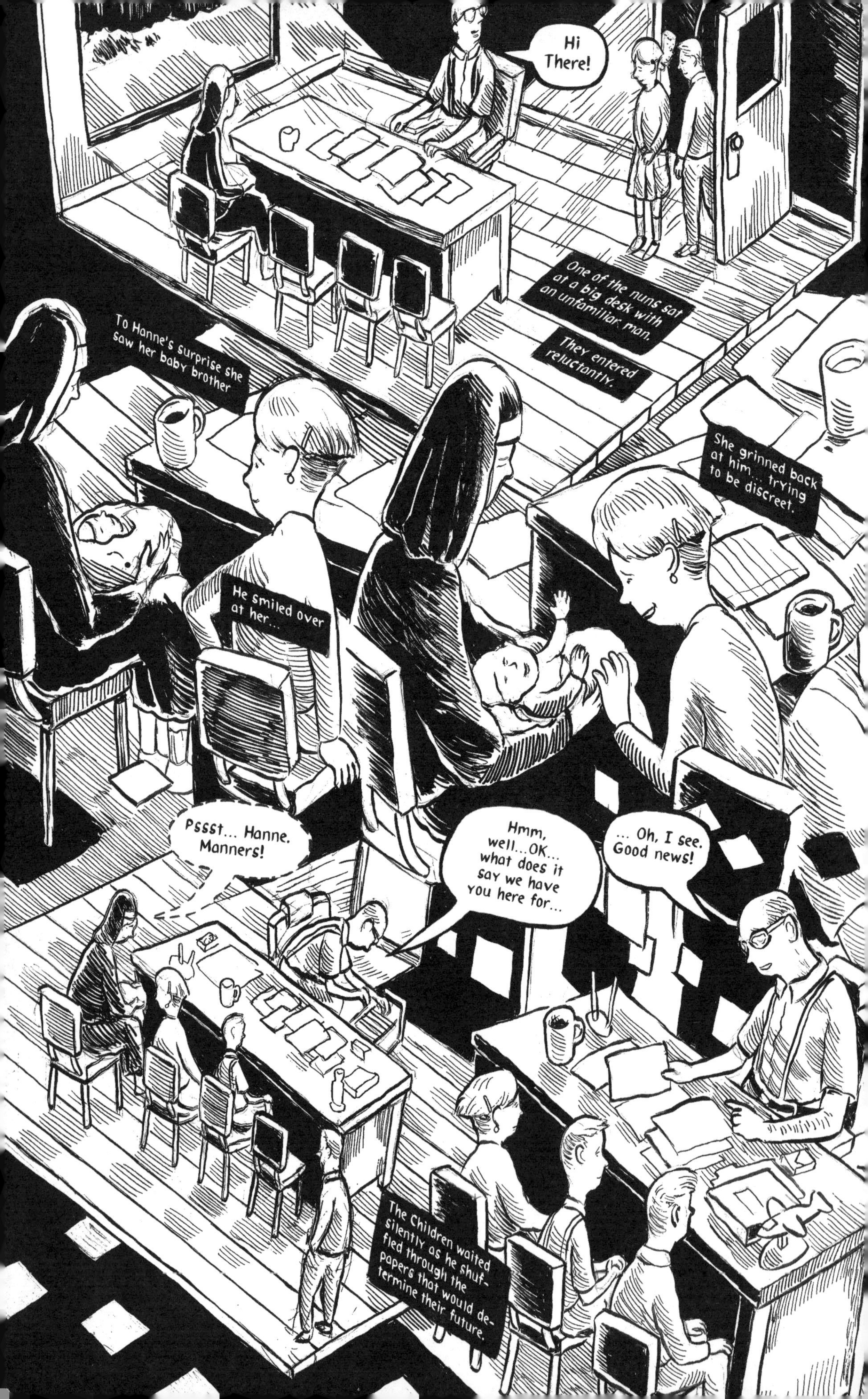
Hi There!
One of the nuns sat at a big desk with an unfamiliar man.
They entered reluctantly.
To Hanne's surprise she saw her baby brother
He smiled over at her...
She grinned back at him... trying to be discreet.
Pssst... Hanne. Manners!
Hmm, well...OK... what does it say we have you here for...
... Oh, I see. Good news!
The Children waited silently as he shuffled through the papers that would determine their future.

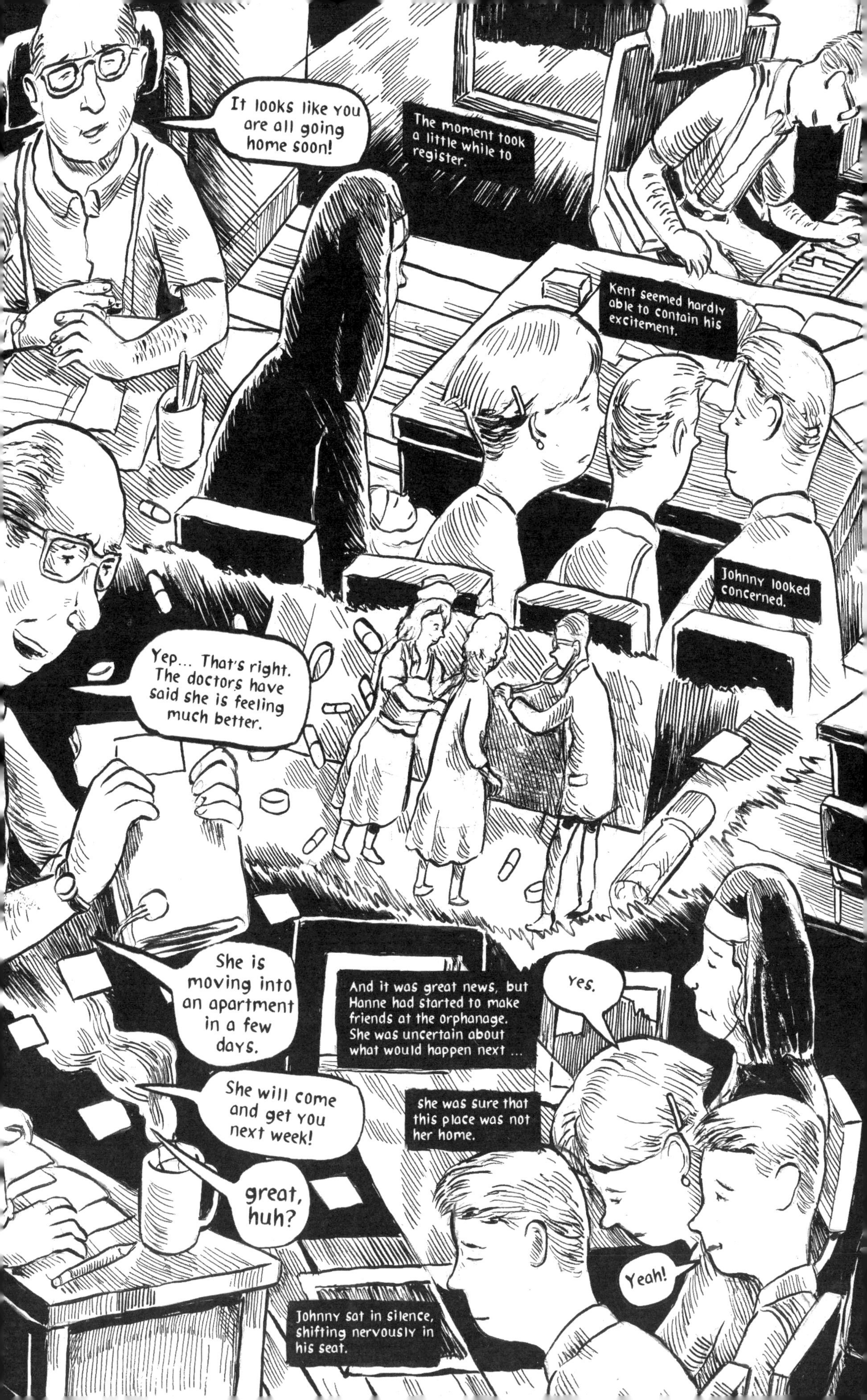
It looks like you are all going home soon!
The moment took a little while to register.
Kent seemed hardly able to contain his excitement.
Johnny looked concerned.
Yep... That's right. The doctors have said she is feeling much better.
She is moving into an apartment in a few days.
And it was great news, but Hanne had started to make friends at the orphanage. She was uncertain about what would happen next ...
Yes.
She will come and get you next week!
she was sure that this place was not her home.
great, huh?
Yeah!
Johnny sat in silence, shifting nervously in his seat.

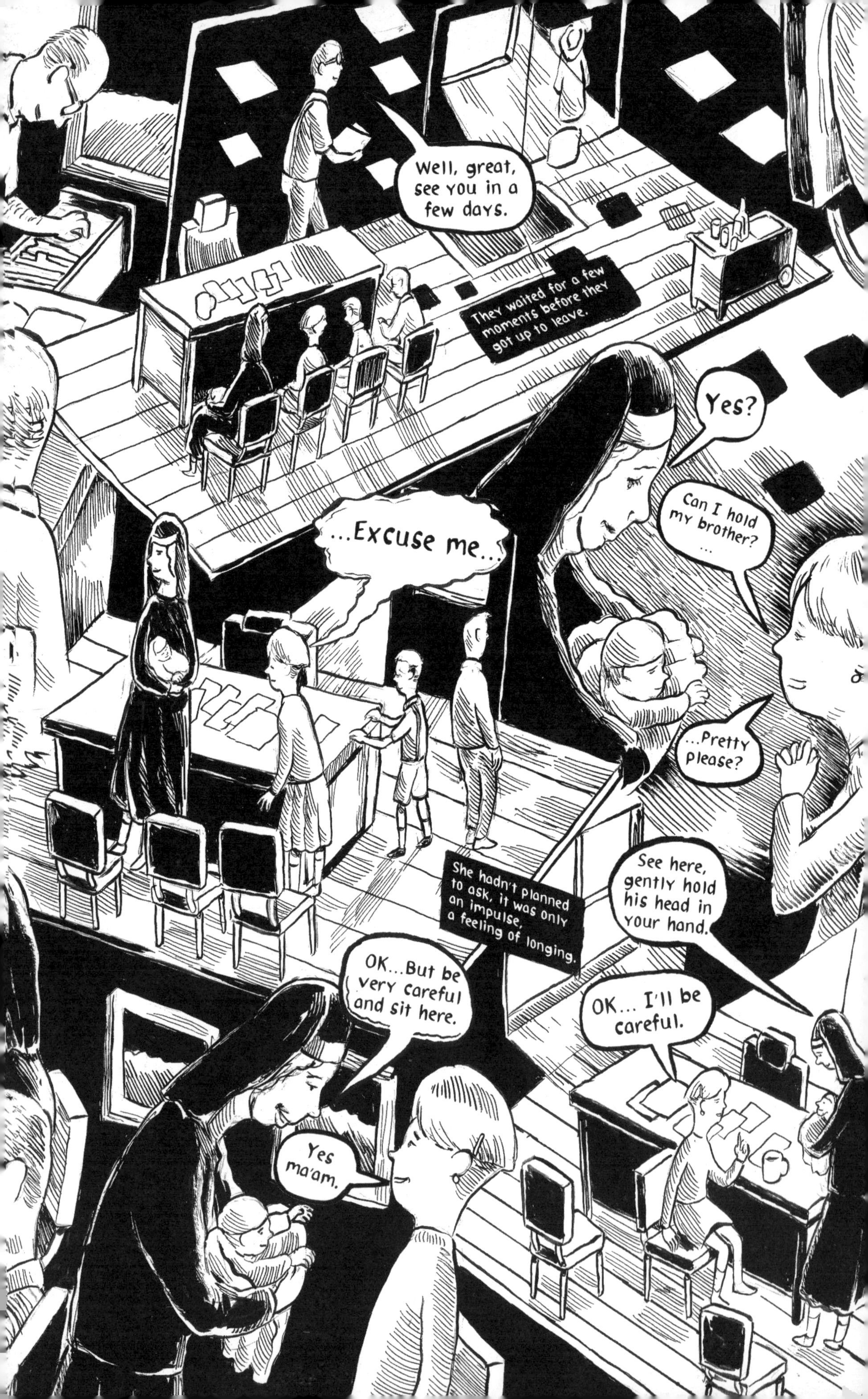
Well, great, see you in a few days.
They waited for a few moments before they got up to leave.
...Excuse me...
Yes?
Can I hold my brother? ...
...Pretty please?
She hadn't planned to ask, it was only an impulse, a feeling of longing.
See here, gently hold his head in your hand.
OK... I'll be careful.
OK...But be very careful and sit here.
Yes ma'am.

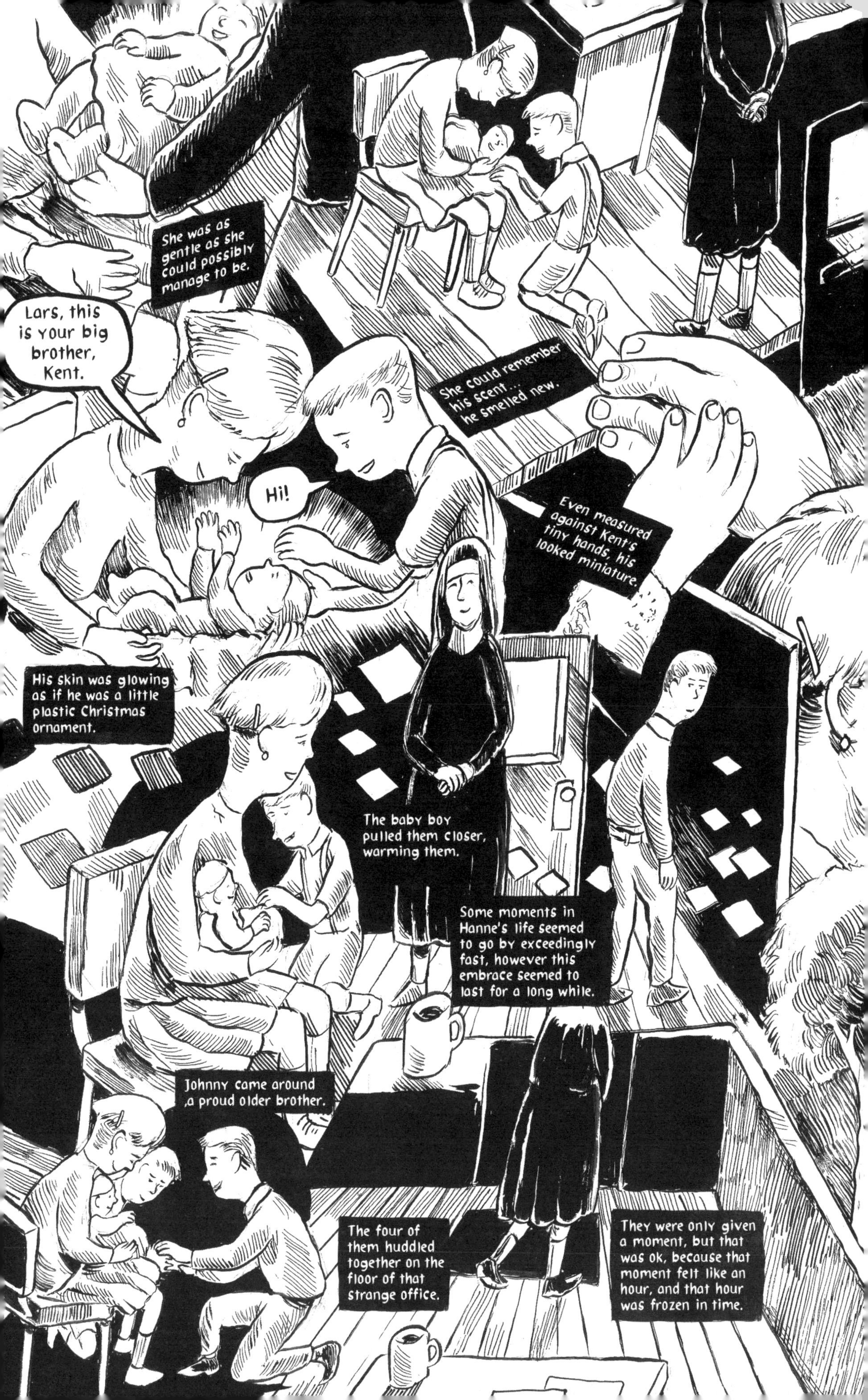

She was as gentle as she could possibly manage to be.
Lars, this is your big brother, Kent.
She could remember his scent... he smelled new.
Hi!
Even measured against Kent's tiny hands, his looked miniature.
His skin was glowing as if he was a little plastic Christmas ornament.
The baby boy pulled them closer, warming them.
Some moments in Hanne's life seemed to go by exceedingly fast, however this embrace seemed to last for a long while.
Johnny came around ,a proud older brother.
The four of them huddled together on the floor of that strange office.
They were only given a moment, but that was ok, because that moment felt like an hour, and that hour was frozen in time.

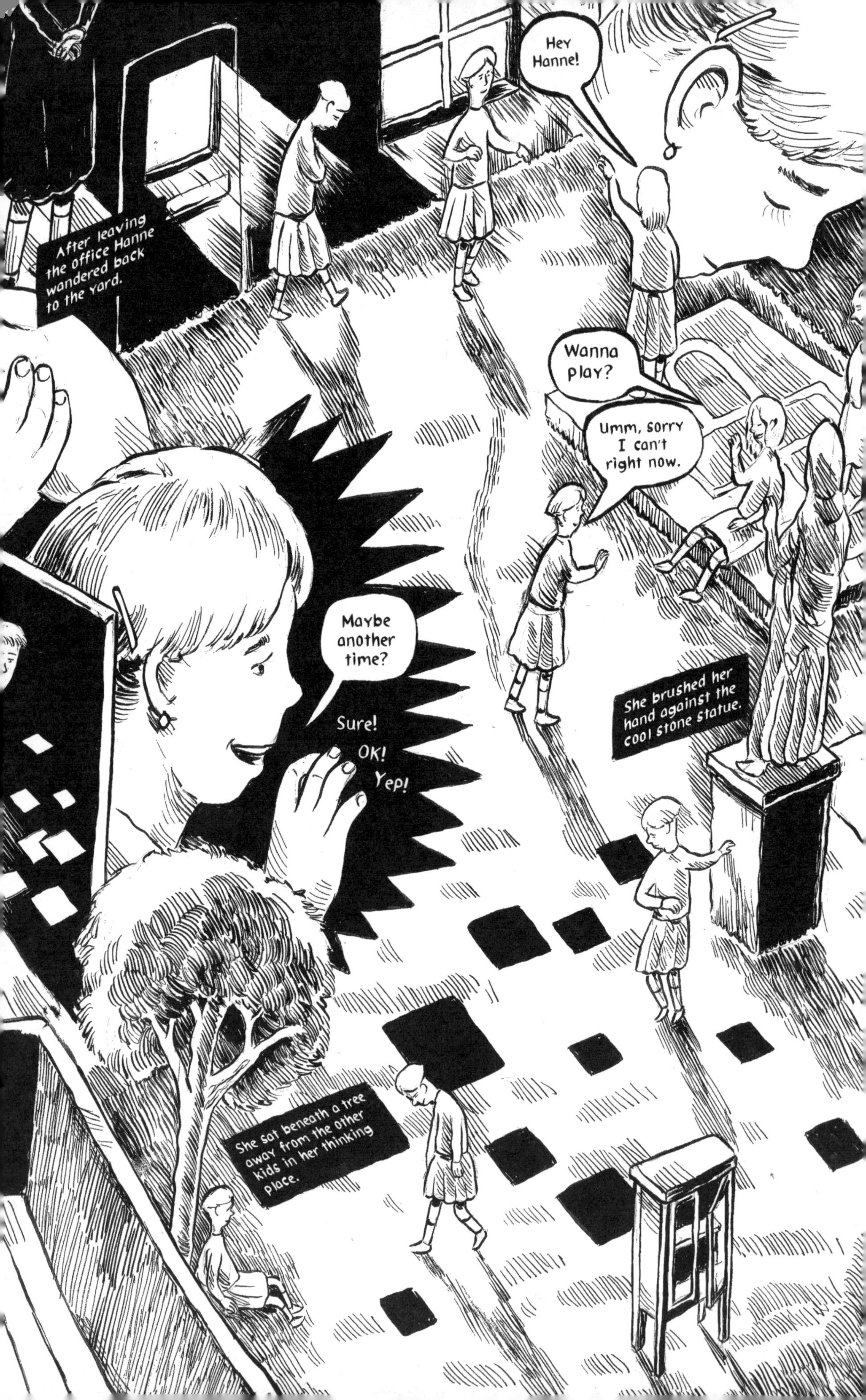
After leaving the office Hanne wandered back to the yard.
Hey Hanne!
Wanna play?
Umm, sorry I can't right now.
Maybe another time?
Sure!
OK!
Yep!
She brushed her hand against the cool stone statue.
She sat beneath a tree away from the other kids in her thinking place.

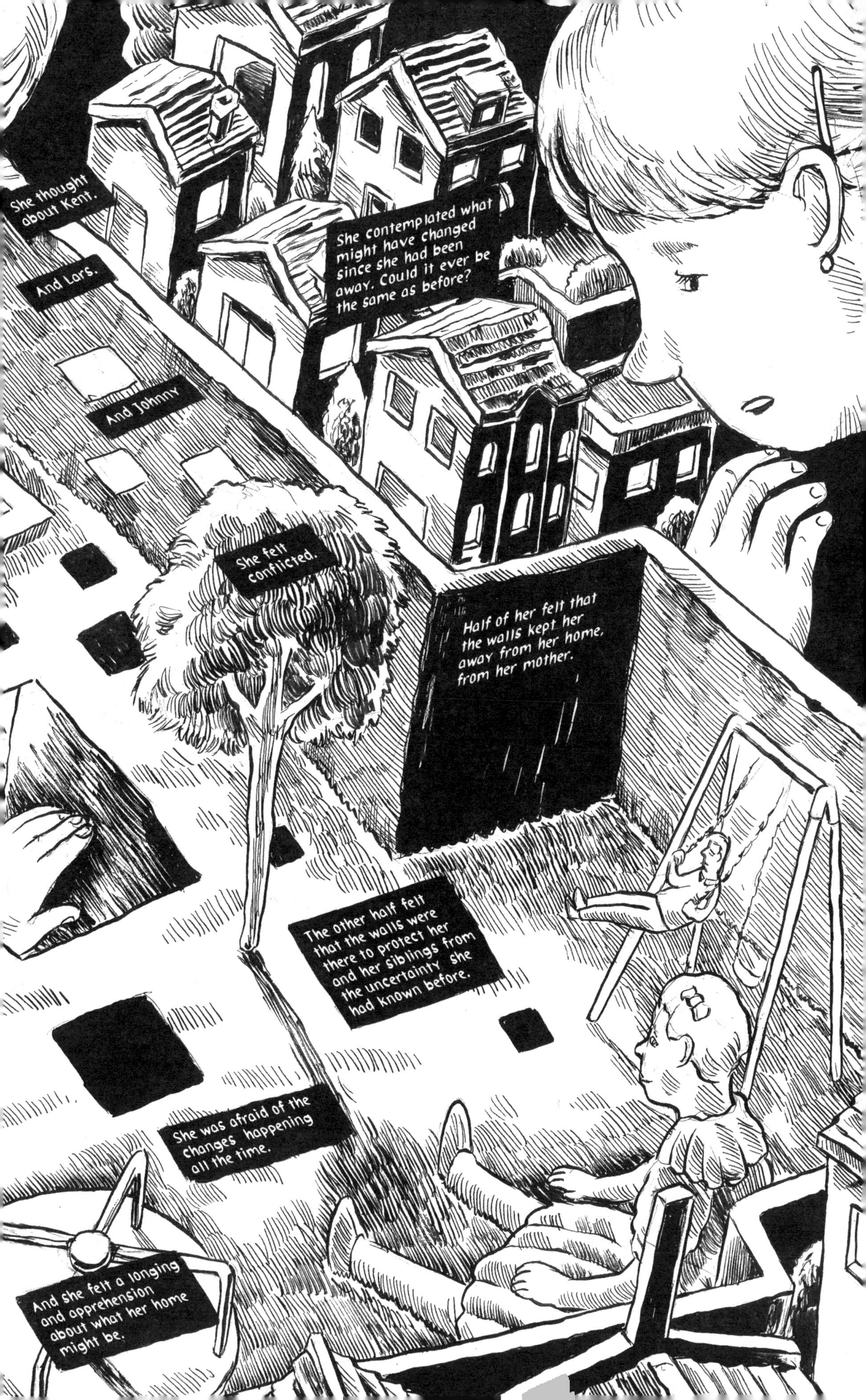
She thought about Kent.
And Lars.
And Johnny
She contemplated what might have changed since she had been away. Could it ever be the same as before?
She felt conflicted.
Half of her felt that the walls kept her away from her home, from her mother.
The other half felt that the walls were there to protect her and her siblings from the uncertainty she had known before.
She was afraid of the changes happening all the time.
And she felt a longing and apprehension about what her home might be.

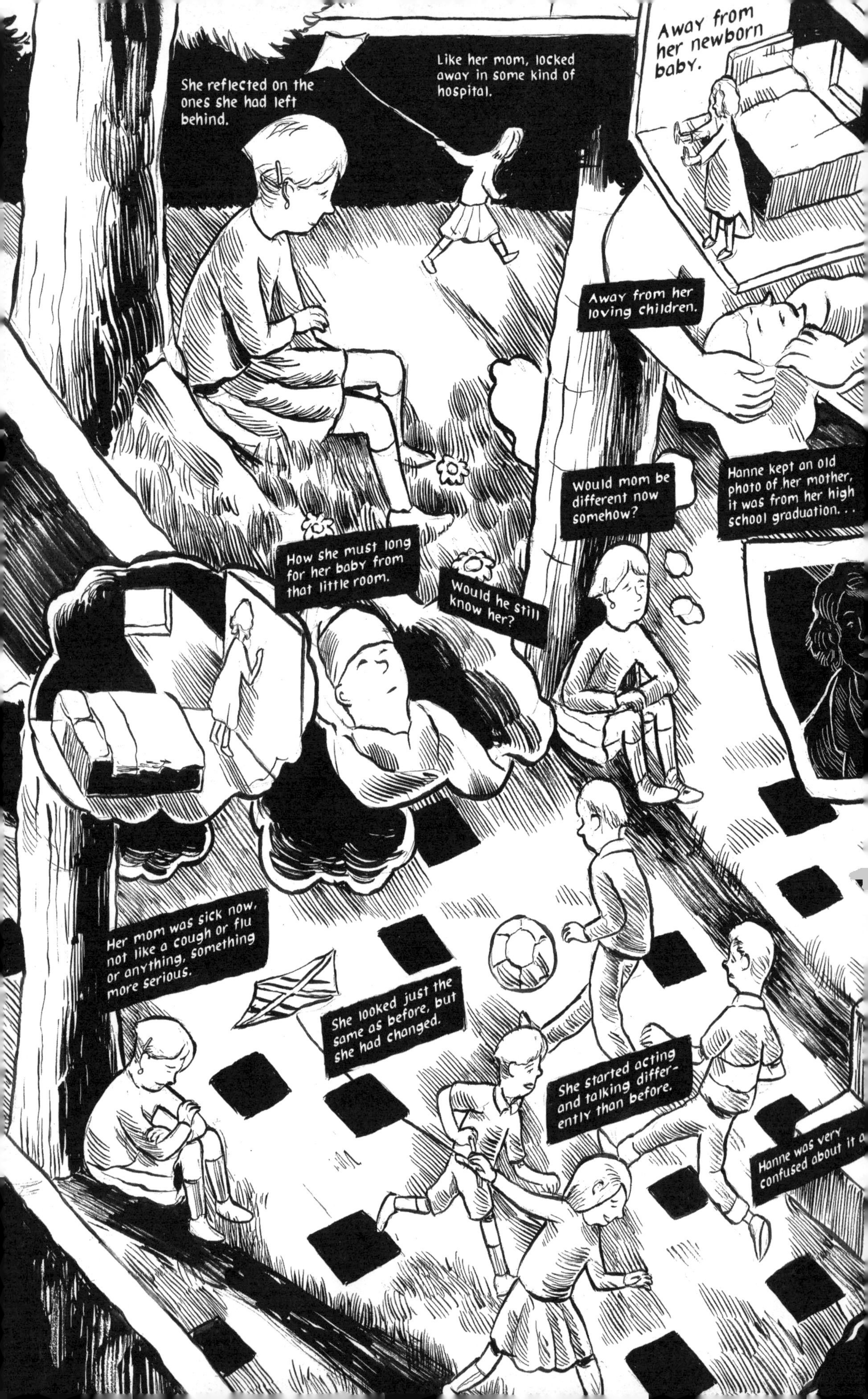
She reflected on the ones she had left behind.
Like her mom, locked away in some kind of hospital.
Away from her newborn baby.
Away from her loving children.
How she must long for her baby from that little room.
Would he still know her?
Would mom be different now somehow?
Hanne kept an old photo of her mother, it was from her high school graduation. . .
Her mom was sick now, not like a cough or flu or anything, something more serious.
She looked just the same as before, but she had changed.
She started acting and talking differ-ently than before.
Hanne was very confused about it a

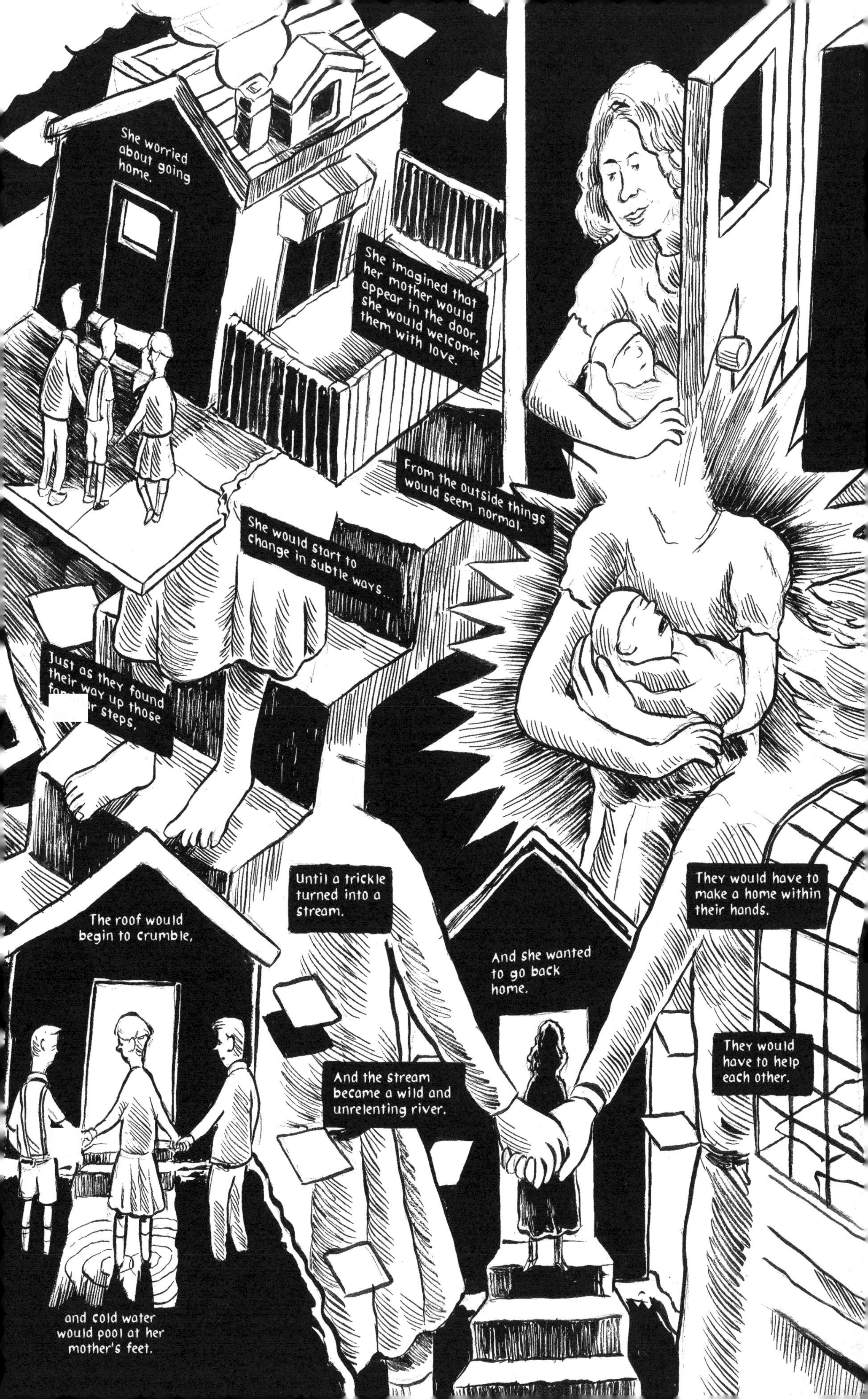
She worried about going home.
She imagined that her mother would appear in the door, she would welcome them with love.
From the outside things would seem normal.
She would start to change in subtle ways...
Just as they found their way up those steps,
The roof would begin to crumble,
and cold water would pool at her mother's feet.
Until a trickle turned into a stream.
And the stream became a wild and unrelenting river.
And she wanted to go back home.
They would have to make a home within their hands.
They would have to help each other.

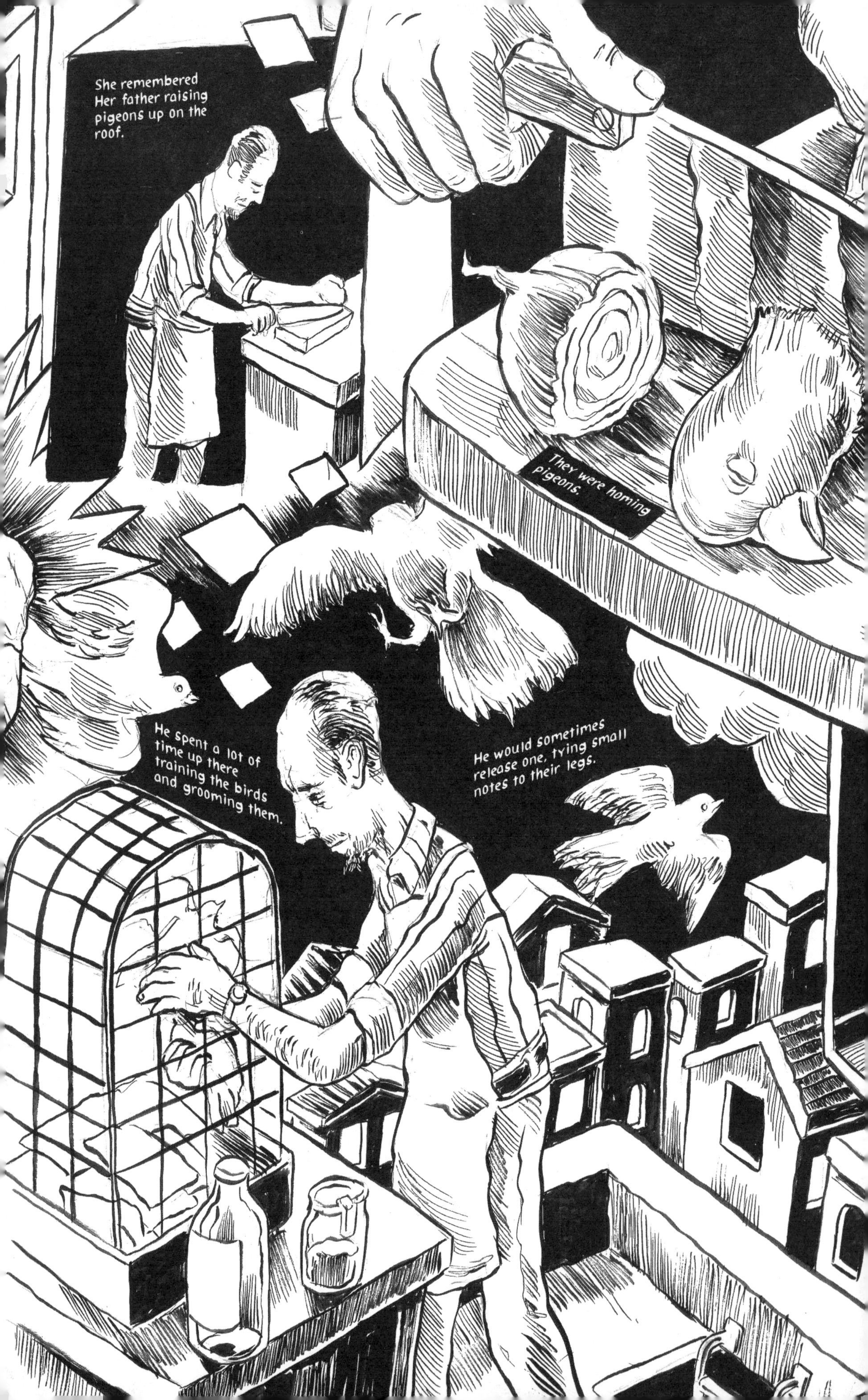
She remembered Her father raising pigeons up on the roof.
They were homing pigeons.
He spent a lot of time up there training the birds and grooming them.
He would sometimes release one, tying small notes to their legs.

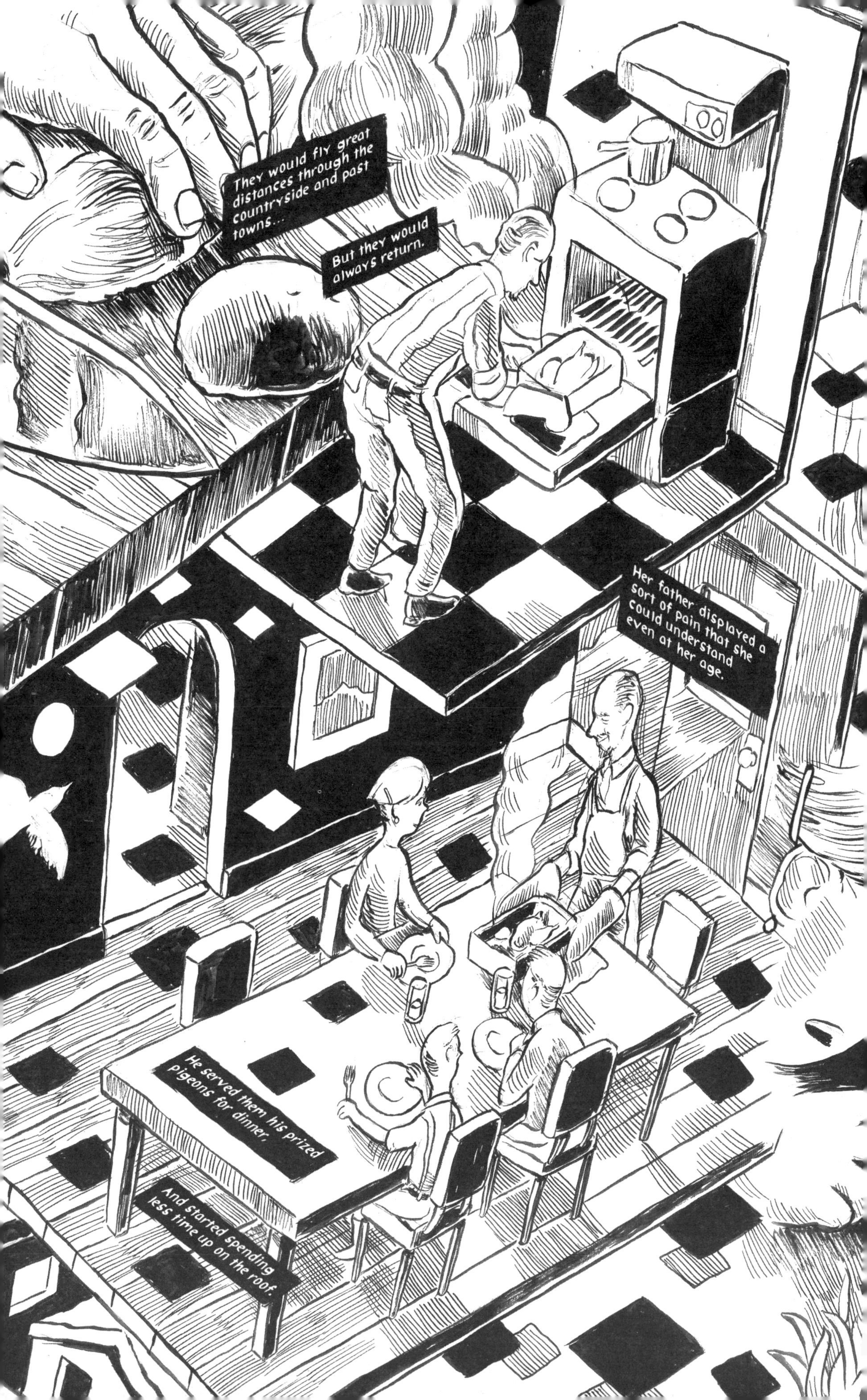
They would fly great distances through the countryside and past towns...
But they would always return.
Her father displayed a sort of pain that she could understand even at her age.
He served them his prized pigeons for dinner.
And started spending less time up on the roof.

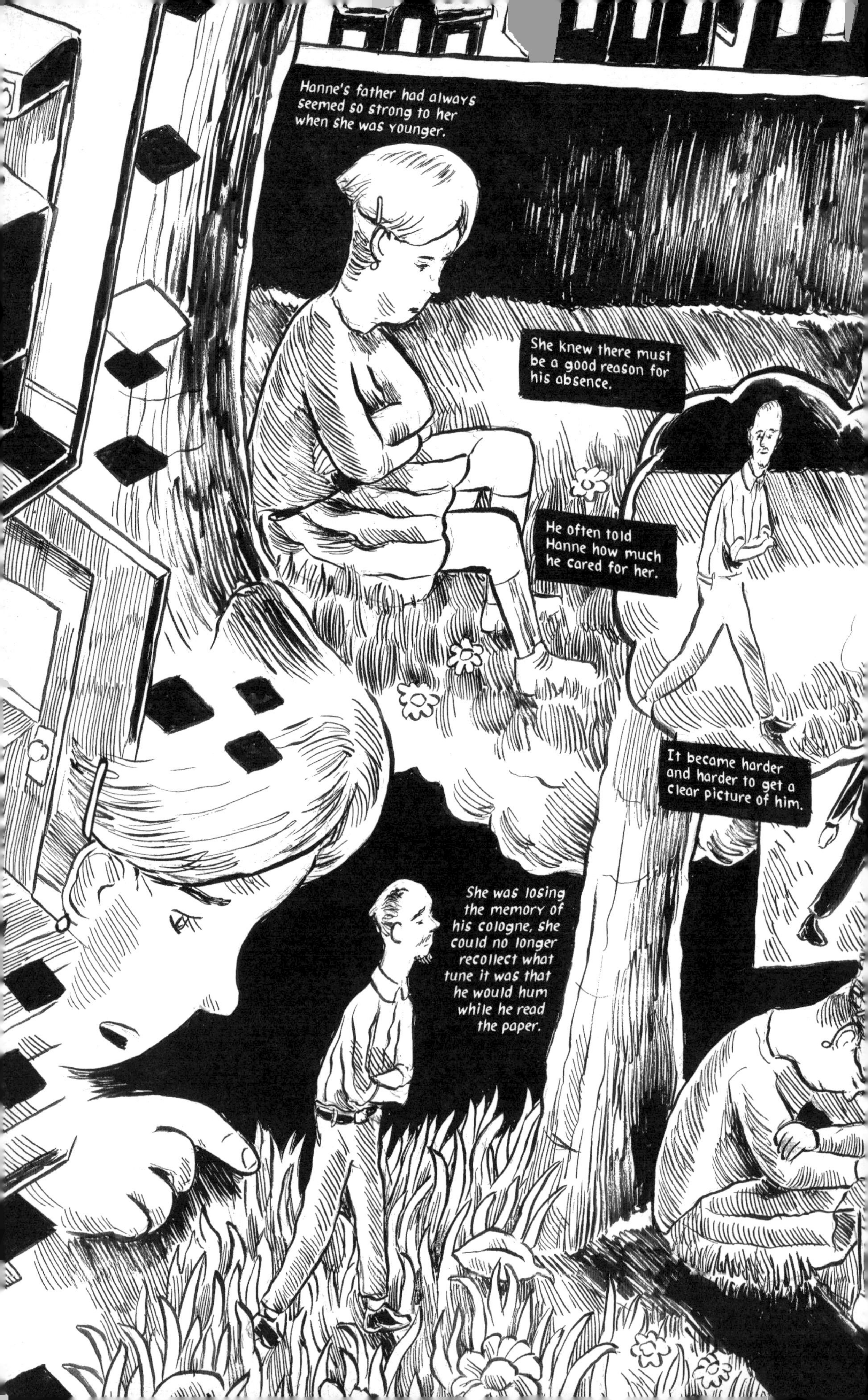
Hanne's father had always seemed so strong to her when she was younger.
She knew there must be a good reason for his absence.
He often told Hanne how much he cared for her.
It became harder and harder to get a clear picture of him.
She was losing the memory of his cologne, she could no longer recollect what tune it was that he would hum while he read the paper.

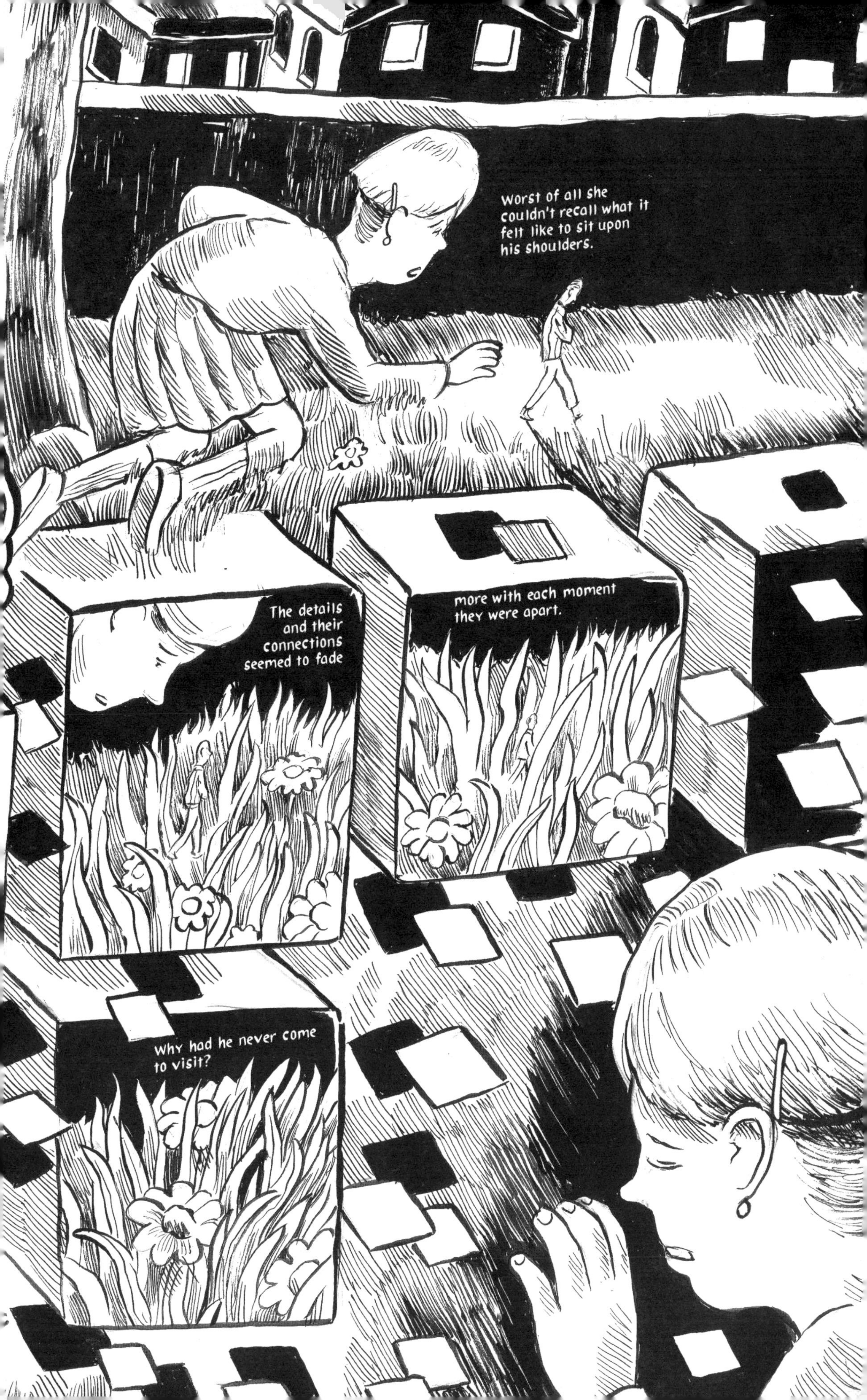
Worst of all she couldn't recall what it felt like to sit upon his shoulders.
The details and their connections seemed to fade
more with each moment they were apart.
Why had he never come to visit?

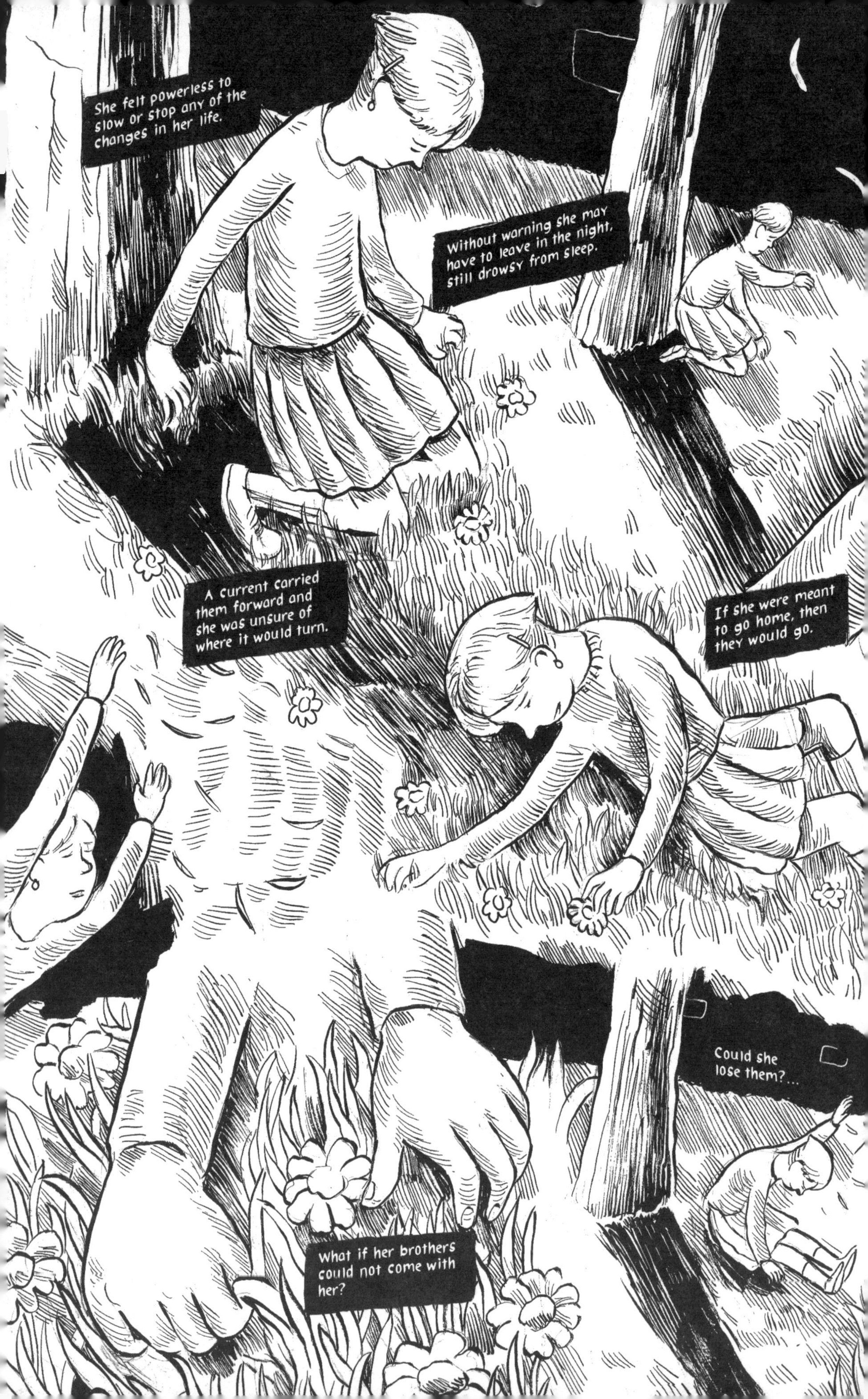
She felt powerless to slow or stop any of the changes in her life.
Without warning she may have to leave in the night, still drowsy from sleep.
A current carried them forward and she was unsure of where it would turn.
If she were meant to go home, then they would go.
Could she lose them?...
What if her brothers could not come with her?

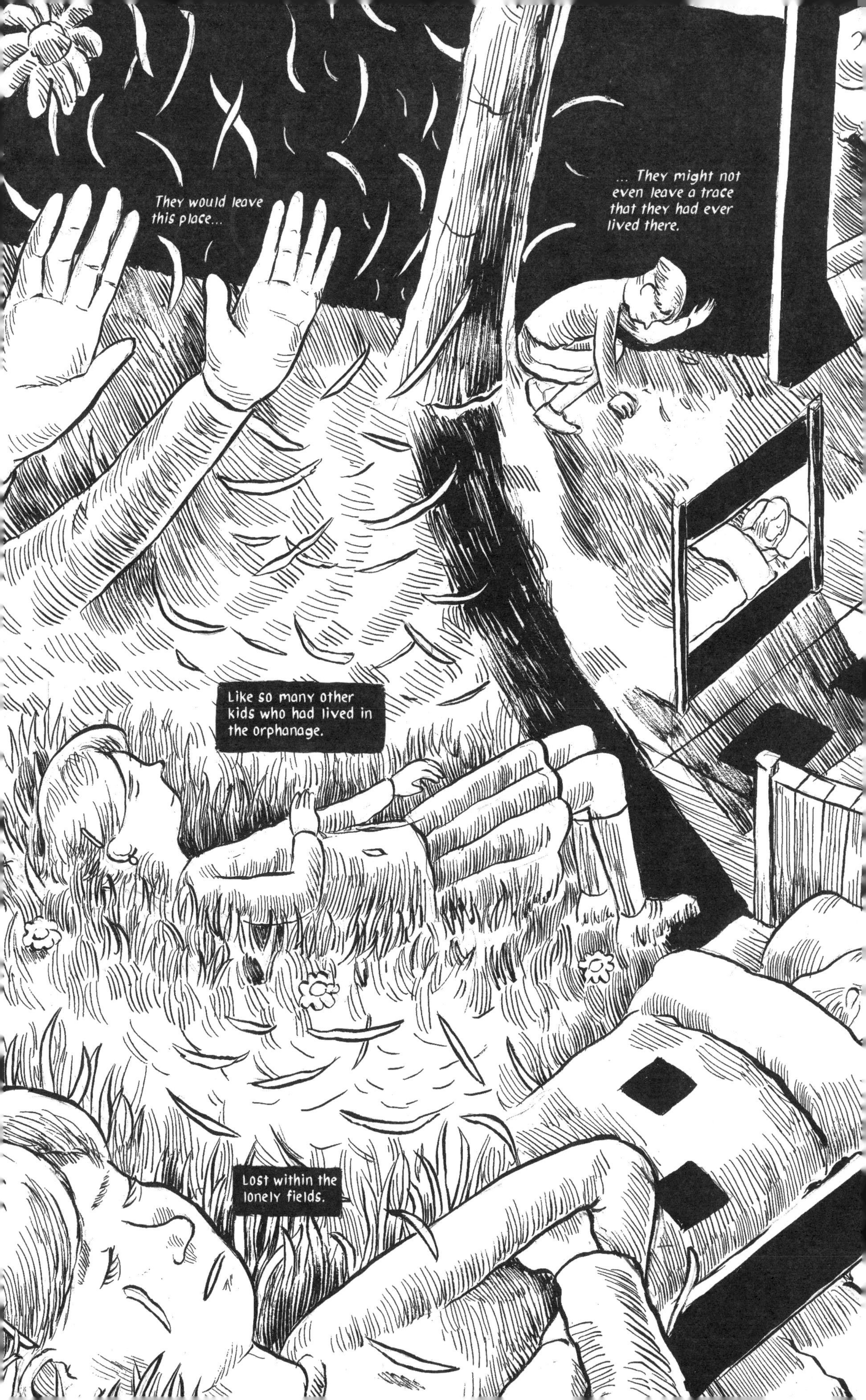
They would leave this place...
... They might not even leave a trace that they had ever lived there.
Like so many other kids who had lived in the orphanage.
Lost within the lonely fields.

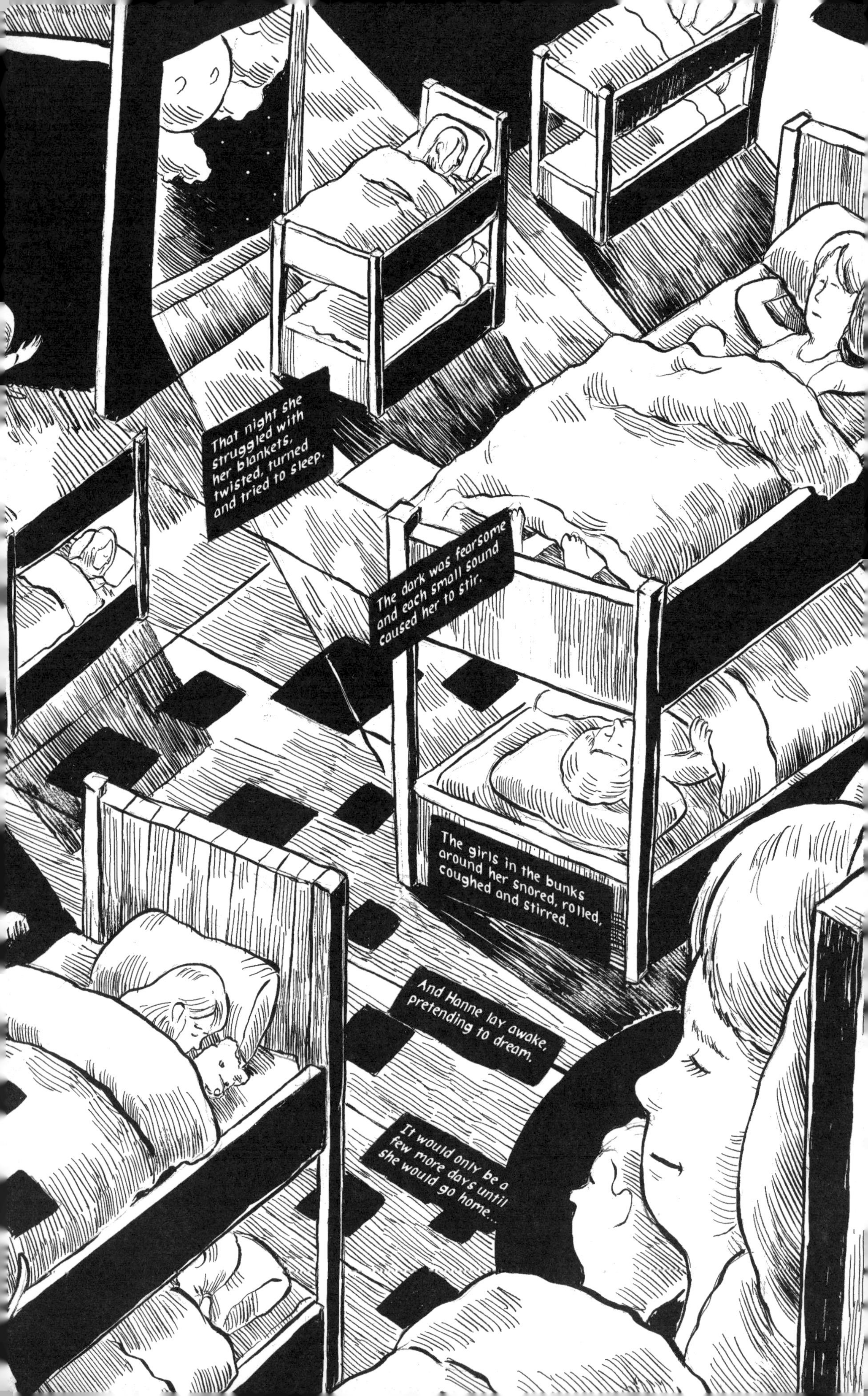
That night she struggled with her blankets, twisted, turned and tried to sleep.
The dark was fearsome and each small sound caused her to stir.
The girls in the bunks around her snored, rolled, coughed and stirred.
And Hanne lay awake, pretending to dream.
It would only be a few more days until she would go home...

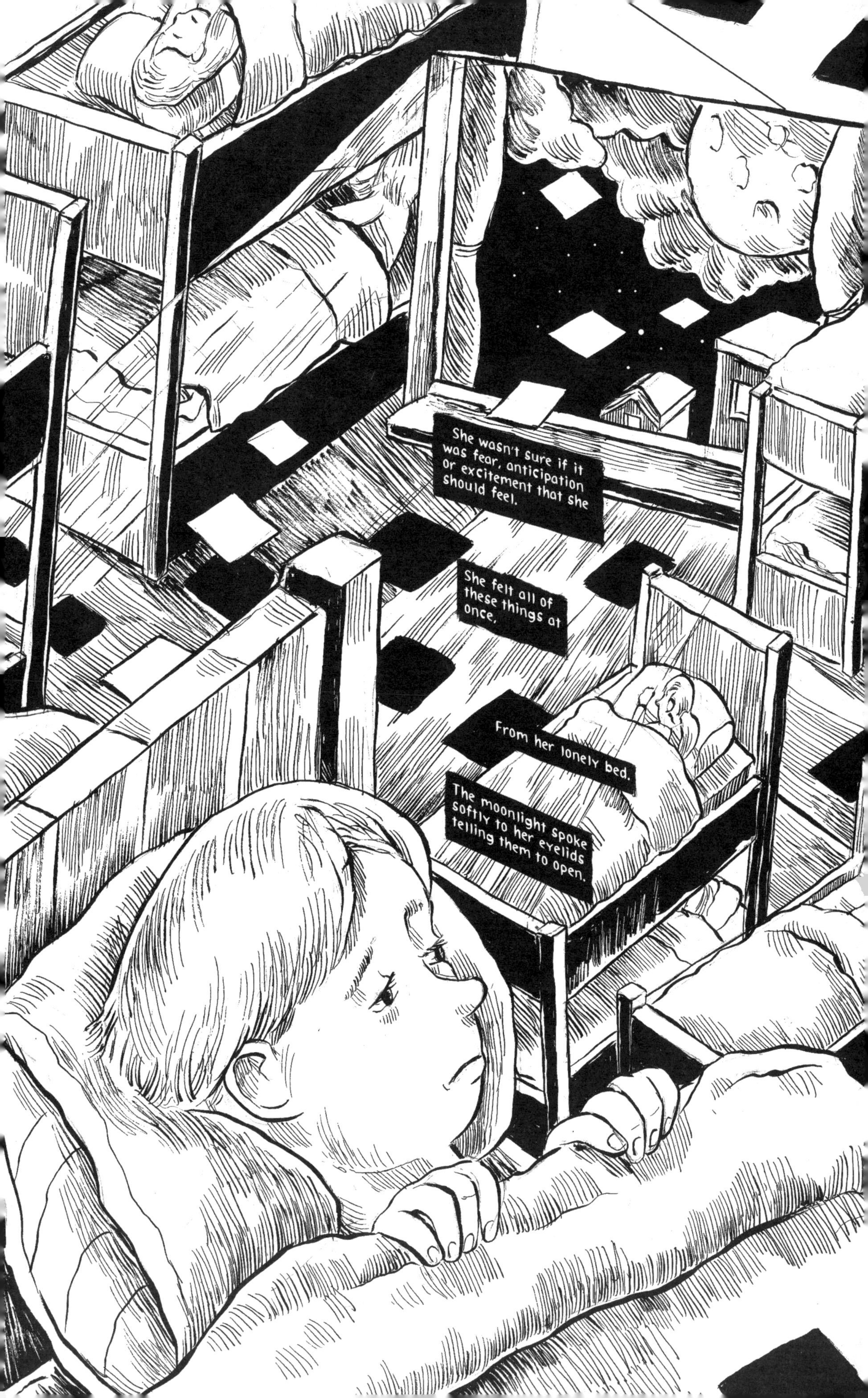
She wasn't sure if it was fear, anticipation or excitement that she should feel.
She felt all of these things at once,
From her lonely bed.
The moonlight spoke softly to her eyelids telling them to open.

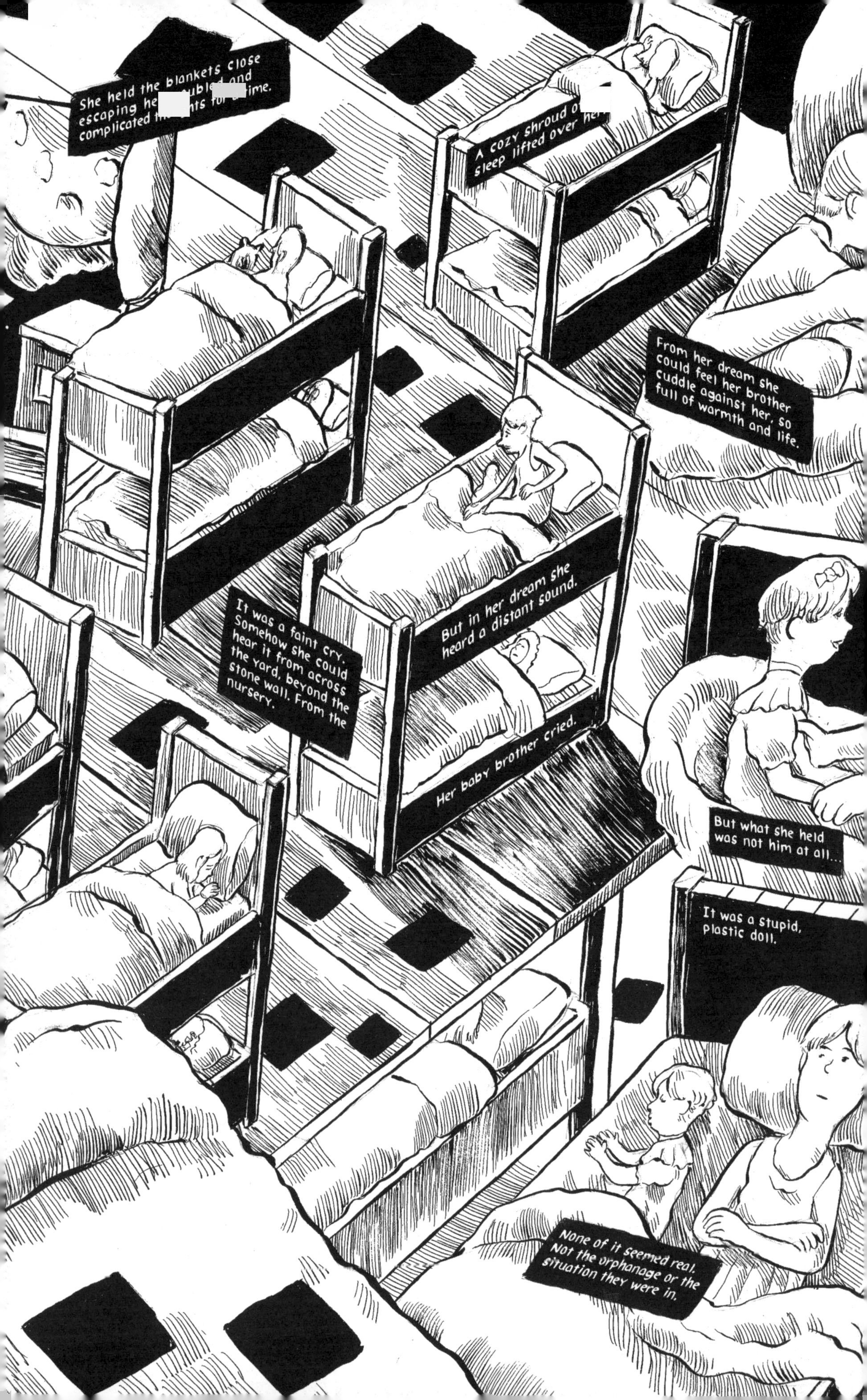

She held the blankets close
escaping he oubled and
complicated th nts for a time.
A cozy shroud o
sleep lifted over her.
From her dream she could feel her brother cuddle against her, so full of warmth and life.
But in her dream she heard a distant sound.
Her baby brother cried.
It was a faint cry. Somehow she could hear it from across the yard, beyond the stone wall. From the nursery.
But what she held was not him at all...
It was a stupid, plastic doll.
None of it seemed real. Not the orphanage or the situation they were in.

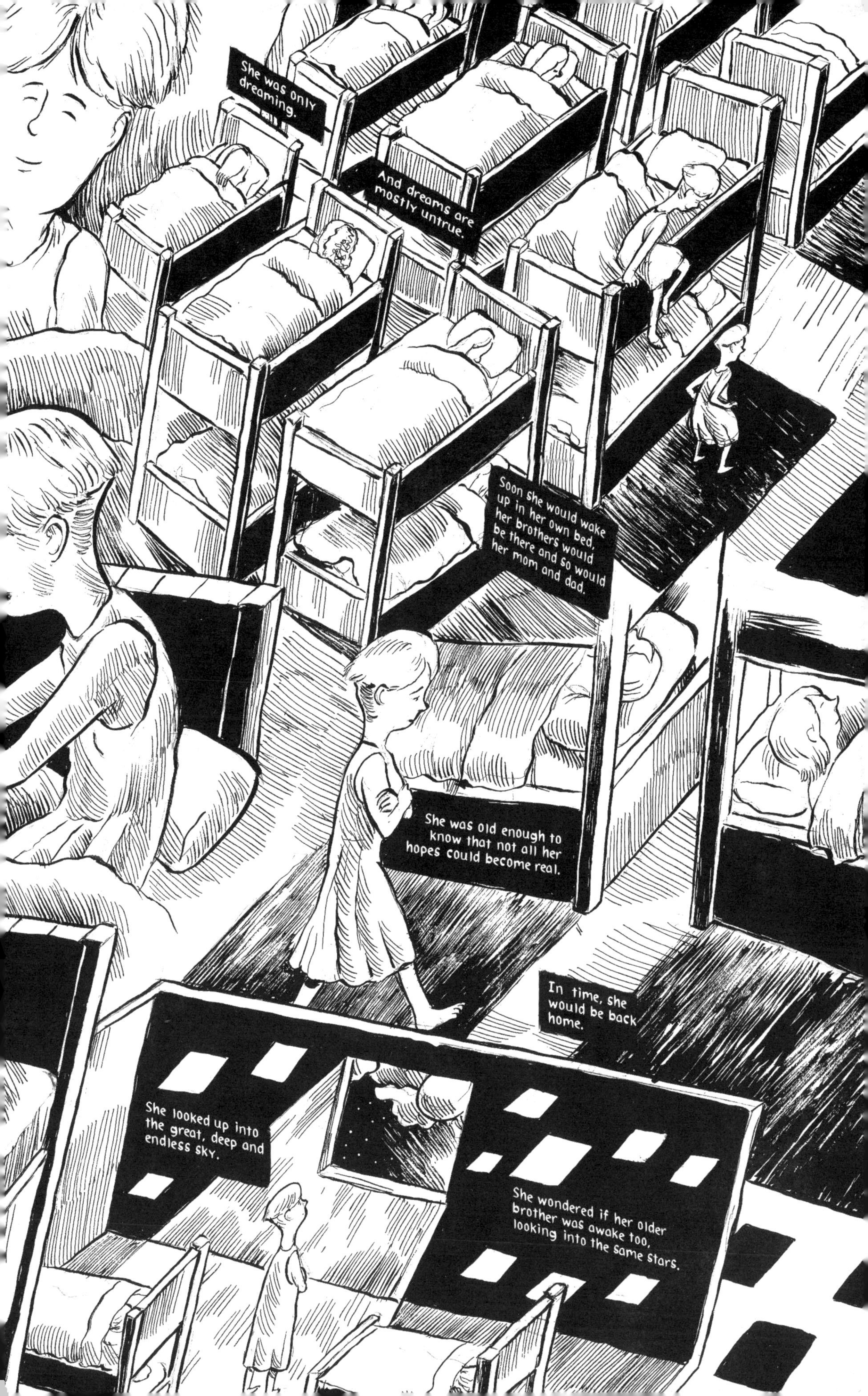
She was only dreaming.
And dreams are mostly untrue.
Soon she would wake up in her own bed, her brothers would be there and so would her mom and dad.
She was old enough to know that not all her hopes could become real.
In time, she would be back home.
She looked up into the great, deep and endless sky.
She wondered if her older brother was awake too, looking into the same stars.

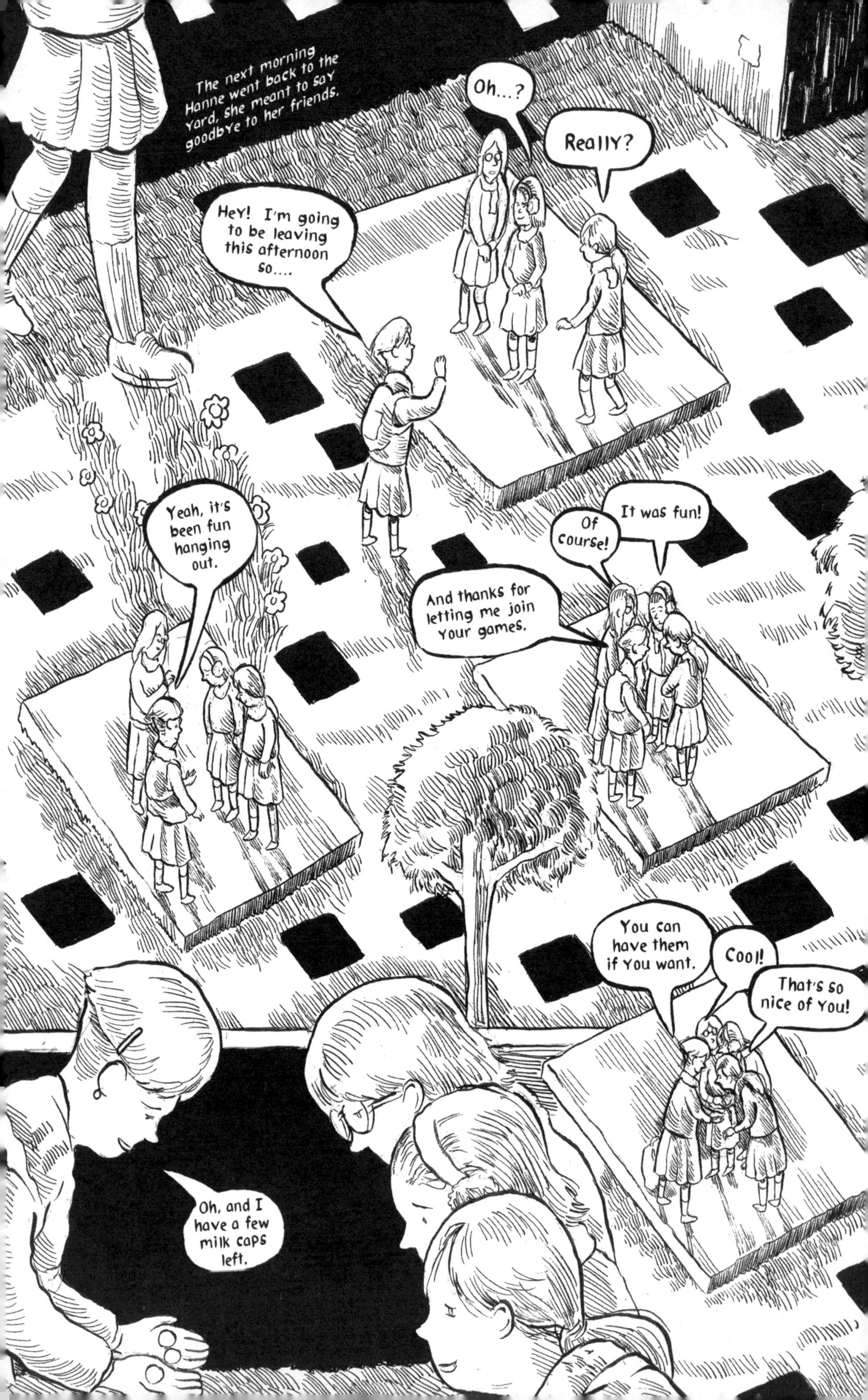
The next morning Hanne went back to the Yard, she meant to say goodbye to her friends.
Oh...?
Really?
Hey! I'm going to be leaving this afternoon so....
Yeah, it's been fun hanging out.
It was fun!
Of course!
And thanks for letting me join your games.
You can have them if you want.
Cool!
That's so nice of you!
Oh, and I have a few milk caps left.

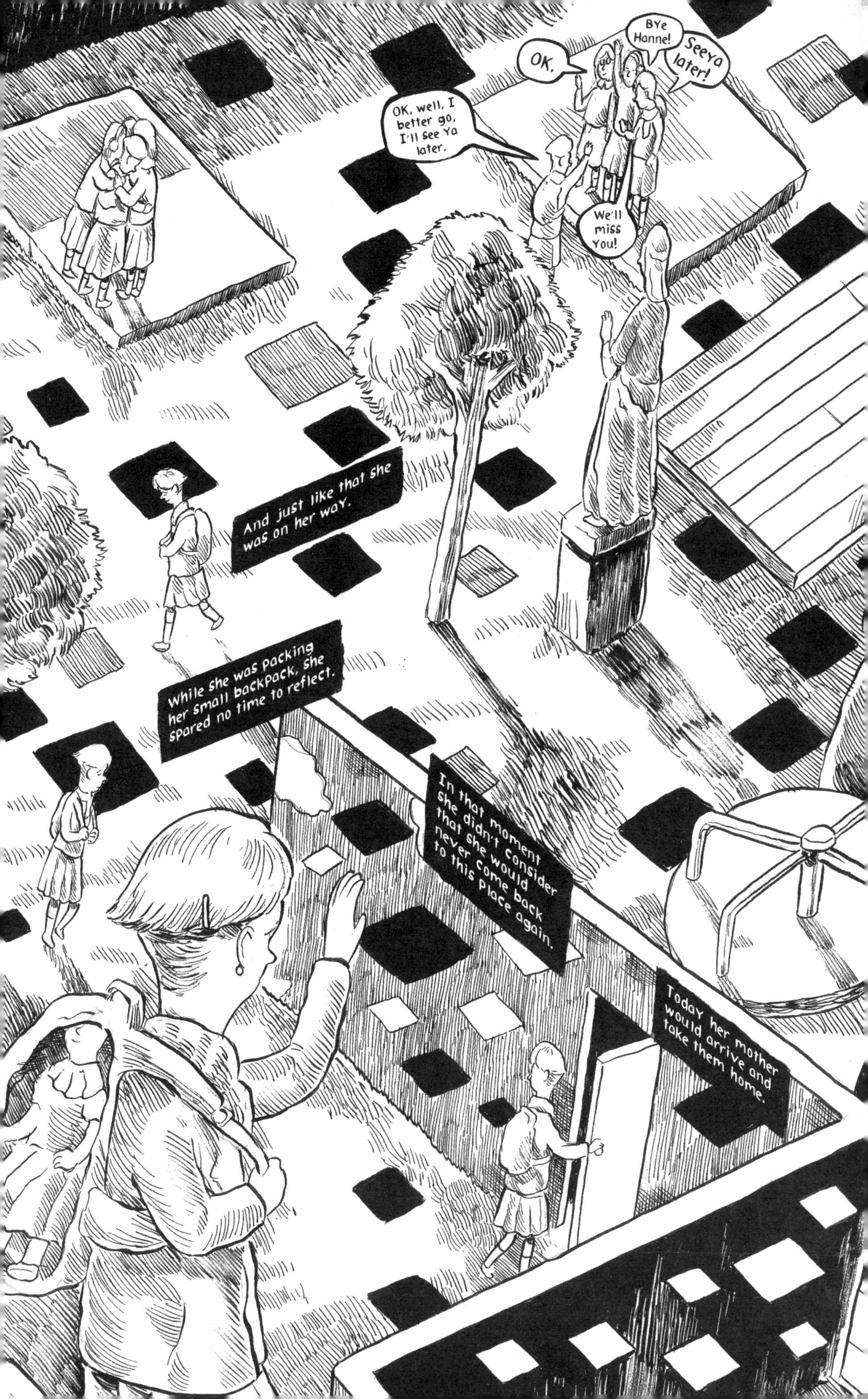
OK.
BYe Hanne!
Seeya later!
OK, well, I better go, I'll see Ya later.
We'll miss You!
And just like that she was on her waY.
While she was packing her small backPack, she spared no time to reflect.
In that moment she didn't consider that she would never come back to this place again.
Today her mother would arrive and take them home.

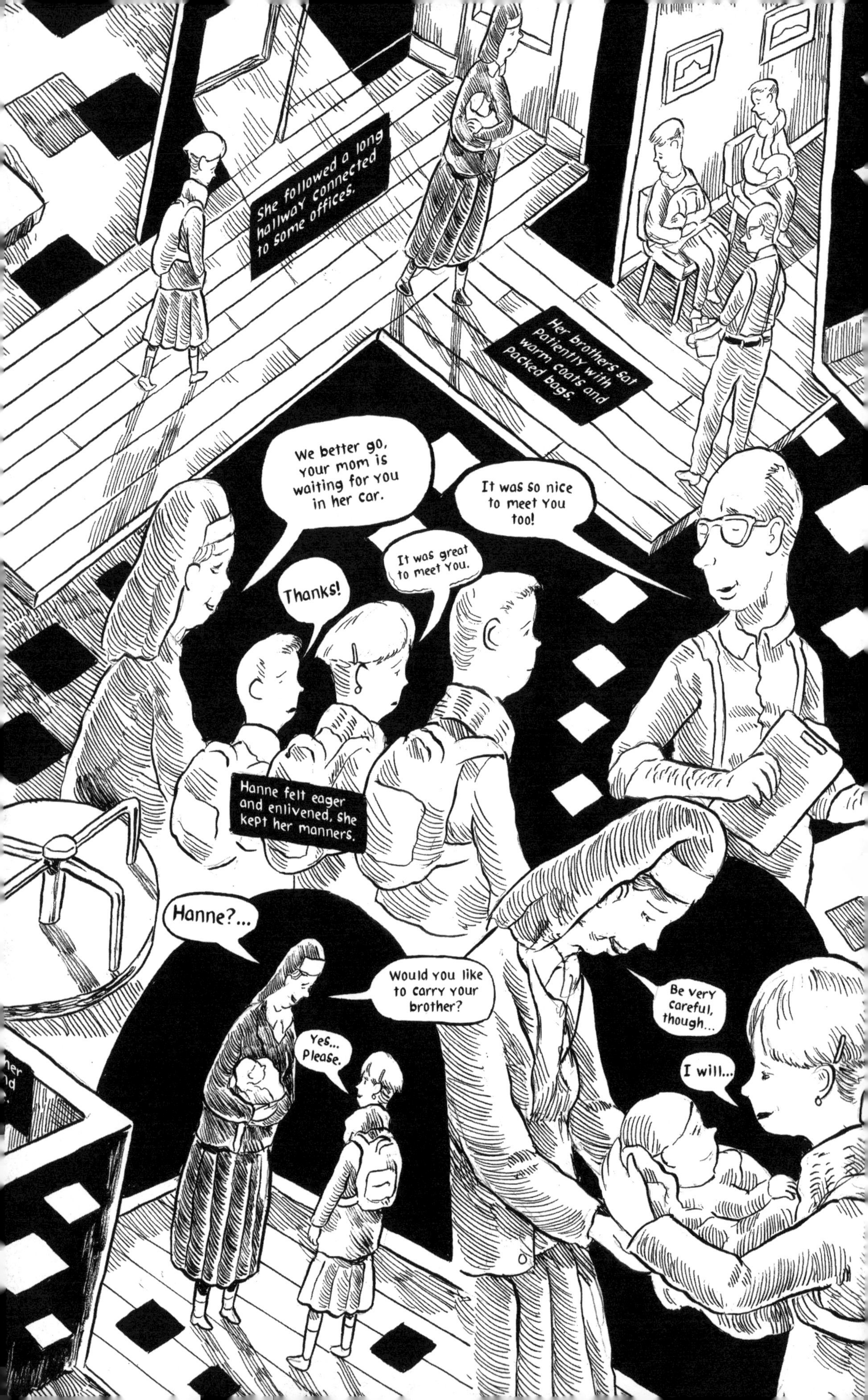
She followed a long hallway connected to some offices.
Her brothers sat patiently with warm coats and packed bags.
We better go, your mom is waiting for you in her car.
It was so nice to meet you too!
It was great to meet you.
Thanks!
Hanne felt eager and enlivened, she kept her manners.
Hanne?...
Would you like to carry your brother?
Yes... Please.
Be very careful, though...
I will...

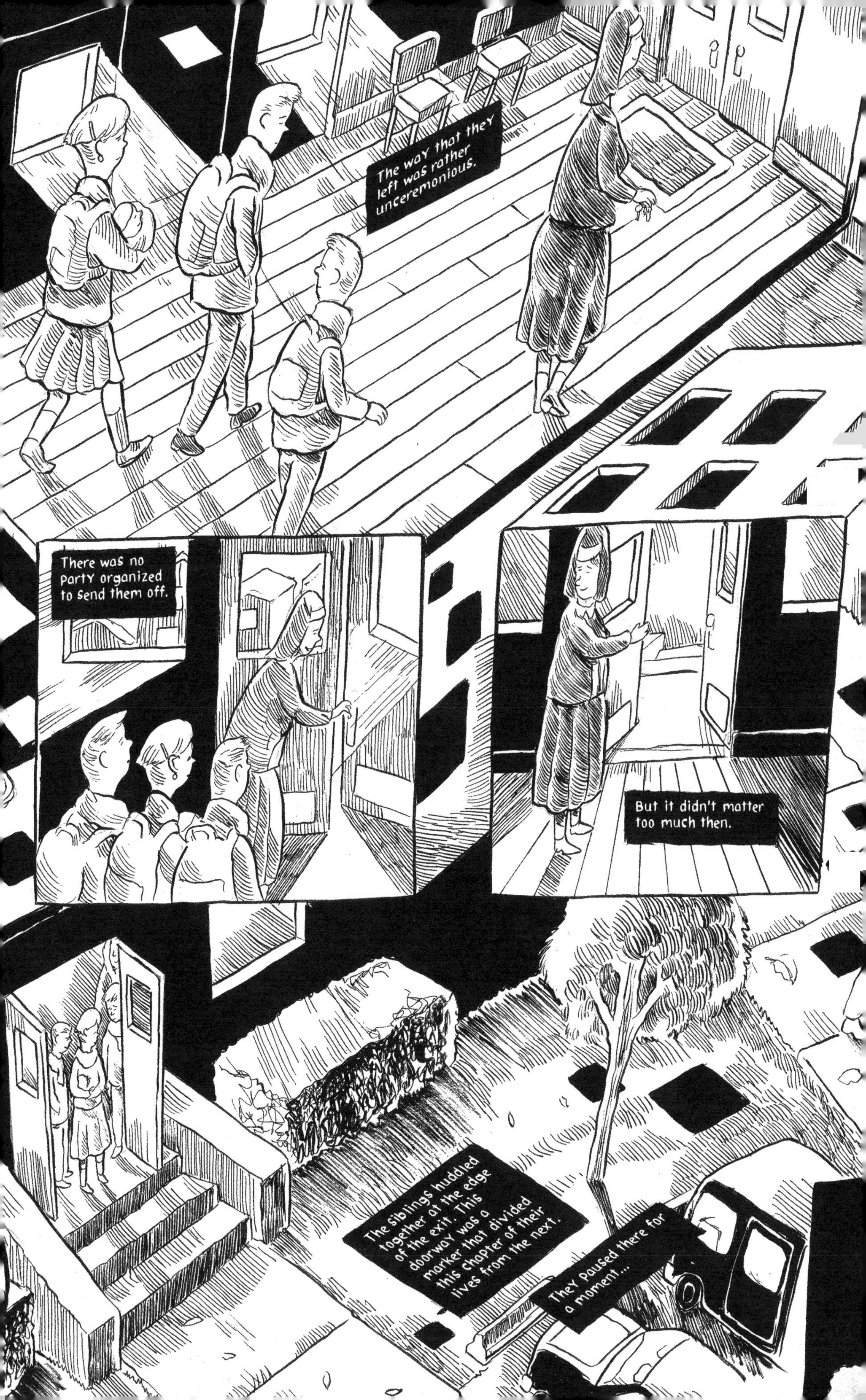
The way that they left was rather unceremonious.
There was no party organized to send them off.
But it didn't matter too much then.
The siblings huddled together at the edge of the exit. This doorway was a marker that divided this chapter of their lives from the next.
They paused there for a moment...

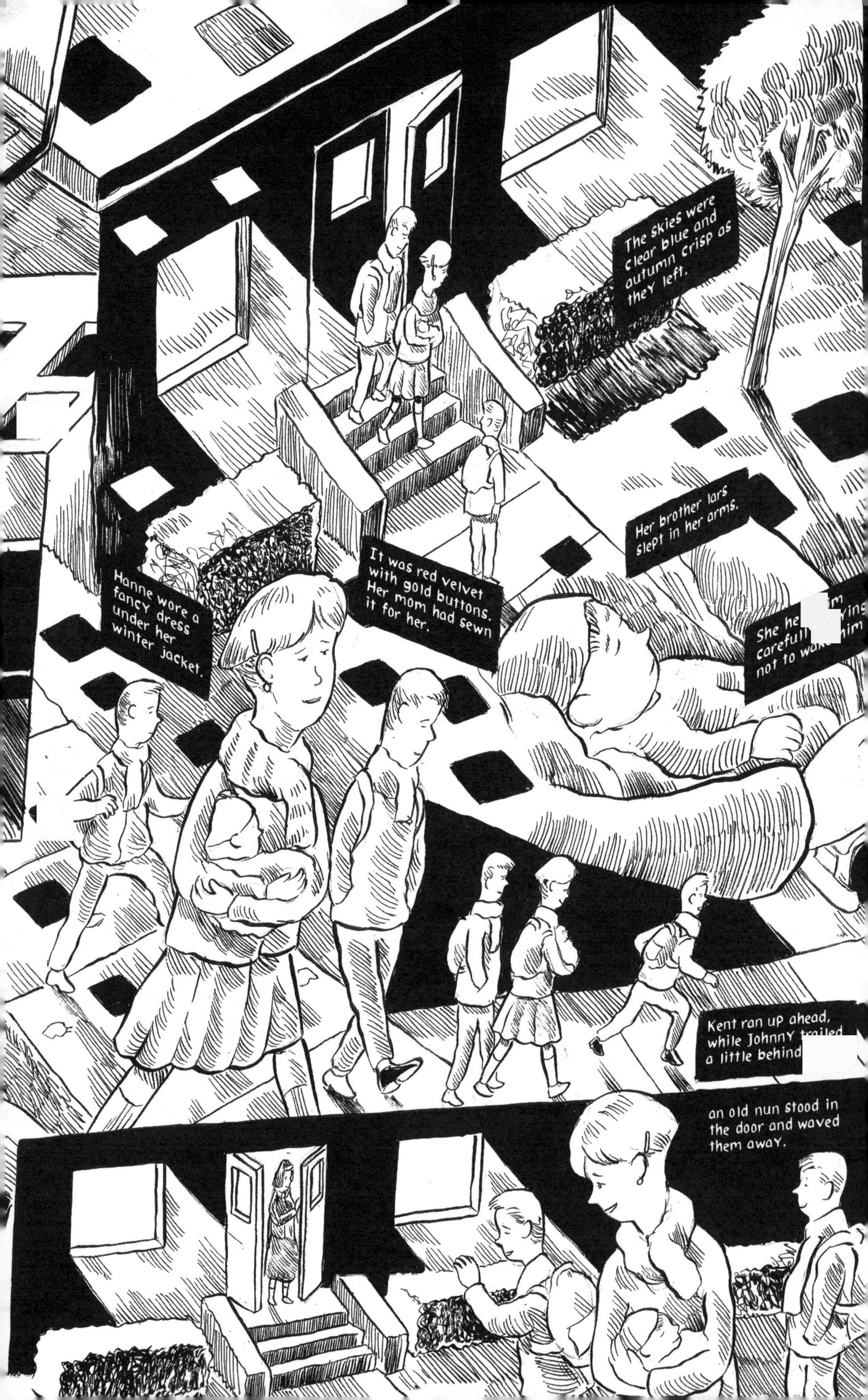
The skies were clear blue and autumn crisp as they left.
Her brother lars slept in her arms.
It was red velvet with gold buttons. Her mom had sewn it for her.
Hanne wore a fancy dress under her winter jacket.
She he im carefull ying not to wa him
Kent ran up ahead, while Johnny trailed a little behind
an old nun stood in the door and waved them away.

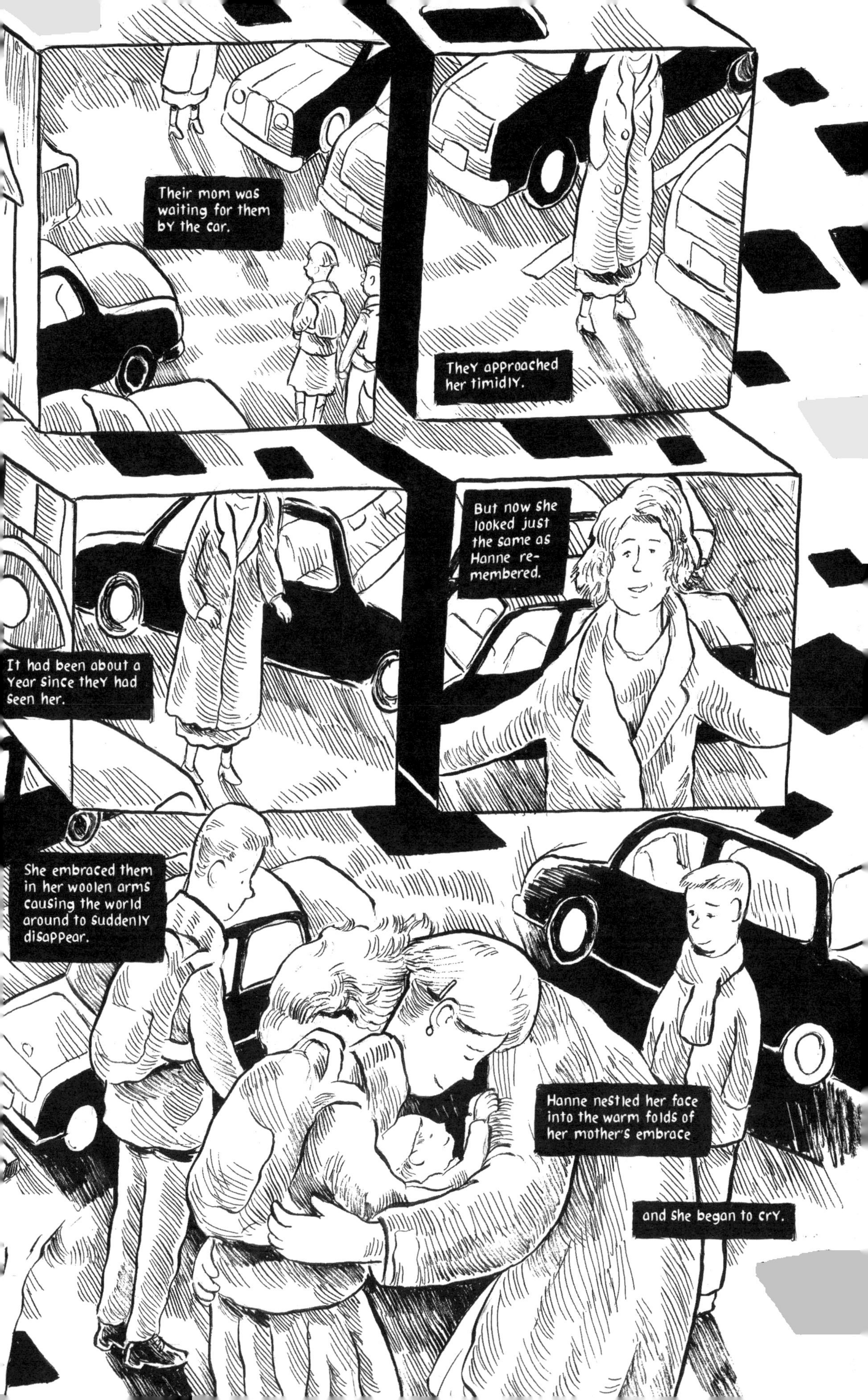
Their mom was waiting for them by the car.
They approached her timidly.
It had been about a year since they had seen her.
But now she looked just the same as Hanne re-membered.
She embraced them in her woolen arms causing the world around to suddenly disappear.
Hanne nestled her face into the warm folds of her mother's embrace
and she began to cry.

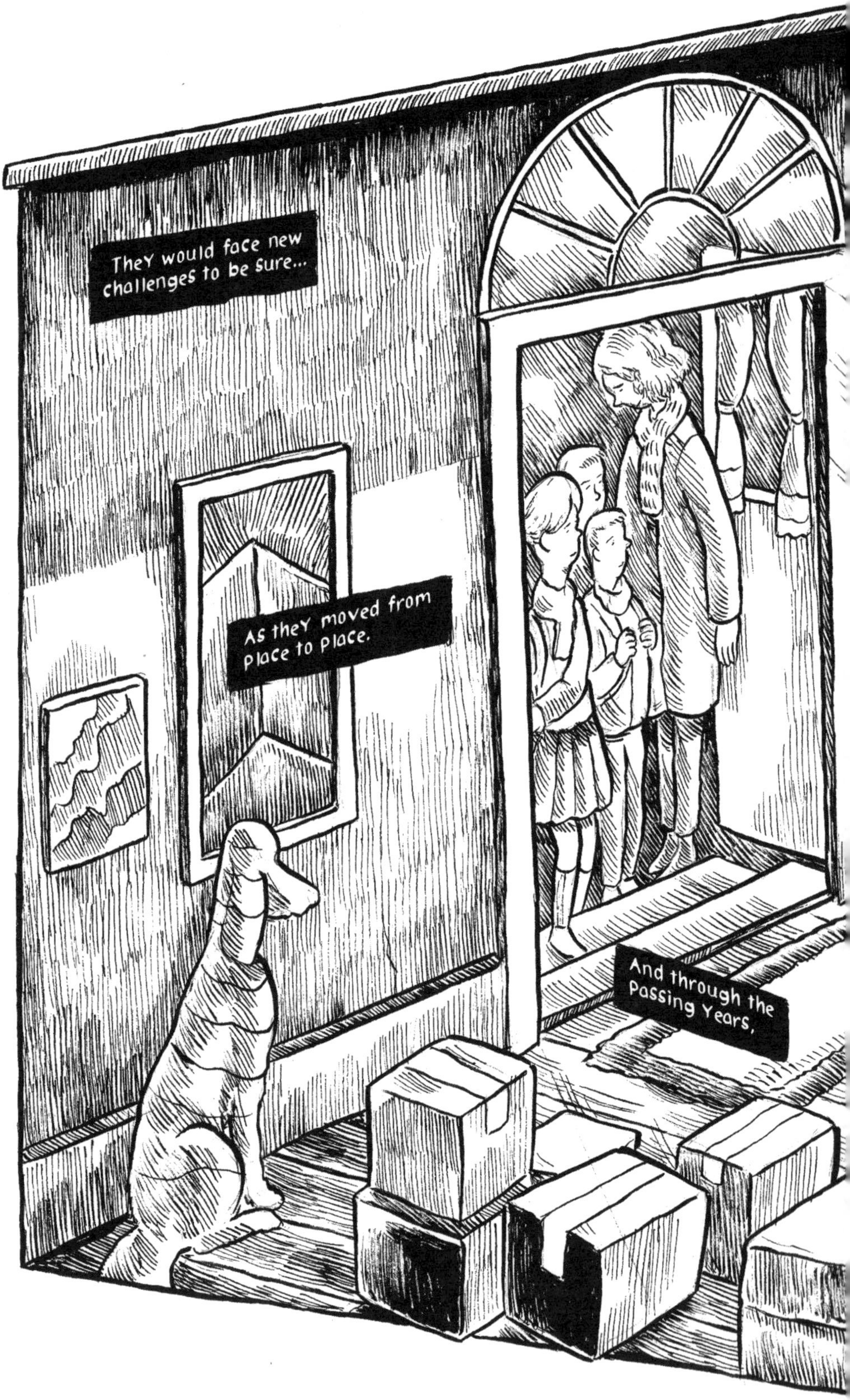
They would face new challenges to be sure...
As they moved from place to place.
And through the Passing Years,

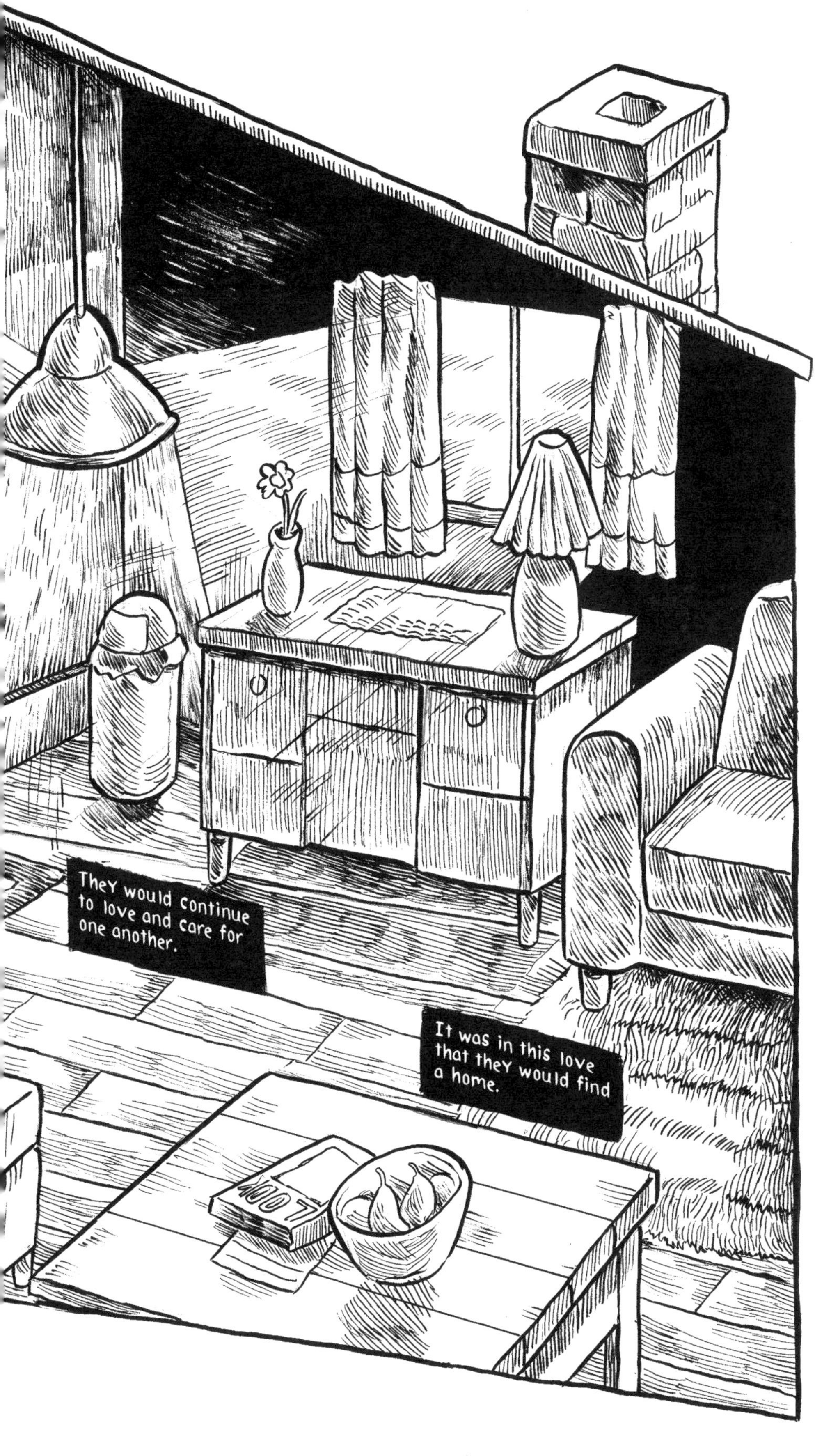
They would continue to love and care for one another.
It was in this love that they would find a home.

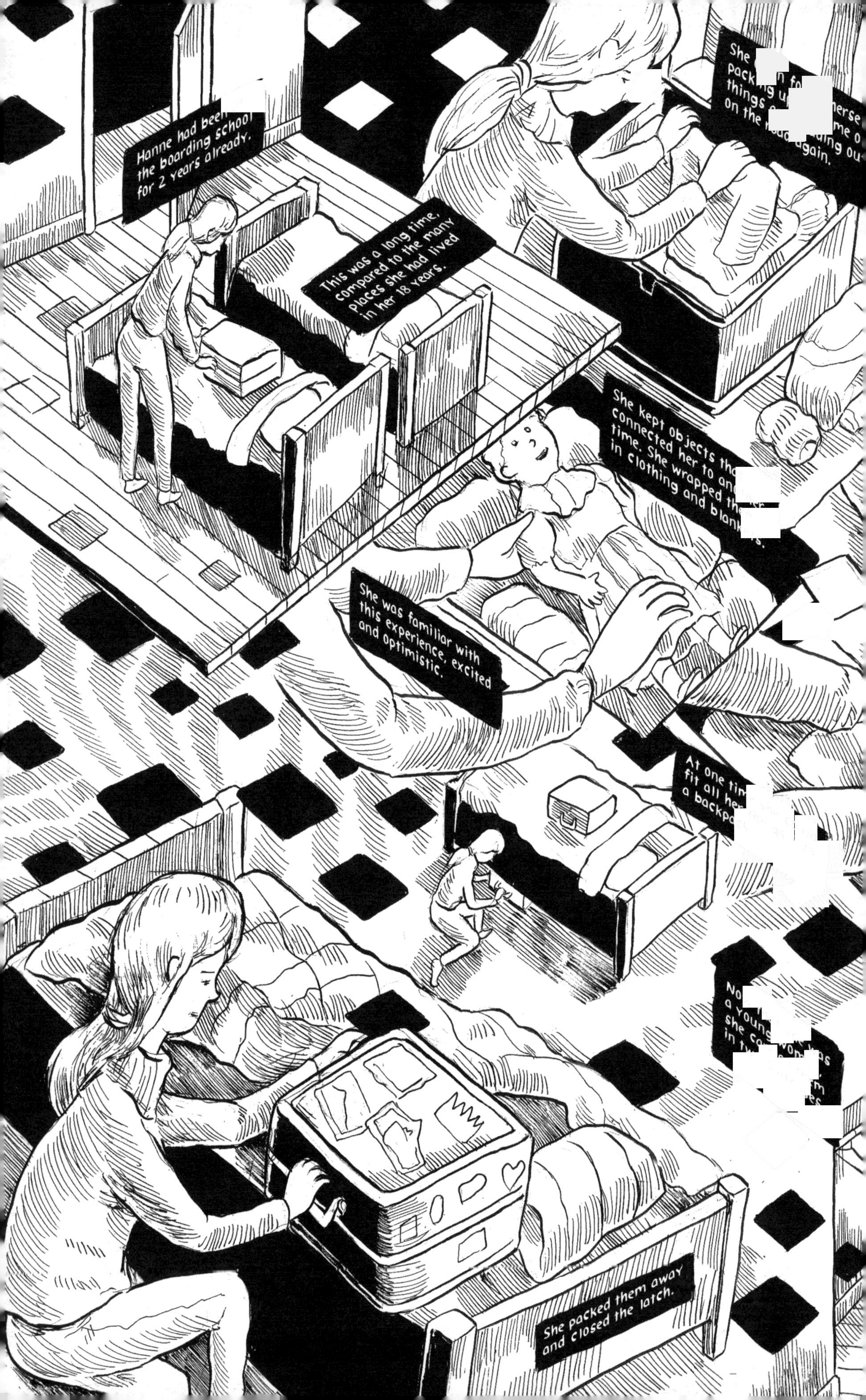
Hanne had been
the boarding school
for 2 years already.
This was a long time,
compared to the many
places she had lived
in her 18 years.
She kept objects
connected her to
time. She wrapped
in clothing and
She was familiar with
this experience, excited
and optimistic.
She packed them away
and closed the latch.

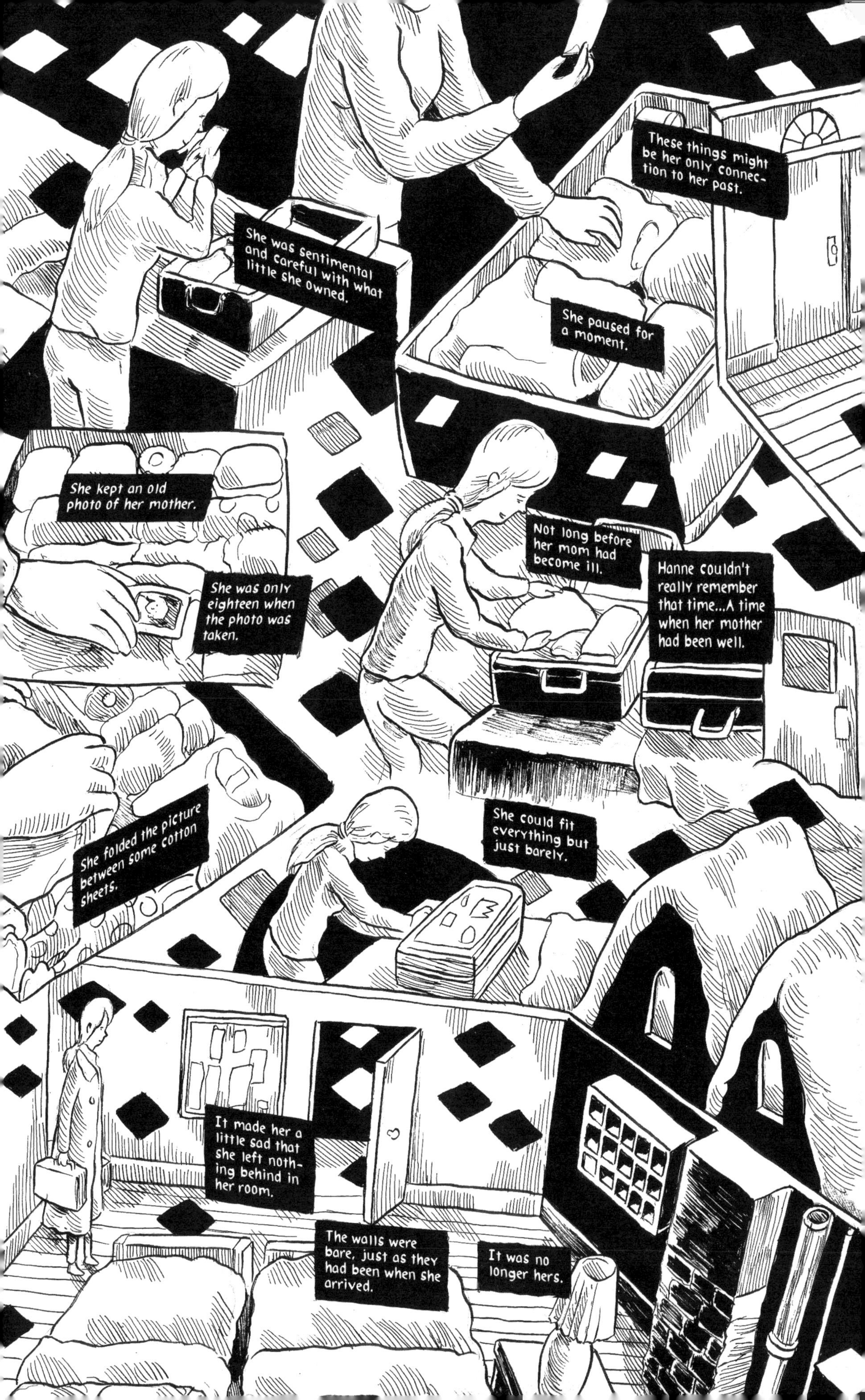
She was sentimental and careful with what little she owned.
These things might be her only connection to her past.
She paused for a moment.
She kept an old photo of her mother.
She was only eighteen when the photo was taken.
Not long before her mom had become ill.
Hanne couldn't really remember that time...A time when her mother had been well.
She folded the picture between some cotton sheets.
She could fit everything but just barely.
It made her a little sad that she left nothing behind in her room.
The walls were bare, just as they had been when she arrived.
It was no longer hers.

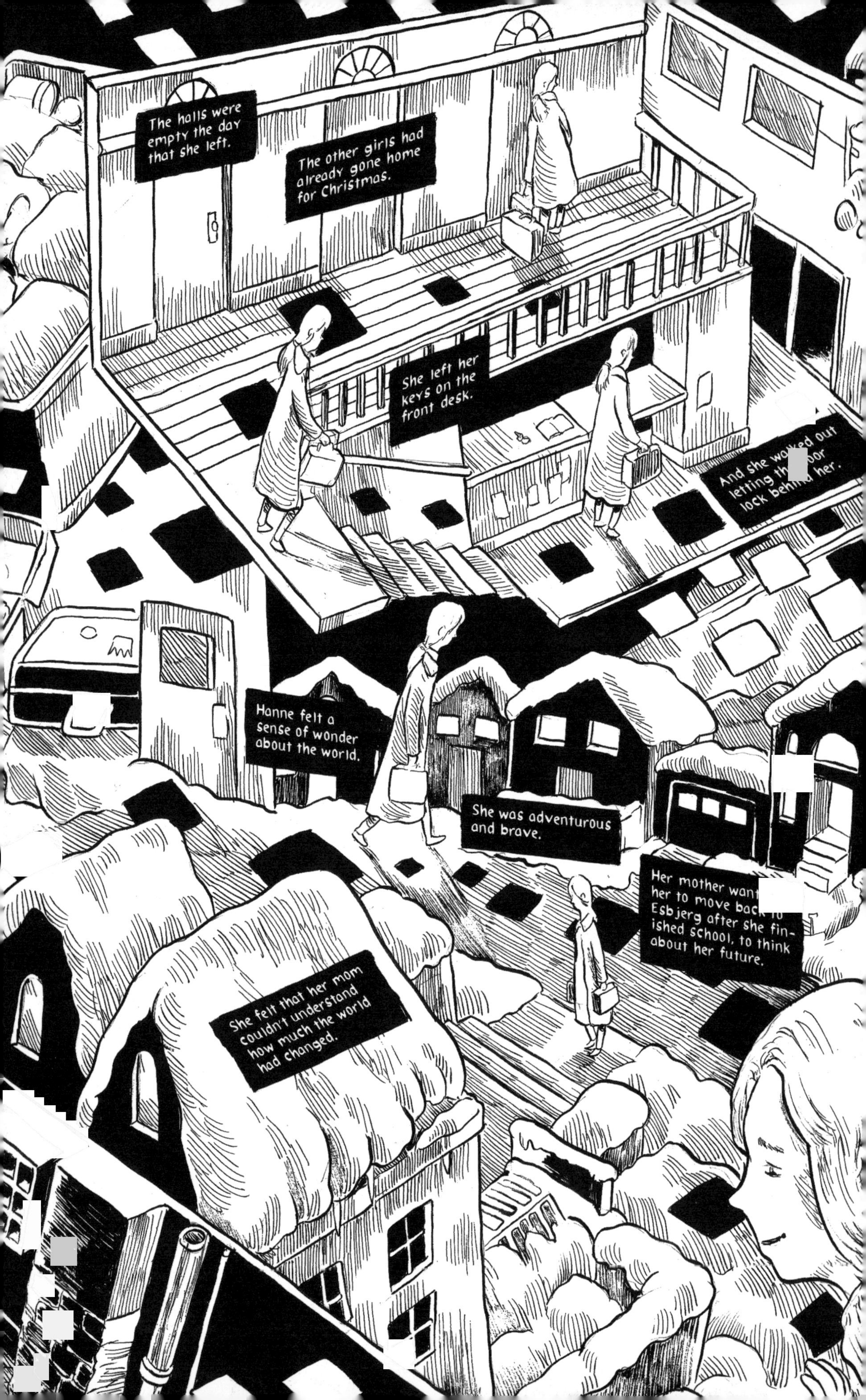
The halls were empty the day that she left.
The other girls had already gone home for Christmas.
She left her keys on the front desk.
And she wa ed out letting th oor lock beh d her.
Hanne felt a sense of wonder about the world.
She was adventurous and brave.
Her mother want her to move bac Esbjerg after she finished school, to think about her future.
She felt that her mom couldn't understand how much the world had changed.

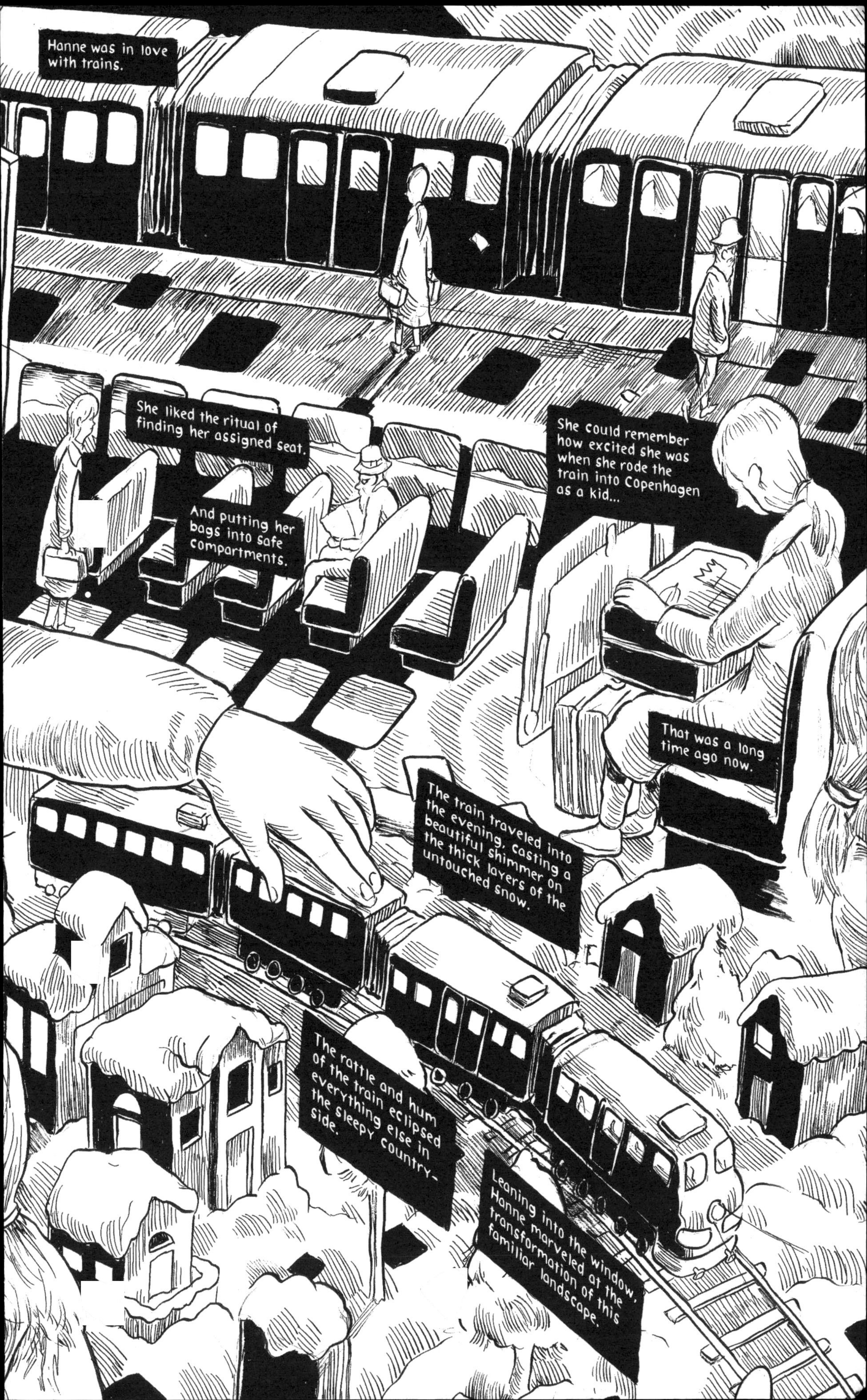
Hanne was in love with trains.
She liked the ritual of finding her assigned seat.
And putting her bags into safe compartments.
She could remember how excited she was when she rode the train into Copenhagen as a kid...
That was a long time ago now.
The train traveled into the evening, casting a beautiful shimmer on the thick layers of the untouched snow.
The rattle and hum of the train eclipsed everything else in the sleepy country-side.
Leaning into the window, Hanne marveled at the transformation of this familiar landscape.

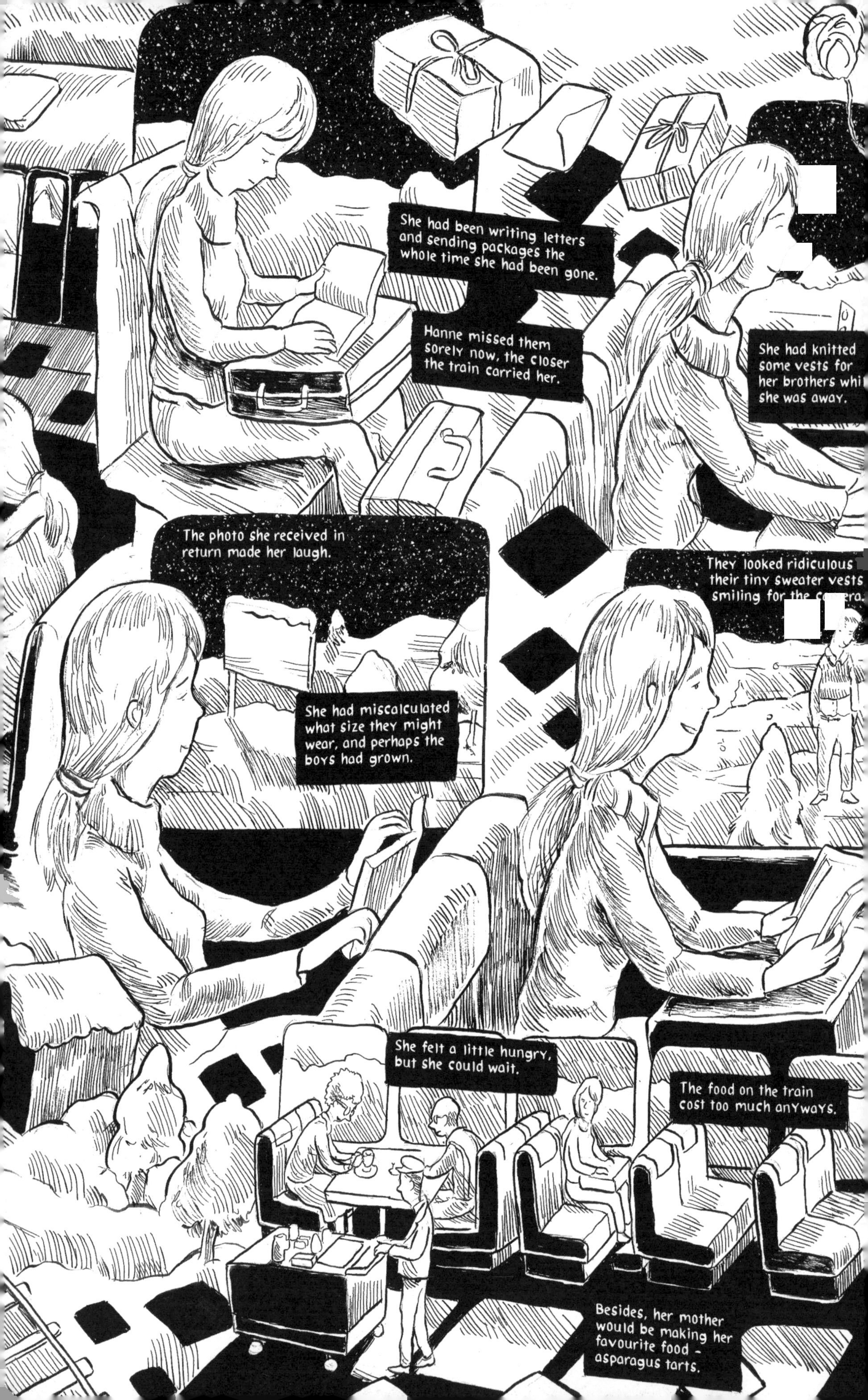
She had been writing letters and sending packages the whole time she had been gone.
Hanne missed them sorely now, the closer the train carried her.
She had knitted some vests for her brothers whi she was away.
The photo she received in return made her laugh.
She had miscalculated what size they might wear, and perhaps the boys had grown.
They looked ridiculous their tiny sweater vests smiling for the
She felt a little hungry, but she could wait.
The food on the train cost too much anyways.
Besides, her mother would be making her favourite food - asparagus tarts.

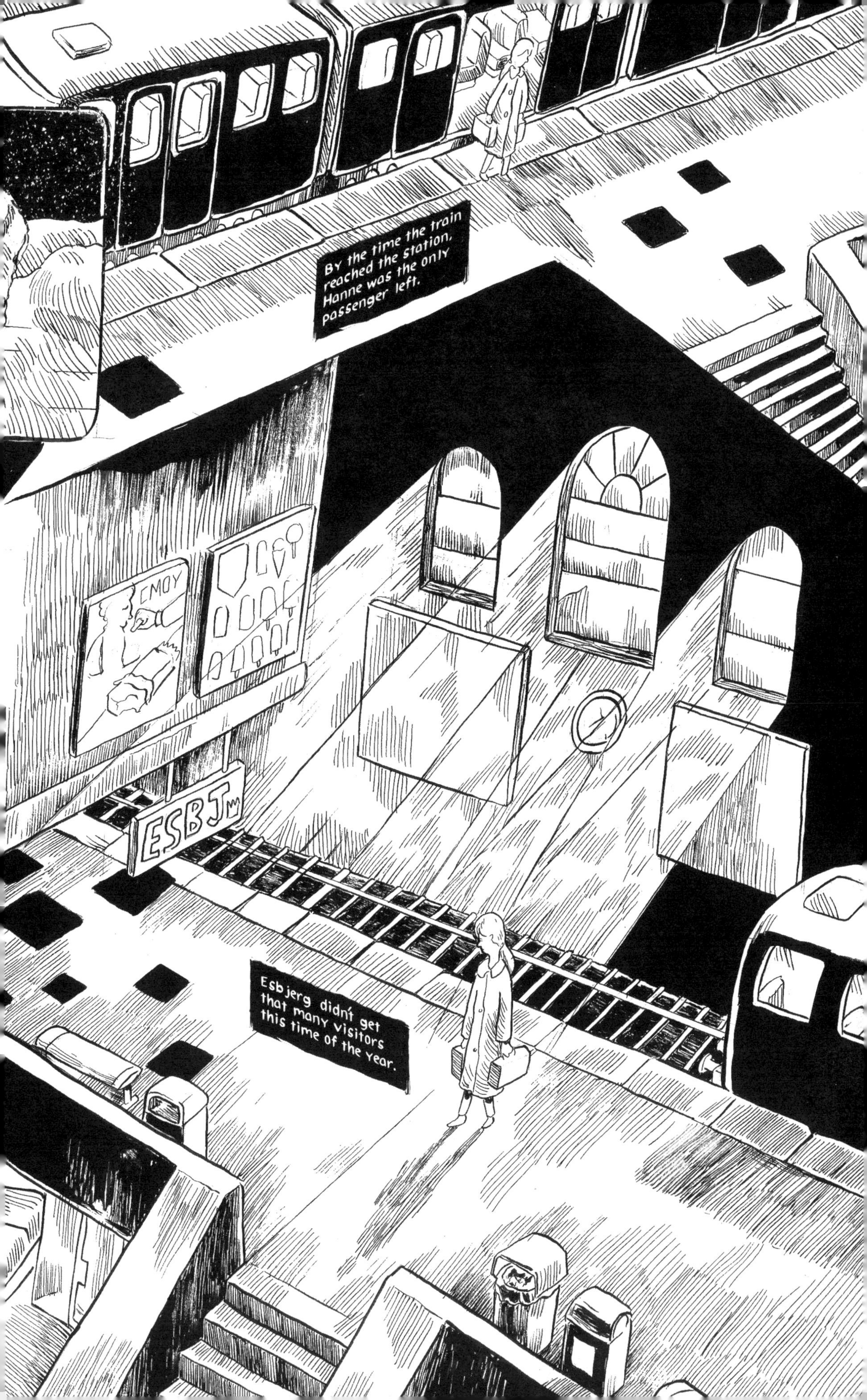
By the time the train reached the station, Hanne was the only passenger left.
ESBJ
Esbjerg didn't get that many visitors this time of the year.

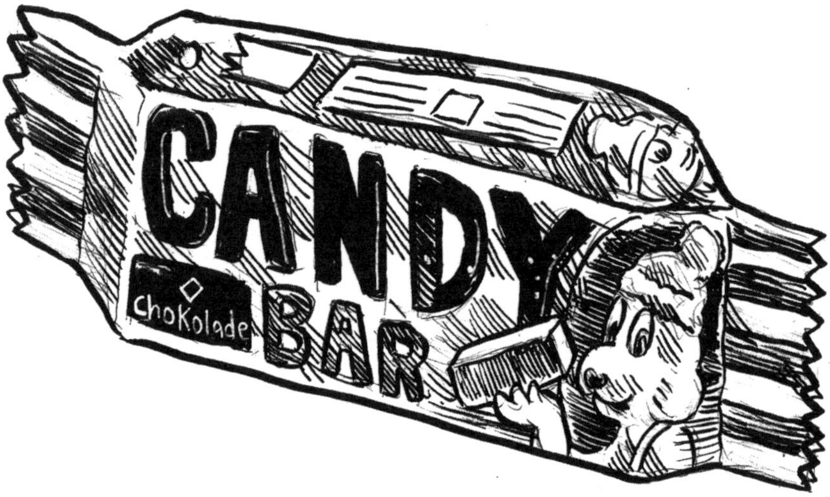
CANDY
BAR
ChoKolade

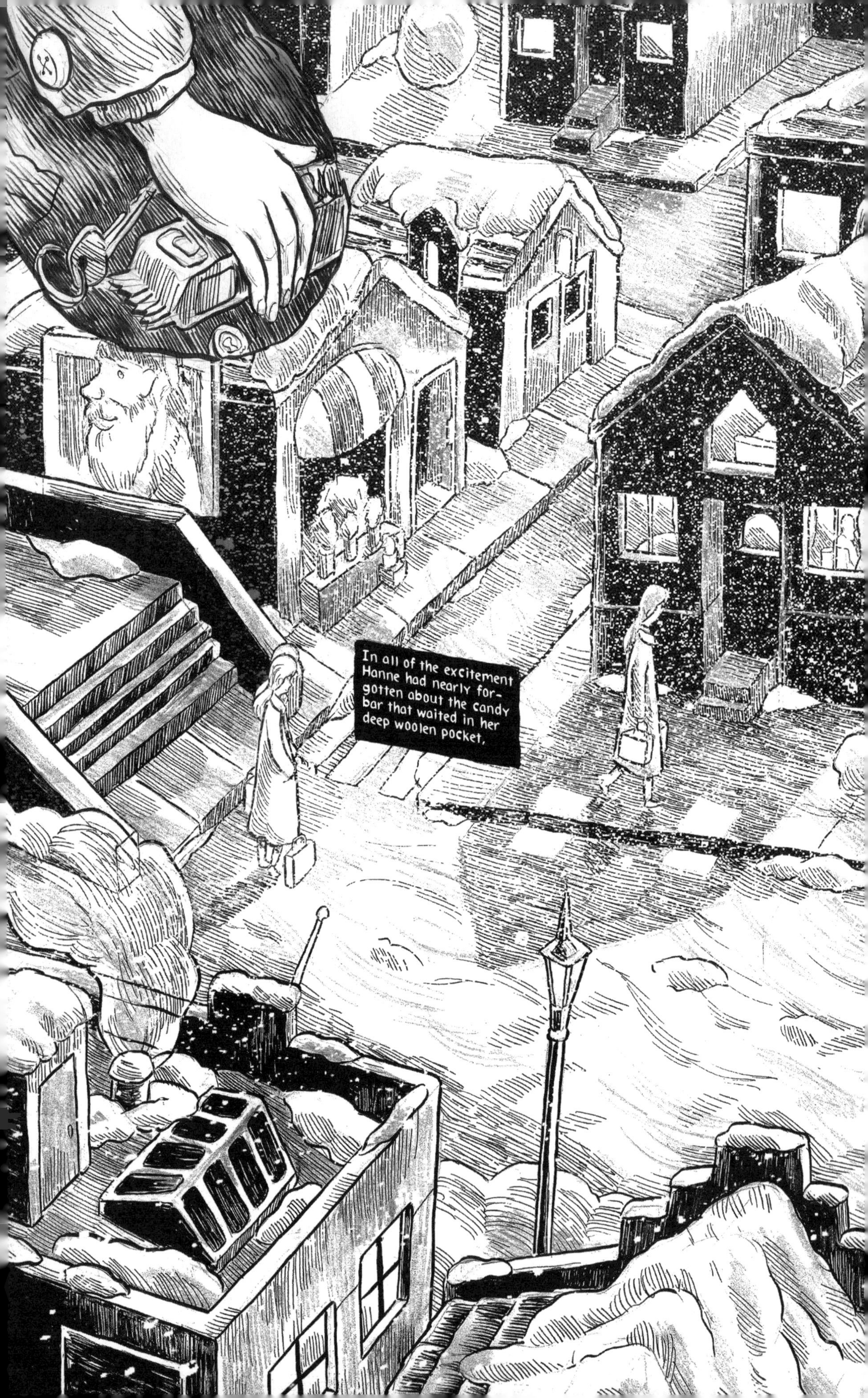
In all of the excitement Hanne had nearly forgotten about the candy bar that waited in her deep woolen pocket.

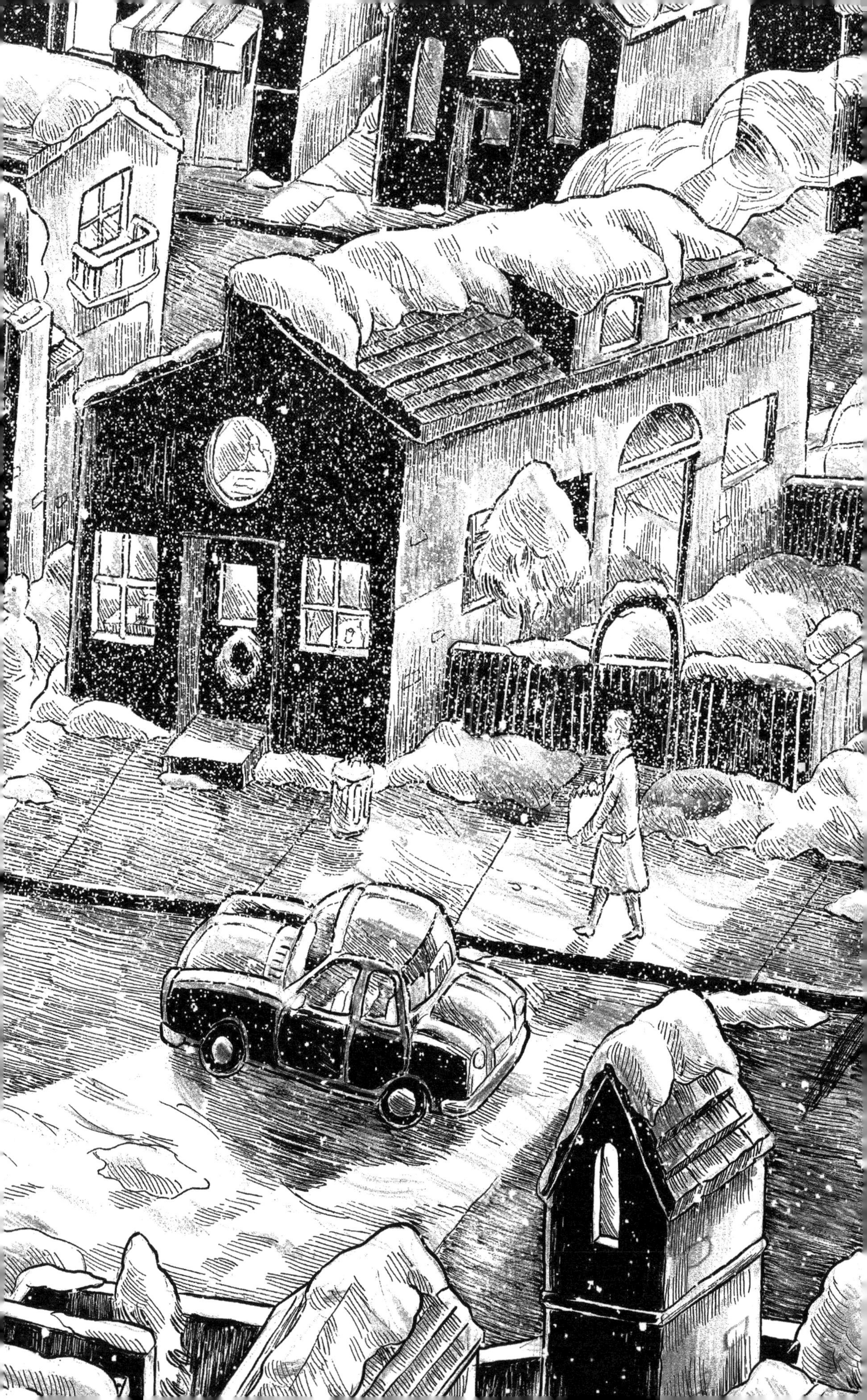

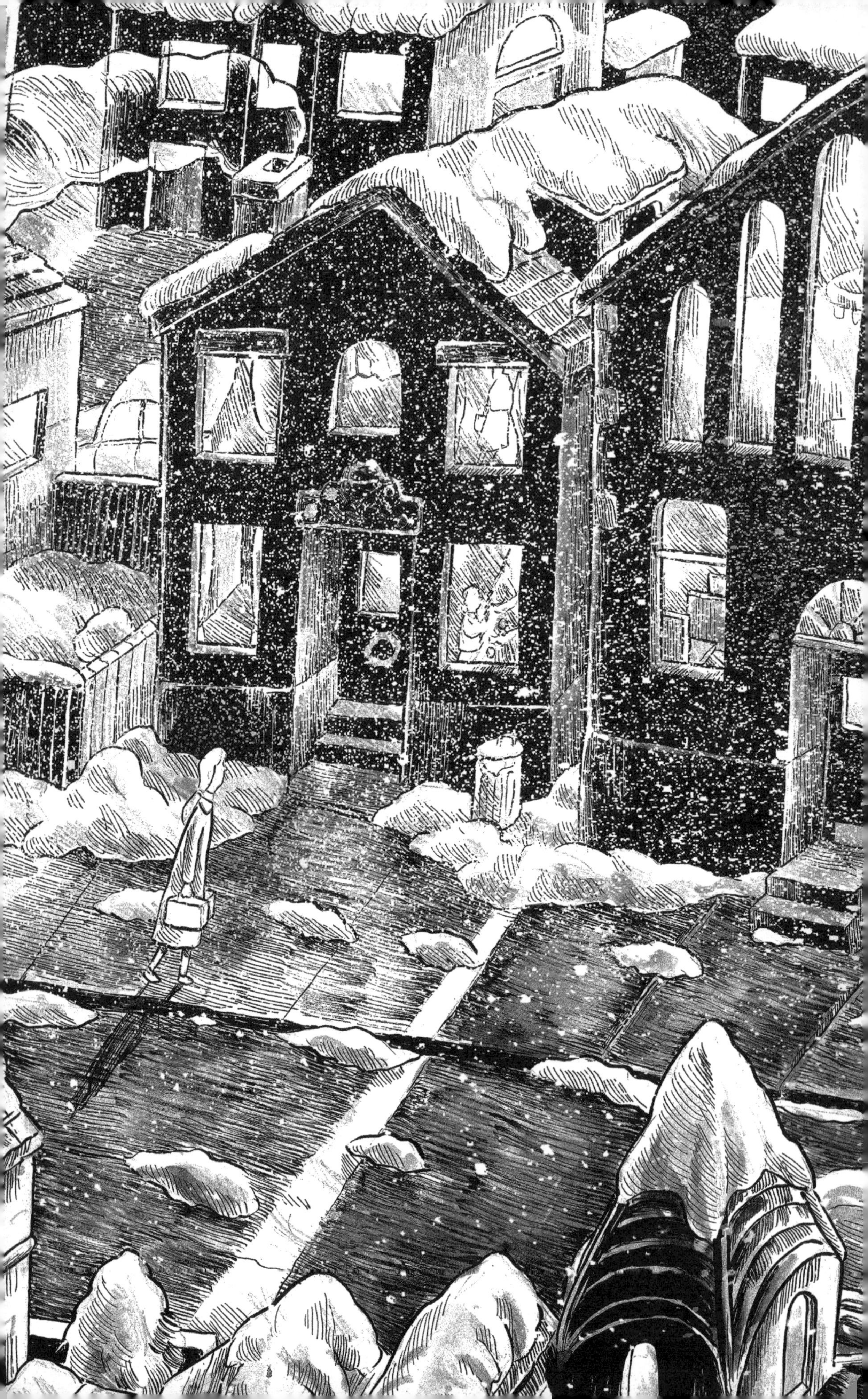

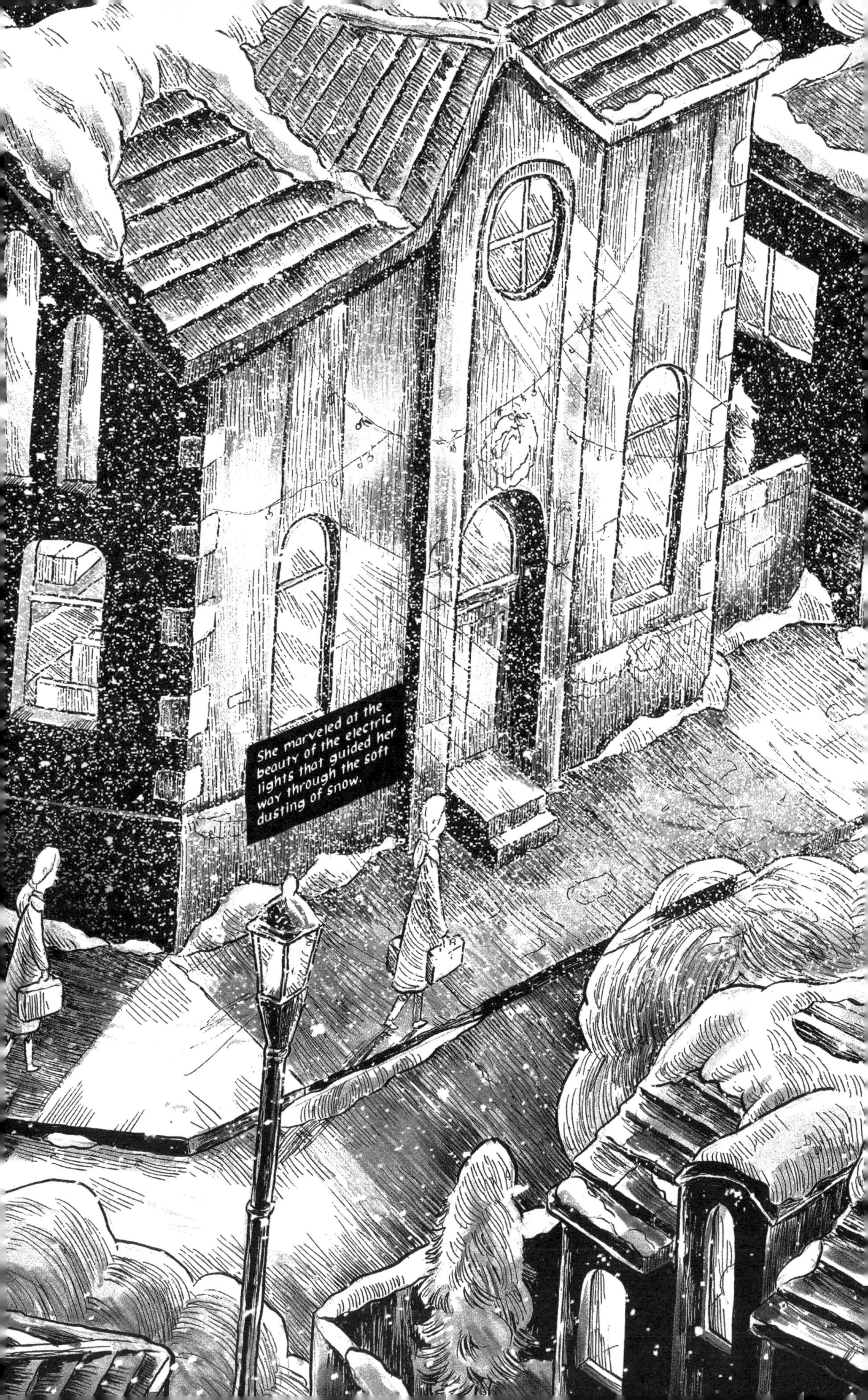
She marveled at the beauty of the electric lights that guided her way through the soft dusting of snow.

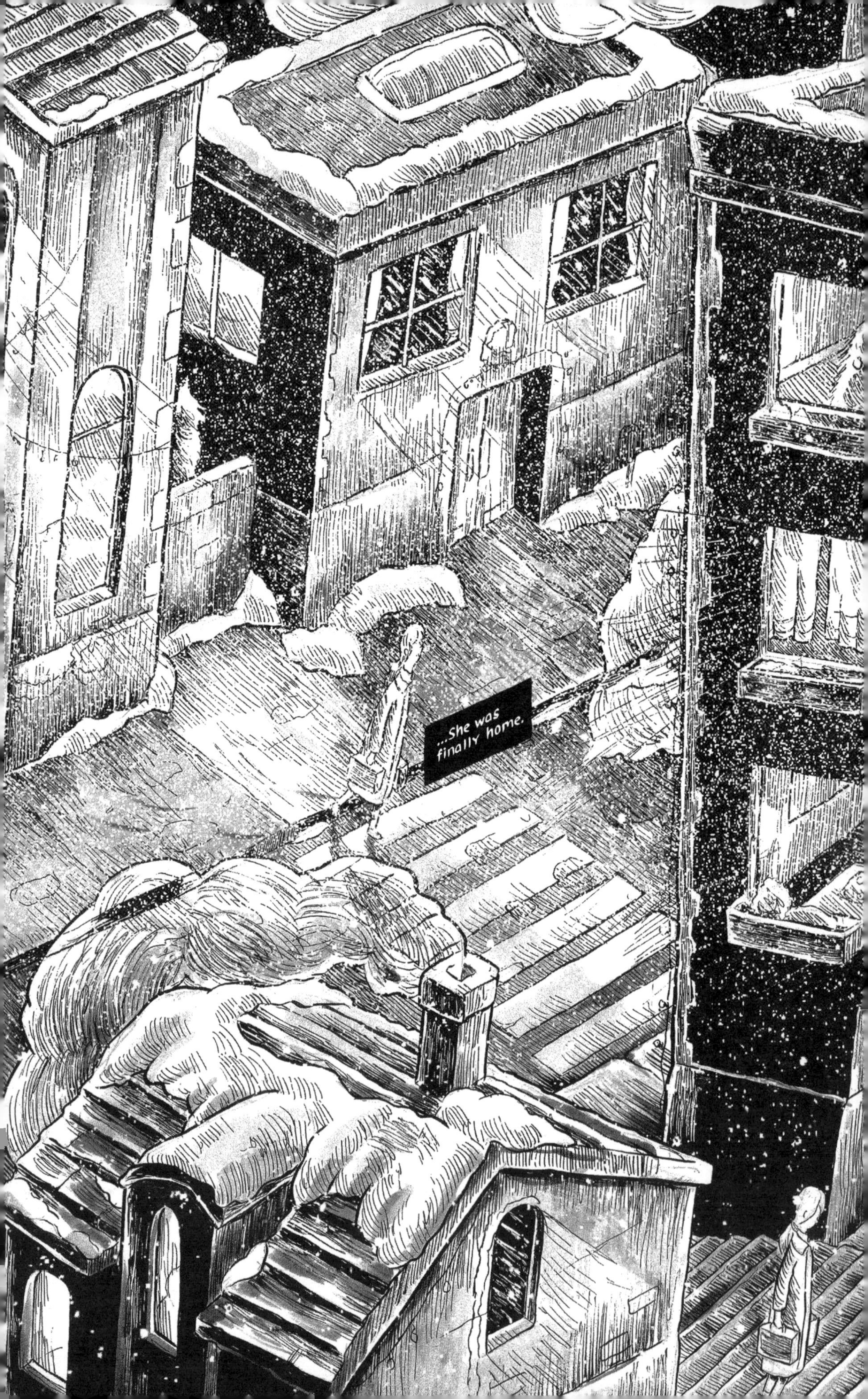
...She was finally home.

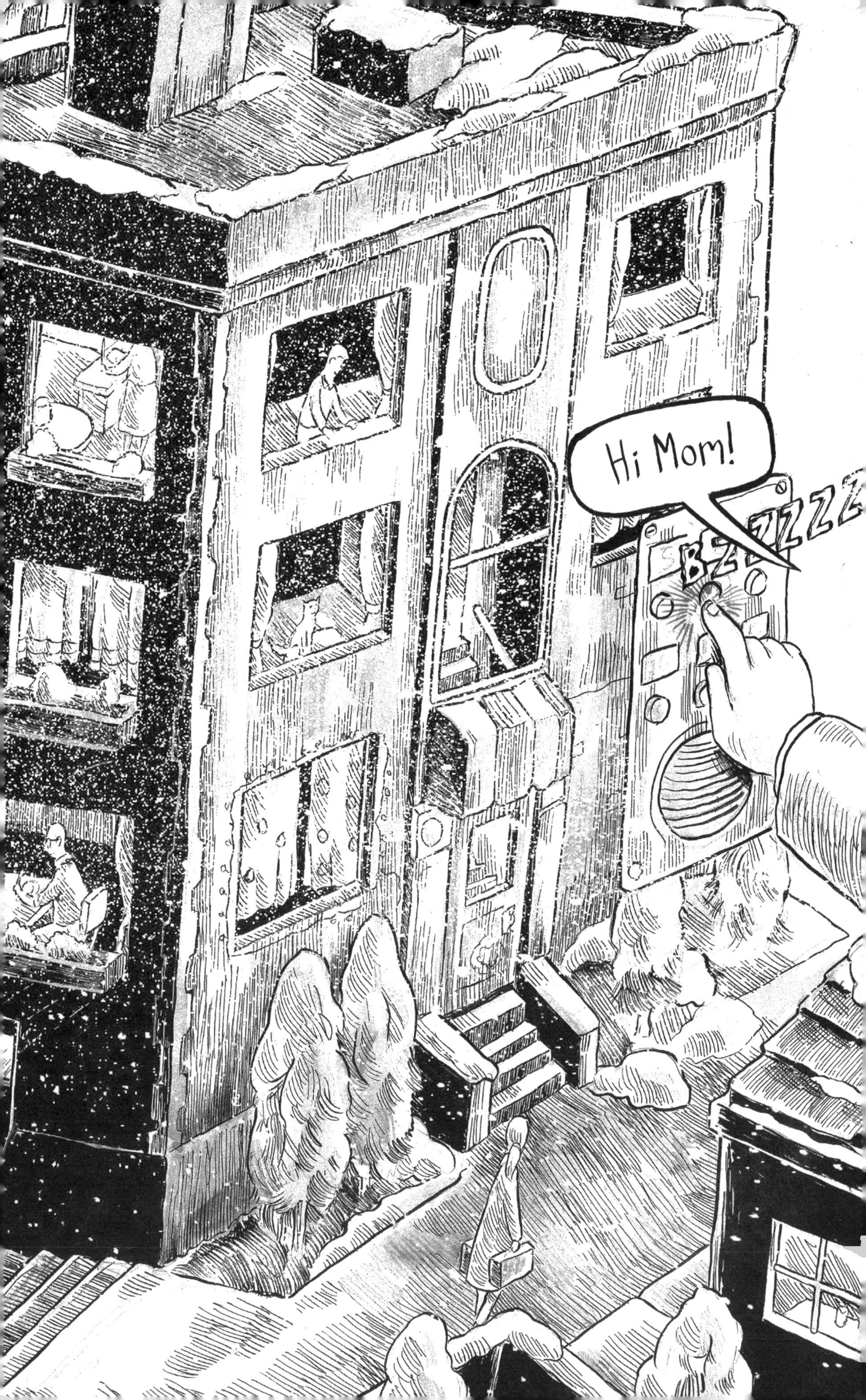
Hi Mom!

Hanne held out her arms and opened herself up to the world.
She hitched rides on freight trucks, finding her way across Europe.
She met like-minded young travellers and camped at a commune in Spain.
It was there she met a young man from Victoria B.C via Holland somewhere.
She held his hand by the light of a fire, the world to them was vast.
They journied together through Egypt, Morocco, and Tunesia.
He left abruptly and went back home to Canada.

They exchanged letters and long distance calls.
She thought of him often, collected coins and saved for a ticket.
Excitedly, she stepped off the plane and they would never be apart.
The young couple saved for a plot of land in the woods near Crofton B.C.
They would construct a house and start a family, they built a home.
Hanne would provide a world of endless possibilities for her kids.
She would give them everything she never had.

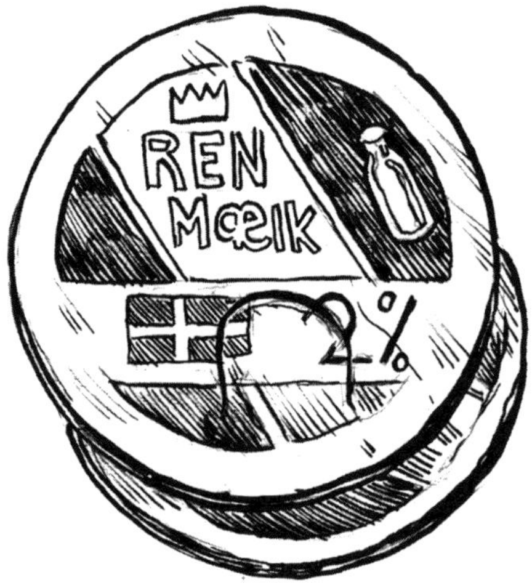
REN
Mælk
2%

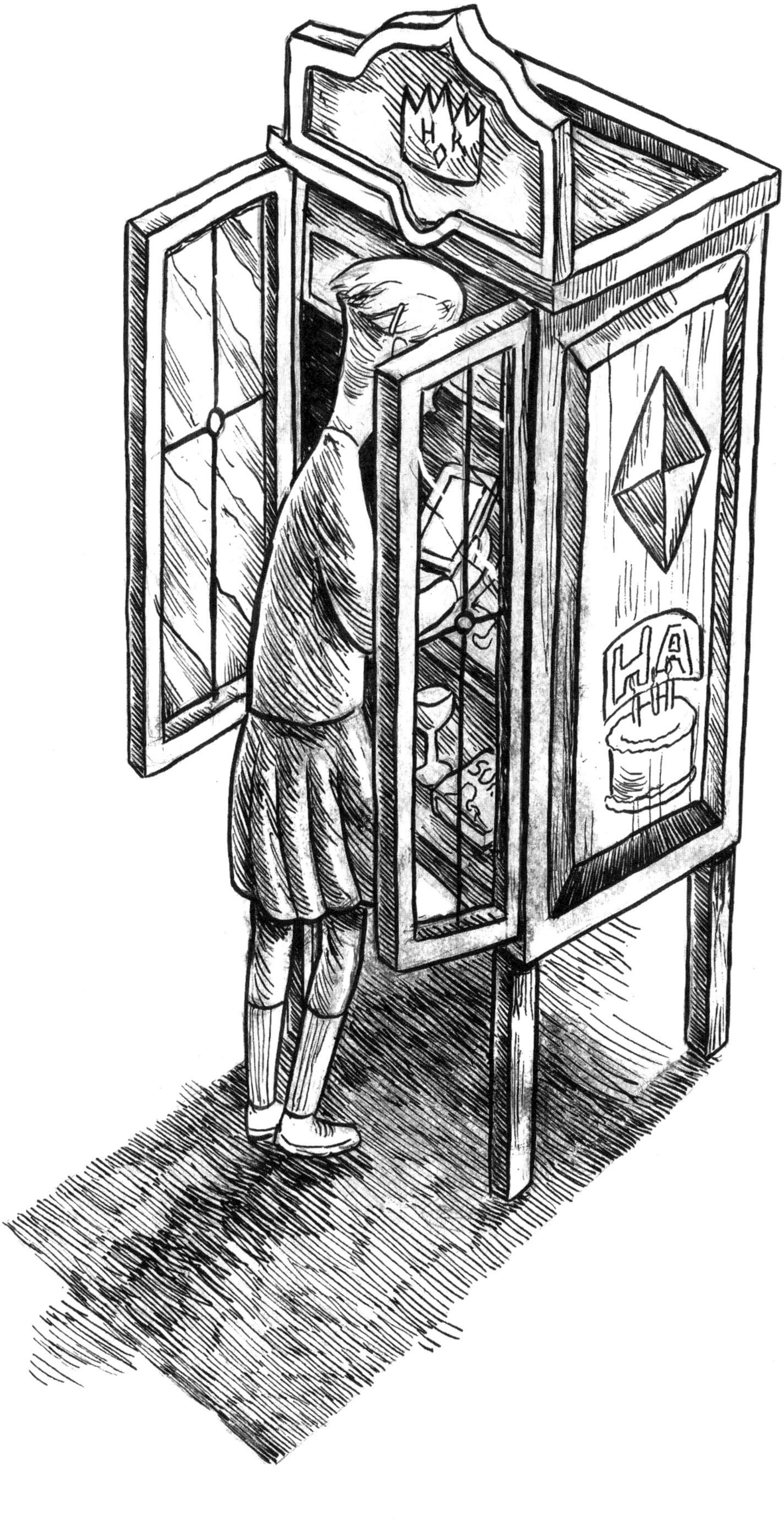
HA

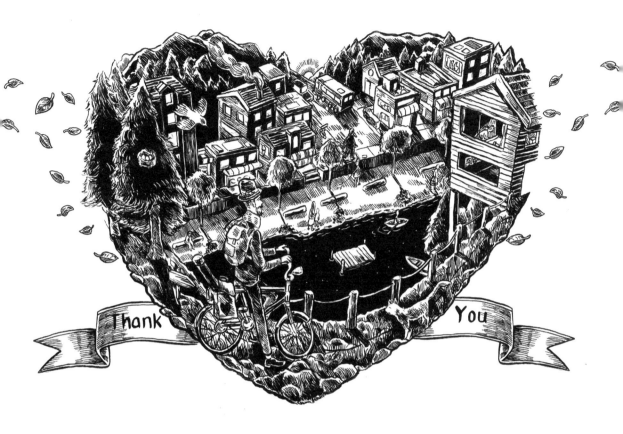

To James Lloyd for being A great mentor and friend.

Thanks to Lynn Johnston for your thoughts, and encouragement.

To Elmira kuznetsova for finding my spelling and punctuation problems.

Thanks To Doris and Robert Yu for opening up your home to me.

To Andy Brown for taking a chance on my work.

To Sarah Sawler for help with promotion of this book and more to come.

To Charles Barnard for opening my mind to new forms and ideas.

To The Kent Harrison Arts Council for a beautiful residency on the lake.

To Ron Mcgrath for your poems, your life, and your vision of a world with love and empathy.

Thanks to Rosa and Mike for being really inspiring friends.

Thank you so deeply to Priscilla Yu for helping me with more than I can describe here.

Thanks to the Canada Council For The Arts for keeping food in the fridge.

And of course thanks a whole lot to my parents; Hanne and Rene Karemaker.

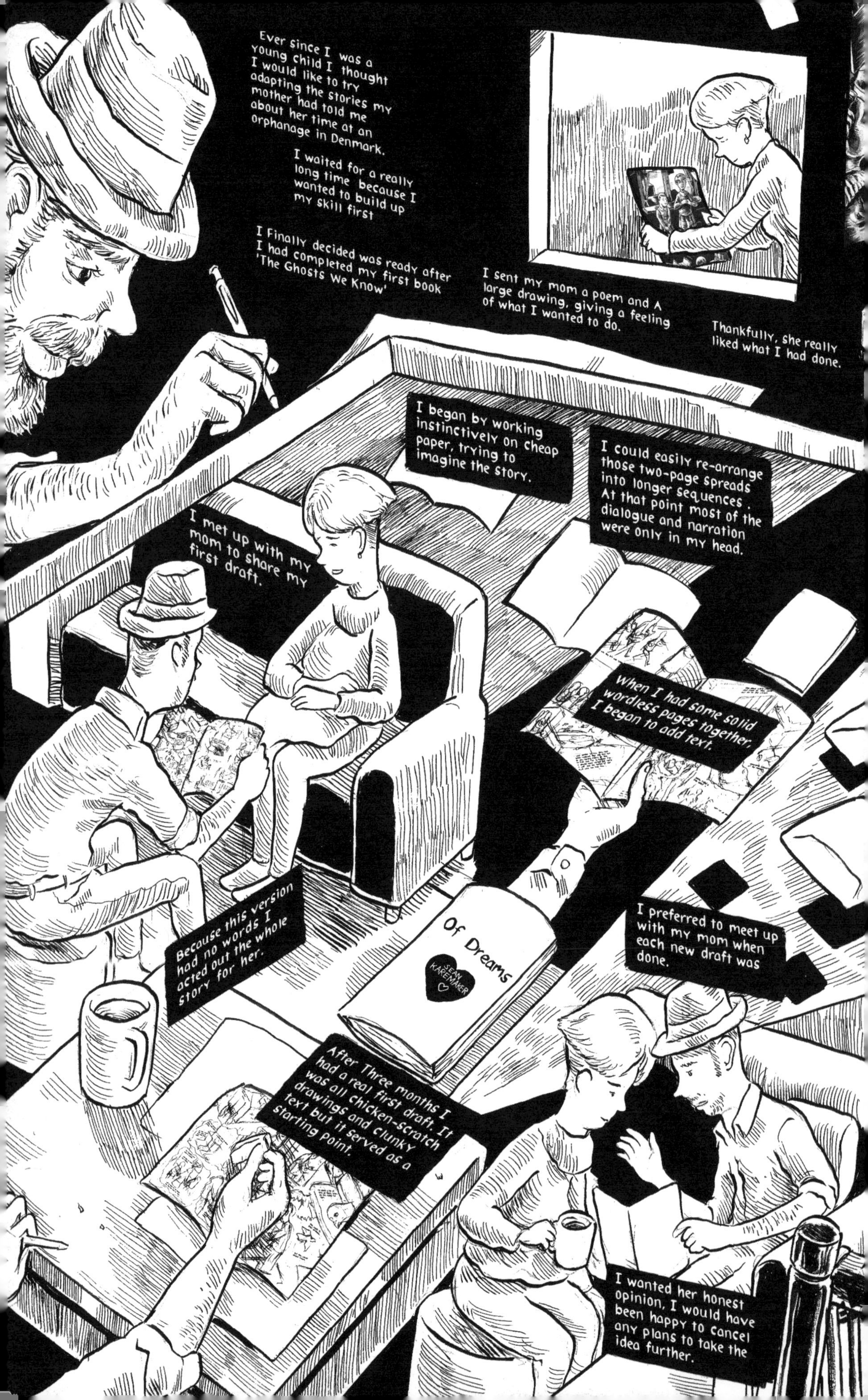
Ever since I was a young child I thought I would like to try adapting the stories my mother had told me about her time at an orphanage in Denmark.
I waited for a really long time because I wanted to build up my skill first
I Finally decided was ready after I had completed my first book 'The Ghosts We Know'
I sent my mom a poem and A large drawing, giving a feeling of what I wanted to do.
Thankfully, she really liked what I had done.
I began by working instinctively on cheap paper, trying to imagine the story.
I could easily re-arrange those two-page spreads into longer sequences. At that point most of the dialogue and narration were only in my head.
I met up with my mom to share my first draft.
When I had some solid wordless pages together, I began to add text.
Because this version had no words I acted out the whole story for her.
Of Dreams
SEAN KAREMAKER
I preferred to meet up with my mom when each new draft was done.
After Three months I had a real first draft. It was all chicken-scratch drawings and clunky text but it served as a starting Point.
I wanted her honest opinion, I would have been happy to cancel any plans to take the idea further.

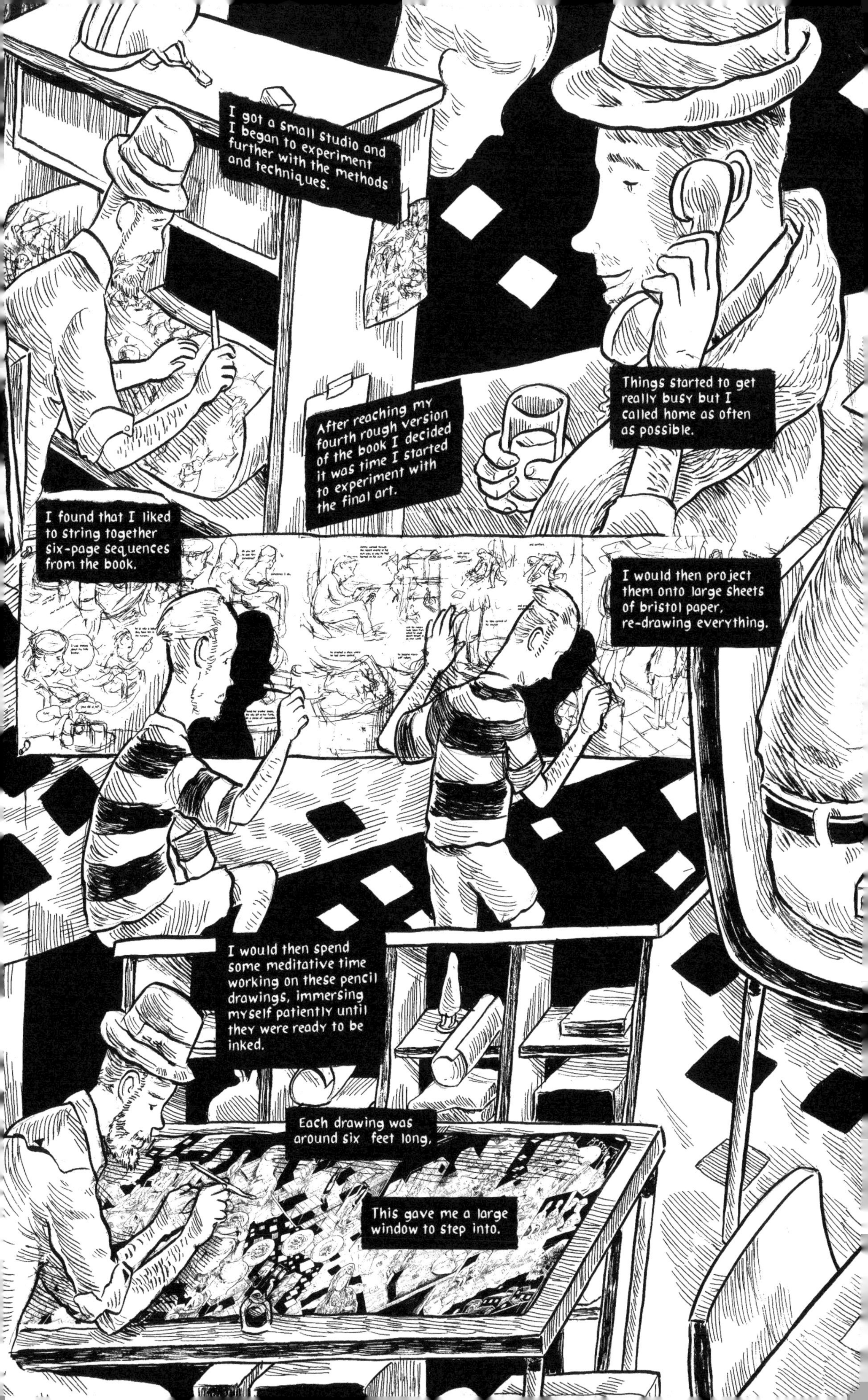
I got a small studio and I began to experiment further with the methods and techniques.
After reaching my fourth rough version of the book I decided it was time I started to experiment with the final art.
Things started to get really busy but I called home as often as possible.
I found that I liked to string together six-page sequences from the book.
I would then project them onto large sheets of bristol paper, re-drawing everything.
I would then spend some meditative time working on these pencil drawings, immersing myself patiently until they were ready to be inked.
Each drawing was around six feet long.
This gave me a large window to step into.

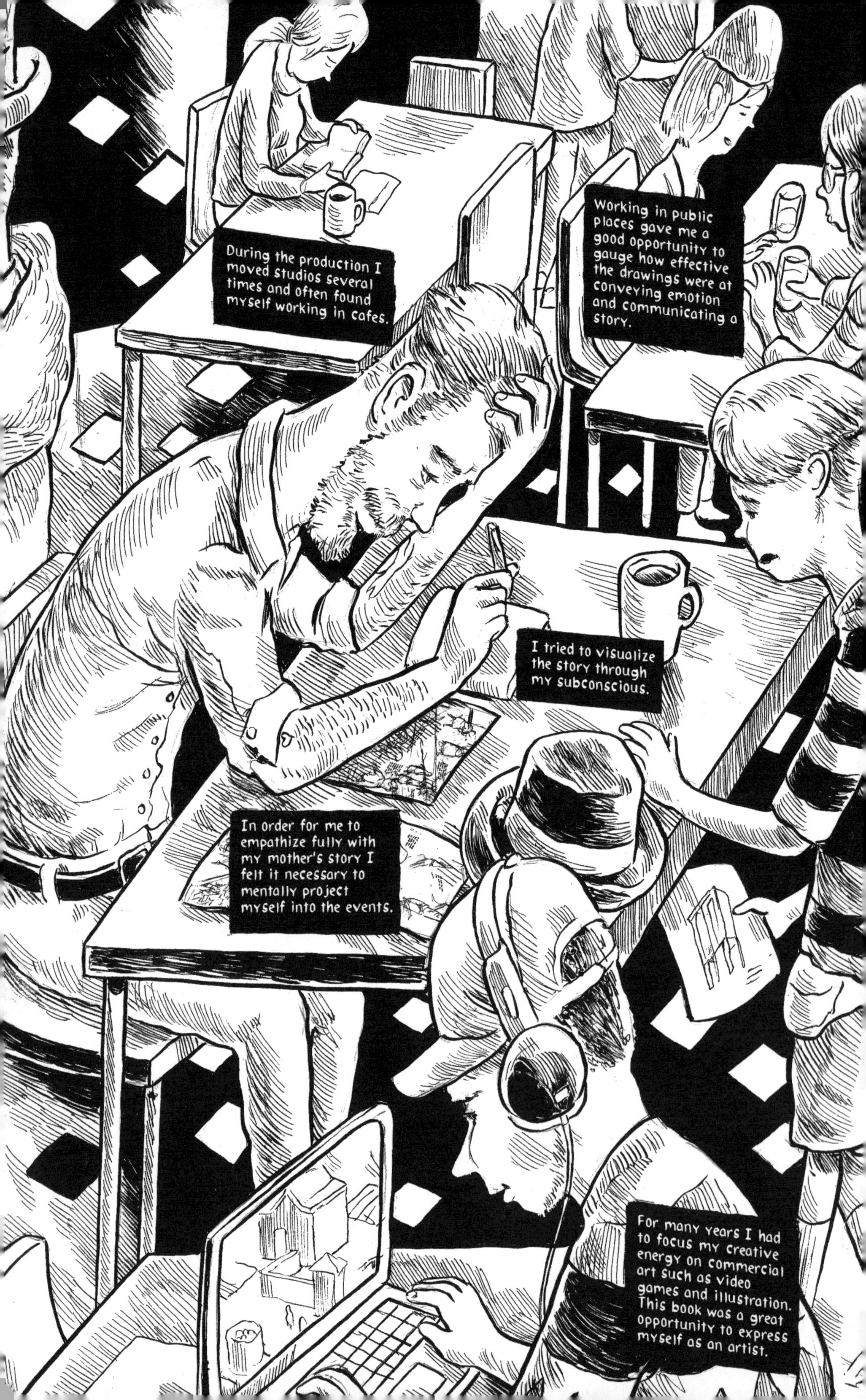
During the production I moved studios several times and often found myself working in cafes.
Working in public places gave me a good opportunity to gauge how effective the drawings were at conveying emotion and communicating a story.
I tried to visualize the story through my subconscious.
In order for me to empathize fully with my mother's story I felt it necessary to mentally project myself into the events.
For many years I had to focus my creative energy on commercial art such as video games and illustration. This book was a great opportunity to express myself as an artist.

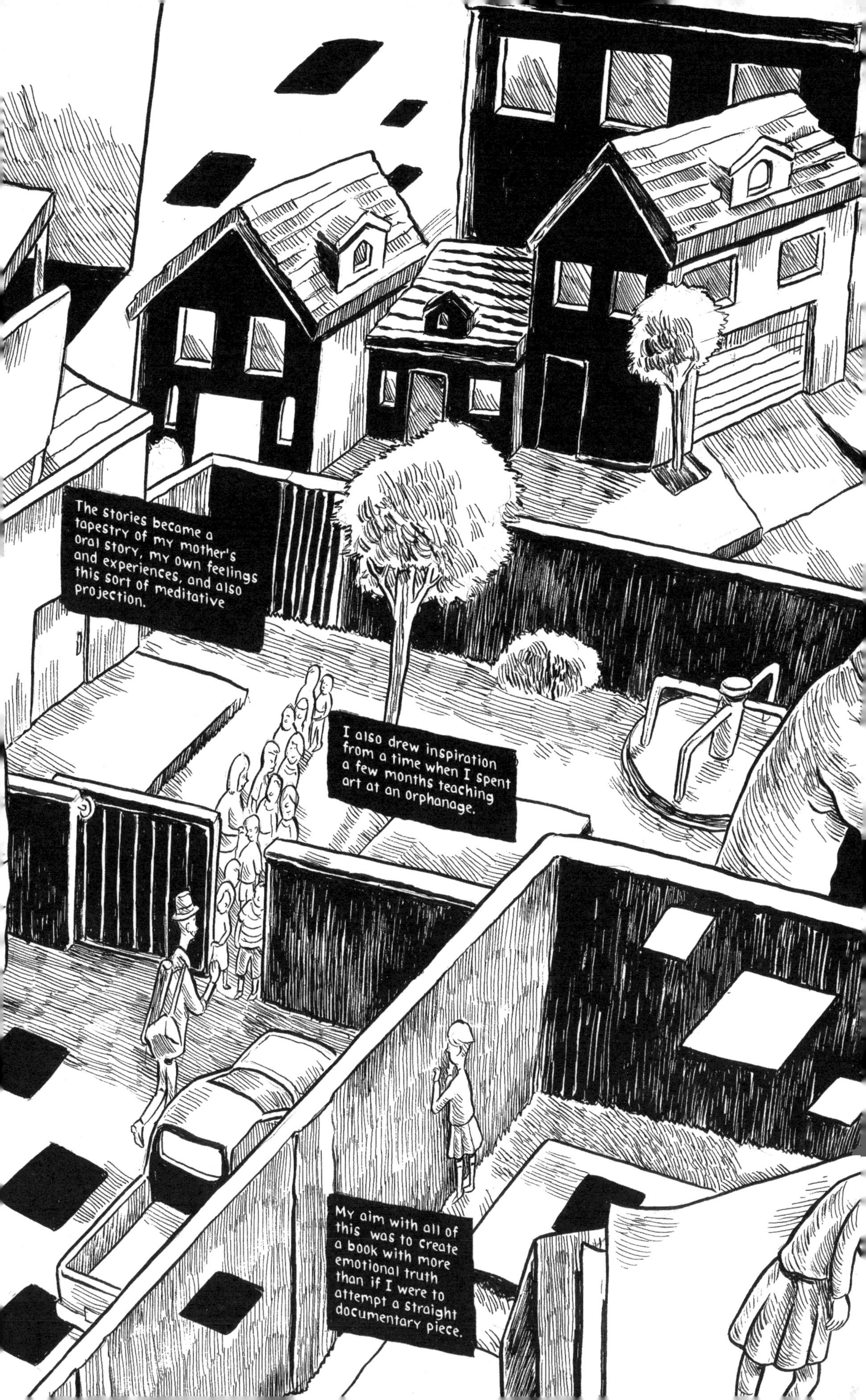
The stories became a tapestry of my mother's oral story, my own feelings and experiences, and also this sort of meditative projection.
I also drew inspiration from a time when I spent a few months teaching art at an orphanage.
My aim with all of this was to create a book with more emotional truth than if I were to attempt a straight documentary piece.

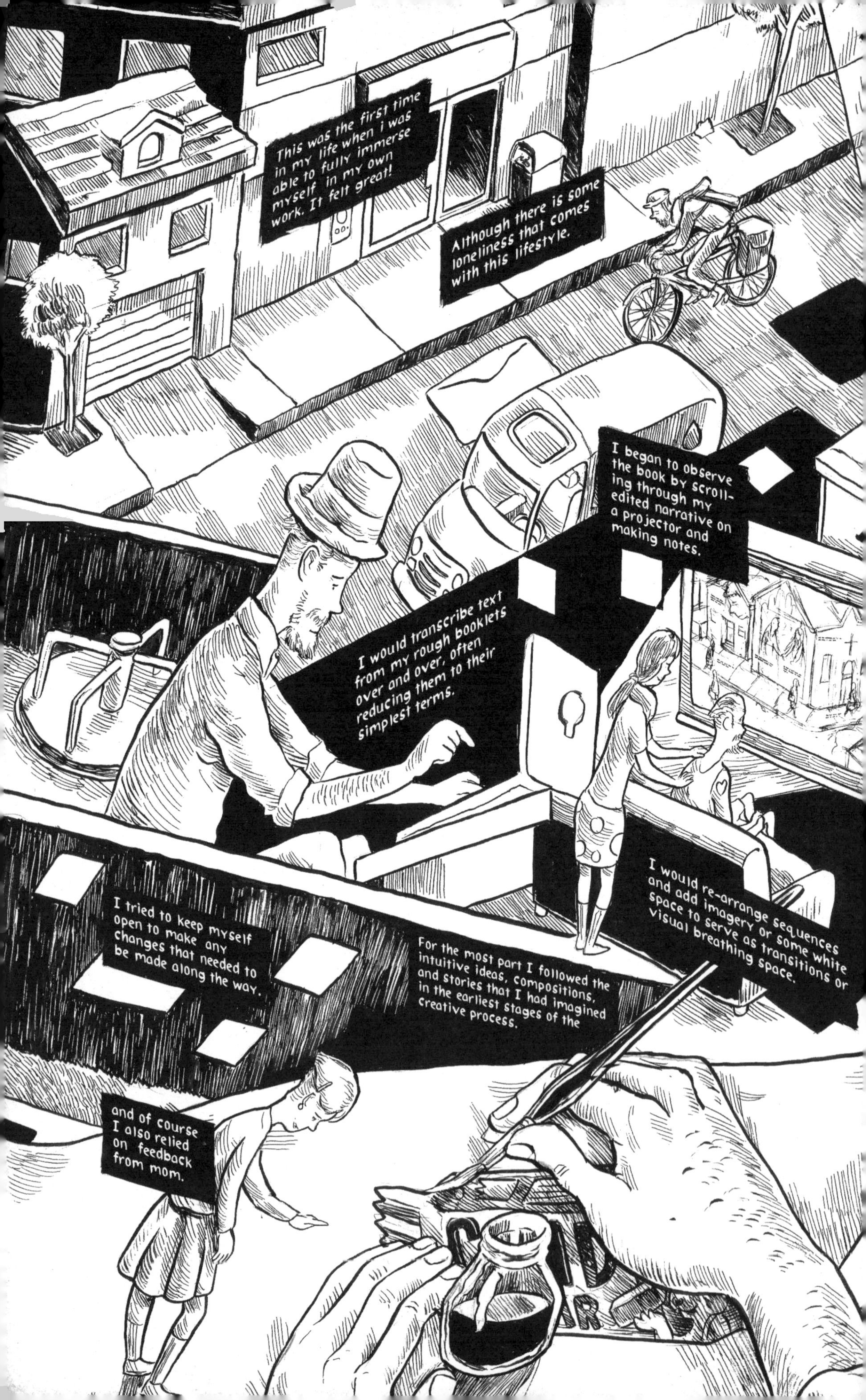
This was the first time in my life when i was able to fully immerse myself in my own work. It felt great!
Although there is some loneliness that comes with this lifestyle.
I began to observe the book by scroll-ing through my edited narrative on a projector and making notes.
I would transcribe text from my rough booklets over and over, often reducing them to their simplest terms.
I would re-arrange sequences and add imagery or some white space to serve as transitions or visual breathing space.
I tried to keep myself open to make any changes that needed to be made along the way.
For the most part I followed the intuitive ideas, compositions, and stories that I had imagined in the earliest stages of the creative process.
and of course I also relied on feedback from mom.

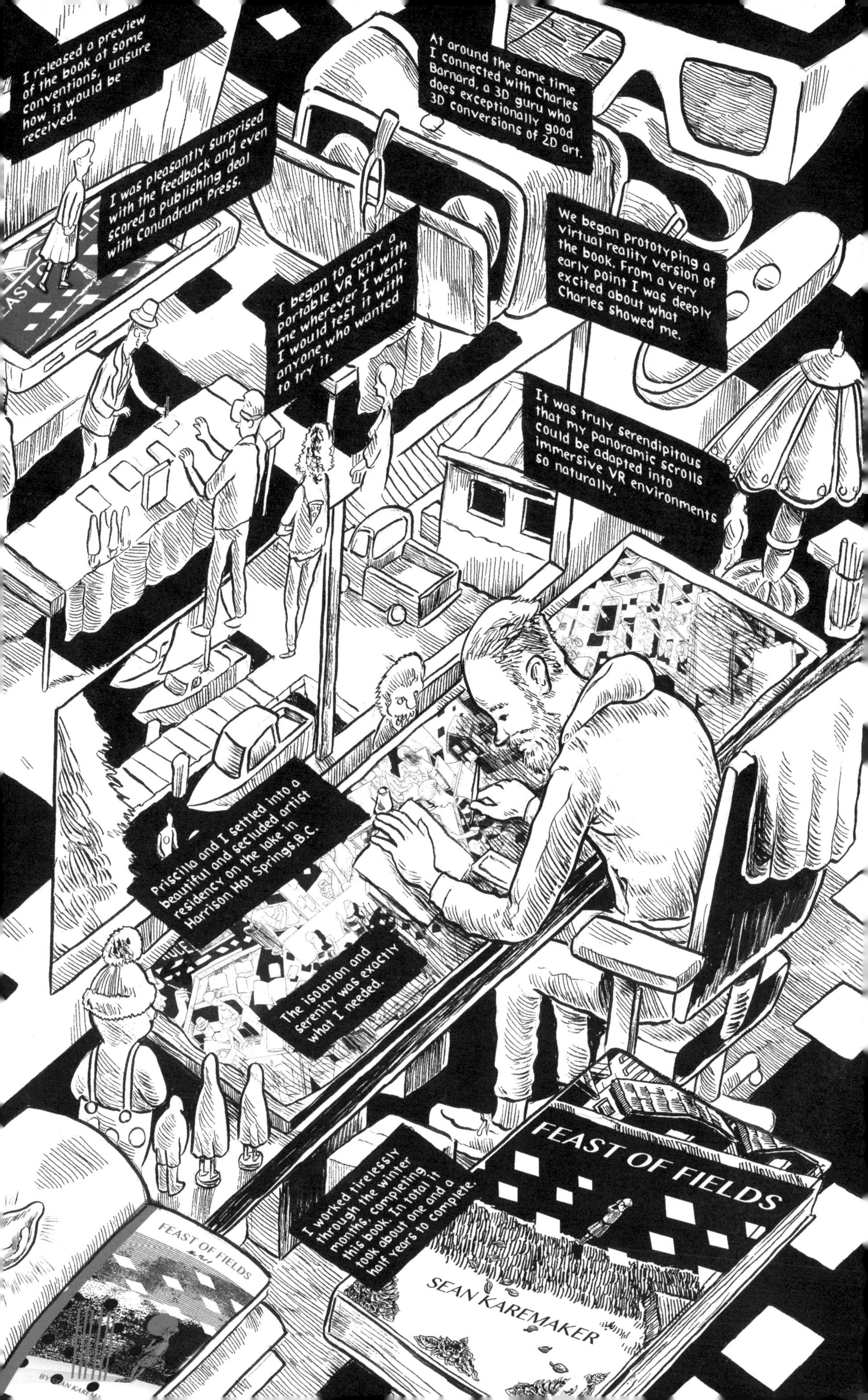
I released a preview of the book at some conventions, unsure how it would be received.
I was pleasantly surprised with the feedback and even scored a publishing deal with Conundrum Press.
I began to carry a portable VR kit with me wherever I went. I would test it with anyone who wanted to try it.
At around the same time I connected with Charles Barnard, a 3D guru who does exceptionally good 3D conversions of 2D art.
We began prototyping a virtual reality version of the book. From a very early point I was deeply excited about what Charles showed me.
It was truly serendipitous that my panoramic scrolls could be adapted into immersive VR environments so naturally.
Priscilla and I settled into a beautiful and secluded artist residency on the lake in Harrison Hot Springs B.C.
The isolation and serenity was exactly what I needed.
I worked tirelessly through the winter months, completing this book. In total it took about one and a half years to complete.
FEAST OF FIELDS
SEAN KAREMAKER
FEAST OF FIELDS

First Edition
Printed by Gauvin Press, Gatineau, Quebec

Published by Andy Brown at Conundrum Press, Wolfville, NS, Canada
www.conundrumpress.com

Library and Archives Canada Cataloguing in Publication

Karemaker, Sean, 1983-, author, illustrator
Feast of fields / Sean Karemaker.

ISBN 978-1-77262-025-2 (softcover)

1. Karemaker, Sean, 1983- --Family--Comic books, strips, etc. 2. Karemaker, Sean, 1983- --Childhood and youth--Comic books, strips, etc. 3. Orphanages--Denmark--Comic books, strips, etc. 4. Mother and child--Comic books, strips, etc. 5. Canada--Emigration and immigration--Comic books, strips, etc. 6. Mental illness--Comic books, strips, etc. 7. Biographical comics. I. Title.

PN6733.K37F43 2018 741.5'971
C2018-900206-9

Conundrum Press acknowledges the financial support of the Canada Council for the Arts, The government of the province of Nova Scotia, and the Government of Canada through the Canada Book Fund toward its publishing activities.

Sean Karemaker would like to acknowledge the generous support of the Canada Council for the Arts and the government of Canada.

Canada Council for the Arts Conseil des arts du Canada NOVA SCOTIA Canada

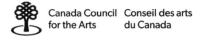

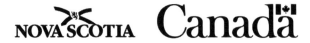